DEVELOPING
VOCAL
SKILLS

SECOND EDITION

THEODORE D. HANLEY
University of California, Santa Barbara

WAYNE L. THURMAN
Eastern Illinois University

39381

HOLT, RINEHART AND WINSTON, INC.

New York · Chicago · San Francisco · Atlanta · Dallas
Montreal · Toronto · London · Sydney

Copyright © 1962, 1970 by Holt, Rinehart and Winston, Inc.

Library of Congress Catalog Card Number: 79–97849

ISBN 0-03-083992-0

Printed in the United States of America

2   3   4   5   6   7   8   9

PREFACE

"The old order changeth, yielding place to new." Trying times, troublous times. Ferment, fervor. Revolt behind the ivied walls and in the streets. Anger, fear, despair, with small oases of tranquility. New heroes and anti-heroes. New religions from old. New musical strains from ancient instruments. New words and old words with new meanings, expanded meanings. "Power," a concept as important to the sociologist as to the astrophysicist. Is "the medium," how the message is delivered, more important or more effective than the message itself?

Clearly a time for the reexamination of traditional disciplines. In our first edition we solemnly announced, "Having observed the limited amount of conversation or formal speaking conducted today in rhyming iambic pentameter, we have denied admission to our book of many old favorites of this type." We thought that to be in step with the times we must make use of the language of the times; today we review our position. We reconsider the advisability of presenting the student with projects in breath control, pitch flexibility, loudness variation, and the like. And we find ourselves more firmly committed to our task-centered orientation than we were six years ago.

"A good man, skilled in speaking" still describes the successful communicator. Ten minutes of unrelieved screaming into the microphone of a public address system may serve to reveal a power advocate's emotional status, may even move prepersuaded audiences to injudicious actions. But thoughtful, disciplined use of the voice and language still has the greater potential for persuading the unpersuaded and modifying the stance of the adamant, provided, we continue to believe, that there is substance and merit in the message.

"Discipline," an old-fashioned word, is perhaps the theme of this book. We have lost none of our enthusiasm for the language of the day— as well as we can reflect it from our student contacts—but we hold with equal tenacity to the belief that it is only through controlled experience in vocal variation, and repetition of that experience to the point of habituation that the language of today or tomorrow can become meaningful and important to the listener.

Thus this revision of our earlier edition stands as a reiteration of our conviction that the communicator owes it to his message, himself, and his listener to present his ideas with all the vocal skill that he can develop in himself and bring to bear on the communication task at hand. We rely on the findings of research laboratories in suggesting approaches and techniques for achieving vocal skill. We endorse reasonable use of the modern idiom, though—conservatively—we remind our readers how passé are now the favored campus expressions of the near past. In short, our revision is an attempt to report our experience with the development of vocal skills in young adults in meaningful and practical terms, appropriate to conditions today.

Specifically, repeating a few lines from the 1962 Preface, "In the informational aspect of the text, concentrated in, but not entirely confined to the first half, we apply data from the sciences of acoustics and anatomy to phenomena of vocal communication, and we present the tools of the phonetician. We have not attempted to provide a fully annotated and exhaustive summary of each area of information, but frequent research references are included where they seem needed to strengthen, expand, or clarify."

"In the operational section of the book we draw upon the information in the previous chapters to expand the student's understanding of each aspect of vocal production as he seeks to improve it. For student practice in breathing for speech and control of pitch, rate, articulation, and quality, we include exercises which we believe to be normal and natural to everyday communication needs of young adults."

"We emphasize careful, discriminating listening to others as a route to critical self-listening. Each operational chapter is designed to heighten the student's awareness of one aspect of his vocal operation and to help him develop conscious control of it. Meaningful summary projects are suggested to relate practice on each isolated factor in vocal output to daily vocal needs, both social and professional."

"We believe the book to be flexible in that an instructor may shorten or lengthen class work on any vocal factor by selective omission or repetition of exercises. Many teachers will want to use the operational chapters almost as prescribed corrective materials for individuals or small groups in a class. We suggest also that the projects we present at the end of each practice chapter might be duplicated or enlarged upon to provide more classroom practice at the discretion of the teacher."

Finally, we reacknowledge our debt to students, professional critics, and our editor. As before, many voices and many blue pencils contributed to the finished product.

Santa Barbara, California   Theodore D. Hanley
Charleston, Illinois   Wayne L. Thurman
October 1969

CONTENTS

CHAPTER
1

THE REMARKABLE THING

Communication—verbal communication—word of mouth; we all do it. Acceptably? Convincingly? Effectively? Not always for any of us, not sometimes for some talkers, never for some; that's why we're writing. Our readers—primarily a group of young men and women in a class "Voice Skills" or "Voice and Diction." Why? They've talked for years and no complaints. Unrealized potential? We can only speculate.

The simple point we're trying to make is that speech skills, like all other human skills, are subject to improvement. We can only speculate about unrealized potential. We can only, by comparison with other young people whose academic and social achievements are somewhat more satisfying to them, suggest that an undeveloped skill, once polished, may yield unexpected by-products. Speech skills vary in degree from person to person. Some people are endowed with better vocal structures than others; some, by virtue of fortuitous environmental influences, learn speech better.

But all are capable of improvement, of building upon their present basic skills.

We believe in the ability of the normal person to change his vocal habits, whatever his external circumstances. If we seem to be classroom oriented, this is not entirely true. You, the individual, are a part of our orientation. With the help of a faithful listener and critic, you are invited to prove to yourself your ability to make desired modifications in your speaking patterns.

A fairly substantial segment of the population gets by on the vocal abilities acquired incidentally during the attainment of an eighth-grade certificate or high school diploma. You would "get by" too, even if you were denied this opportunity to develop vocal skills. Perhaps you're one of the lucky ones who will do much better than just get by simply on native speech proficiency. But the odds are that you will not be content to coast, and with reasonable effort on your part and the guidance of your instructor, you will emerge from the course having made substantial improvement in no fewer than four speech attributes. Objective records we have kept over a period of years on classes similar to yours support this contention.

However, the attainment of speech attributes isn't "The Remarkable Thing" alluded to in the chapter heading. Really, the remarkable thing is that you, your classmates, and mankind in general are able to communicate by voice at all. Through the eons man has adapted an oddly assorted set of organs to perform some unlikely acoustical feats. These feats, when combined in various ways, have come to be associated with meanings, objects, events, and ideas as the sounds are perceived by the human ear.

We shall write briefly in this chapter, and at greater length in later ones, of the vocal propagation, transmission, and auditory reception of information—the act of vocal communication.

To return to the odd assortment of organs and the unlikely sounds they emit, we can describe the structures principally involved in speech production as

a pair of sacks into and out of which air can flow;

two bands of muscle alternately advancing toward and retreating from each other;

an irregularly shaped Y-tube opening into a vaulted chamber and an irregularly walled, divided cavity;

a writhing muscular mass of tissue that, from moment to moment, changes in size and shape like an enlarged, speeded-up amoeba;

a curved row of wedge-shaped small bones; and

another pair of muscle strips that curl and twist and flap about in front of the cavity they encircle.

These organs, in the order described, are the lungs, the vocal cords, the throat cavity connecting with mouth and nose, the tongue, the teeth, and the lips. An odd assortment, indeed. If you were designing a communications instrument, would you select these for components? Would anyone?

Before we dismiss this biological complex entirely, with a shrug at the apparent haphazardness of the system, we need to remind ourselves that all these structures are carrying a double load. Not only do they function with astonishing coordination to emit sequences of interpretable tones and noises; they also play vital roles in the sheer biological survival of the individual. The lungs provide for the interchange of gases without which life becomes predictably shorter. The vocal cords assist other structures in preventing the intrusion of foreign objects—from dust particles to chicken bones—into the lungs. Teeth, tongue, and the throat cavity are active in preparing and delivering the fuel that keeps the whole system running. Even the lips participate in this survival system by assisting in the management of food and drink as well as their other well-known functions. In short, to use a phrase which was coined so many years ago that it has achieved an honored cliché status in the field of vocal communication, speech is an *overlaid function* on the organs involved. The older and perhaps more primitive function of each organ is to participate in some vegetative activity as breathing to maintain life or chewing a morsel of food that is eaten for the same purpose. In the long history of man, speech, we believe, was an accidentally or incidentally learned pattern of behavior, an overlaid function.

However, though overlaid, speech is not to be thought of as a secondary function. Communication by word of mouth is so basic a part of modern living that socioeconomic survival is almost as dependent upon the speech organs as biological survival. Try going through one day, through just the hours from eight to five, without speaking. Put yourself momentarily in the position of the person who somehow loses the power of speech. Your short-term, voluntary speechlessness may be a thought-provoking experience for you. When you emerge from it, you'll not discount the importance of this activity, overlaid function or not.

Considering the wide and obvious differences between the two main functions of the speech organs, it is not surprising that sometimes there is incompatibility of function localized in a single region. The harassed parent, mindful equally of her child's manners and possibility of his inhaling a mouthful of peanut butter, cries, "Don't talk with your mouth full!" Here is conflict between biological function (mastication) and communication. A movie actor helplessly coughs his way through the scene he thought would catapult him to stardom. Conflict again—biological function (rejection of an unwanted substance from the respiratory mechanism) versus speech function. We need not concern ourselves greatly with this conflict of function except to make a mental note that unless the speaker has learned remarkable control over his vocal organs, biological function usually overrides speech function.

And what of the sounds these organs produce? Considered simply as acoustical events, they are a rather pleasant sequence of tones periodically interrupted by snorts, hisses, and pops. The tones are mainly vowel sounds, whereas the interrupting noises are consonants, nasals like *m* and *n,* fricatives like *s* and *z, f,* and *v,* and plosives like *p* and *b.* At least we who speak American English, one of the Indo-European tongues, are spared the clicks and grunts which enliven the conversations of tribesmen in some remote corners of the world. Still, our speech sounds do have elements of the unlikely, as we have suggested before. If we were to start from scratch, building a language on no preconceived notions or experiences, it seems probable that we would do a different, if not a better, job of it.

The acoustical feats of the speech organs do not stop with the production of some thirty-five to forty-five recognizable speech sounds; the mechanism also is capable of modifying the pitch and loudness of the sounds, of shortening or prolonging syllables or longer units, and even of varying the quality or timbre of the tones from harsh or strident through agreeable to rich or mellow. Indeed, without this acoustical capability, vocal communication would have all the persuasiveness, all the capacity to convey feeling, all the human, personal effectiveness of a chattering brass telegraph key.

Somewhat earlier we made reference to man's acoustical accomplishments, his control over the several attributes or dimensions of sound. Most of the time, without conscious effort, he is able to manipulate his voice signals up and down the *pitch* range, strongly or softly in the *loudness* dimension, rapidly or slowly as to *time,* and, to a limited extent, more or less richly or mellowly in the attribute of *quality,* or *timbre.* Thus he produces a sequence of linked acoustical events, each modulated or controlled in at least two perceptible characteristics. Moreover, this control, though on a subconscious level, is an absolute necessity if the thought of the speaker is to be conveyed adequately to and through the receiving apparatus of the listener. Any incoordination in the speaker's bioacoustical mechanism, any inappropriate rise or fall in one of the vocal attributes, introduces the probability of some listener error.

Not very much has been said so far about this listener, but his role in the act of communication is a significant one. There are those who assert, rather dogmatically we feel, that in the absence of a listener there can be no sound. Certainly in his absence the act of speaking may lose much of its significance. What is the listener's role, then? He provides the stimulus for the act of communication either by communicating himself or simply by his presence as an inviting potential link in a communications chain. He serves also, very importantly, as a kind of meter, revealing to the speaker his relative success or failure in transmitting information. The listener responds or does not respond and either the action or the failure to act conveys something to the speaker. When a response does occur it may be a minimal thing, a postural shift or change of facial expression. Or, quite the contrary, the response may be proof positive to the message initiator that he was heard and understood through verbal agreement or disagreement by the listener-become-speaker with what was just said. Thus a model or pictorial representation of the act of speaking desirably includes in it a listener. Whether this important feature is present or not, we may look upon the task of the speaker in electromechanical terms as the act of encoding thought into acoustical symbols, or translating intellectual, neurological events into the physiological act of shaping a succession of sounds to which meaning long ago was assigned. These sounds are transmitted through some physical medium such as the air or a telephone circuit. Eventually the sound-symbols reach a destination, normally the auditory system of the listener (see Figure 1.1). There the message is decoded, "understood," and a purposeful, meaningful event has taken place.

Such an event occurs so often and the messages encoded and decoded are usually so commonplace that we give little thought to its remarkable nature. Consider, for a moment, the statistical possibilities of the situation. In Figure 1.1 the speaker thought and encoded from a very large number of alternatives, the word "top." (If his control had faltered on only the initial consonant, he could have said "bop," "cop," "fop," "hop," "lop," "mop," "pop," or "sop." He might even have selected an initial consonant such as "z" and encoded a nonsense word. There were equal possibilities for error on the vowel and the arresting consonant that terminated the monosyllable.) The word then passed through the medium, was received and perceived by the listener, who correctly decoded it from the same store of alternatives. If a simple three-letter word is so fraught with error potential, how nearly infinite must be the chances for error in just a sentence or paragraph. At the same time we must recognize that while there are, numerically, increasingly greater chances for error in longer speech samples, there are also greater safeguards *against* error. Why is this so? Because phonetic or verbal context often will supply, for the listener, sound elements incorrectly produced or even omitted. The person on the receiving end of the message " 'am" probably assumes that he has heard the first person singular of the verb "to be." In the sentence, "Pass the 'am and eggs," however, he mentally supplies the missing initial consonant *h*, selecting it out of his list of phonetic probabilities as the one most appropriate to the context. So we see how it is that for every sequence of speech sounds we produce there are many, many possibilities for error, situations where the smallest slip of the tongue could lead to large misunderstanding. But we see also how our linguistic usages and hundreds upon hundreds of sound and word associations serve to protect

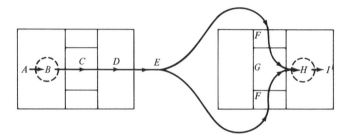

Figure 1.1. Symbolic diagram of human communication. The message originates as an idea in the storage area, the brain (*A*) of the speaker, is encoded in the same unit (*B*), conducted by the neurological system (*C*) to the speech mechanism (*D*), where it is put into acoustical symbols that pass through a medium (*E*), and are received by the listener's ears (*F*). It is then carried by his neurological system (*G*) to the brain, decoded (*H*), and the idea is perceived by the brain (*I*).

us from error. We are reassured to learn that the most likely of a given set of alternatives usually is the correct choice to make.

Scholars who deal theoretically and experimentally with vocal communications refer to the *redundancy* of language—a useful and most appropriate term. If the redundancy could be eliminated, or even reduced, communication efficiency would be materially enhanced, but so would the likelihood of error be increased.

We must recognize that misinterpretation is possible even when there has been perfect production and perception of the phonetic elements of the message. Such factors as stress and intonation themselves contribute to the ultimate understanding or misunderstanding of a message. Finally, the *set* of the listener, his anticipation of a message of particular content, may be markedly influential in determining how a pattern of auditory events is interpreted.

In the preceding paragraphs some of the language and elementary ideas of *communication theory* found their way into this general discussion of the remarkable aspects of vocal communication. This theoretical framework, itself a subsection of a larger body of theory called *information theory,* has figured largely in recent research and critical thinking about language, learning, and the transmission of ideas. Though the finer and more abstract points of information theory seem to have little immediate relevance in a voice and diction text, we believe that some of the concepts which have arisen out of work done in this field can be very useful to us here. For example, the concept of the speech mechanism as a closed cycle servosystem, developed by Grant Fairbanks[1] from earlier speech models, and the cybernetic theory of Wiener may be most helpful in explaining how language is learned, how the production of speech sounds is controlled, why there are errors and vocal inefficiencies, and how new vocal patterns may be substituted for old ones. In brief and greatly simplified review, the servomechanism theory postulates a center in the brain in which comparison can be made of the intended outgoing message (thought) with the actual physiological and acoustical characteristics of the message relayed by the body's sense organs as it is being produced. Figure 1.2 illustrates this "feedback" sequence of events. In this automatic comparison of the intended with the accomplished, sometimes there are discrepancies, and the mechanism, self-triggered, directs an error signal to a mixer, where input and error signals are combined and sent to the appropriate speech effectors (respiratory system, vocal cords, tongue, lips, and so on). Thus, in the same way that the automatic pilot keeps an airplane on course, we believe that the speech servomechanism controls vocal output. The original process of "learning to talk" consisted of establishing patterns for the control center. Speech defects are viewed as bad patterns originally learned; hence, for example, the error signal sent out when the speech mechanism starts to produce "th" instead of "s" is only the standard "message not complete," rather than "mistake in message

---

[1] An article by Dr. Fairbanks is listed in the bibliography at the end of this chapter. A book by Edward D. Mysak, similarly structured and containing an expanded structuring of the model, also is listed. Not more than a half-dozen footnotes will be found in this book, but the student with scholarly inclinations is encouraged to sample the readings recommended at chapter ends. In later chapters there will be textual references to experimental and linguistic phoneticians, included to provide an element of authority for certain conclusions we have reached. The degree to which you, the student, will be held responsible for associating the name of the speech scientist with his findings or opinions must be decided by your instructor.

unit" error signal. Speech defects are viewed also as the result of interference—"noise"—introduced into the receptor system, preventing adequate review of the output. The interference may be actual noise in the environment, which overloads the receptors, or it may be malfunction in one or more parts of the review system. When our hearing sense is impaired,

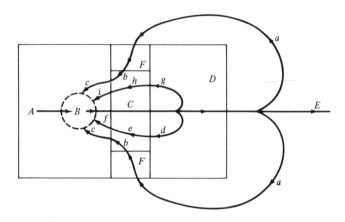

Figure 1.2. Feedback and comparison and correction in the human communicator. The signal originates in the storage area, the brain (*A*), and is encoded into an intended message also in the brain (*B*). It is then carried neurologically (*C*) to the speech mechanism (*D*) where acoustical events are created in the conducting medium (*E*). Feedback occurs at (*a*), (*d*), and (*g*). The sound goes through the medium (*a*) to the ears (*F*), where the signal is reintroduced to the neurological system (*b*) and carried to the brain (*c*). There comparison occurs between the actual and intended signals and correction is instituted. Kinesthetic feedback (*d*) and tactle feedback (*g*) also go from the speech mechanism by the neurological system (*e*) and (*h*) to the brain (*f*) and (*i*), where they contribute to comparison and correction. External feedback from the listener also has a major contribution to make in the establishment and regulation of vocal patterns.

even temporarily, we are more prone to make speech errors. When the senses of touch and movement are dulled in the tongue, as with a dentist's anesthetic, sounds which depend on skilled tongue movements are clumsily formed and may lose identity. Speech sounds originally learned under conditions analogous to these are likely to be faulty.

The task of the instructor of a speech improvement course, in this feedback frame of reference, is similar to that of the director of a play or a practicing speech pathologist: to supply the student with new, sharper, better patterns against which outgoing messages can be compared and also to reduce any interfering "noise" that may be present in the system.

Noise, we are sure you recognize, may come from many sources. It may be noise in its most common form, acoustical disturbance in the environment, drowning out meaningful sounds in the ear. It may be physiological—some defect in the central nervous system. It may be psychological, the result of "nerves" or stage fright in the speaking situation, or, in the extreme case, hysterical deafness. A person made sensitive to the possibilities usually can find ways to eliminate or sharply reduce the noise in his feedback system. It is with the other aspect of the servosystem that this book will concern itself primarily: the substitution of new and better comparison patterns for old. For every major vocal attribute we shall attempt to bring your present speech habits, or patterns, to your conscious level; then we will give you an opportunity to compare those habits with other vocal procedures that may be superior. After that, to change or not to change will be your decision.

Within this theoretical framework for vocal control, we will suggest that if you are to provide yourself with better speech, you can do it most efficiently and economically as a five-stage operation:

1. The first stage is to learn what to listen for in speech, namely, the bioacoustic attributes or variables.

2. Next, you should begin to listen critically to other people, in order to develop an auditory awareness of the various speech characteristics.

3. Stage three requires that you listen critically to yourself, to develop accurate, objective self-evaluation of speech characteristics. Thus you become aware of the patterns existent in your speech servosystem. It is at this stage that external feedback becomes most important. Listening critically to your classmates, your friends, and especially your instructor can help you to recognize your vocal assets and the attributes of voice that are not working actively for you.

4. Next, experiment with your vocal output, first as suggested by your instructor and later on your own. Both external and internal feedbacks are significant at this stage. Again, the critical ear of your instructor can be reinforced by the ears of other interested persons. In the final analysis, however, it is your own feedback system that must be trained to compare the accomplished act with the intended one and report the comparison accurately to you.

5. Finally, you must habituate, by repetition, improved characteristics

of your delivery until the pattern is so sharply etched that your vocal controls are automatic.

In Chapter 2 you will get started on the first stage of this operation, descriptive analysis of sound in general and vocal sound in particular. Specific vocal attributes will be discussed briefly and a plan for "hearing out" pitch, loudness, time, and articulation factors (the second stage) will be presented, along with a scaling technique to provide you with a means of comparing the poor with the good, the good with the excellent. We have placed a listening assignment at the end of Chapter 2, the objective being to initiate in you a state of auditory alertness as suggested in stage one, above. Your instructor will decide whether he wishes you to undertake a listening task as suggested there.

This brings us, at last, to the concluding section of this introductory chapter—the plan of the book. It seems only fair that you should know what lies ahead. You will discover that the primary objective of the text is to provide you with a sequence of vocal tasks designed to lead you into better control over your vocal delivery. Hence on a page-by-page analysis you might discover that the bulk of the book could be called "operational" material.

Under the heading "operational," we include the listening assignments previously mentioned. There will be one or more of these associated with each of the vocal attributes to which your attention will be directed. There will also be vocal exercises. Though disguised to the best of our ability, though made as true to life and as interesting as we can make them, there will be vocal exercises. Just as the piano virtuoso spends hours daily in finger training and the champion athlete achieves and maintains his status with endless repetitions of the movements of his sport, so must the skilled speaker, actor, and speech pathologist work regularly to bring about the infinitely fine adjustments of the vocal mechanism that mean the difference between mediocrity and excellence. Exercises alone, however, do not quite bring the communicator to the peak of his skill. As the athlete requires the contest and the pianist the concert, the communicator requires the stimulation of the audience to achieve his ultimate goals. We feel most strongly about the culminating assignments for each of the operational chapters, to be found in the section titled *Student Projects*. These we call Performance Assignments; they are opportunities for the student, with his classmates as his audience, to demonstrate his acquired skills and controls. We hope you will find these assignments challenging and, upon the completion of each, will feel the sense of accomplishment that they are designed to yield.

At fairly regular intervals, usually preceding operational sections, we have placed what we term, for want of a better name, "content" materials. Why? To add weight to the next? No, we include some elementary acoustics, anatomy and physiology, and a section on phonetic symbolization because we believe that efficient use of the vocal mechanism depends, in part, upon understanding the mechanism and the basic laws governing the propagation and transmission of sound. Moreover, certain vocal procedures will be suggested to you that have been demonstrated in controlled research to have merit. Relevant research findings have a place in our text, we feel; hence we have included them. An understanding of the academic background materials is basic for those of you who plan further study of speech or communications from any frame of reference. Since our experience is that a substantial majority of students in a class such as this will be found later in other speech classes, we deliberately contribute fundamental information on which you can build.

As you undertake the modest learning experiences we designed for you, we hope you will take the work and yourselves seriously, but not too seriously. Vocal communication is part skill and part art, and it is accomplished best by those who participate in it pleasurably. When speech becomes unrelieved drudgery, however technically well executed, it loses flavor and character. Work at the assignments, but have a little fun, too.

RECOMMENDED READINGS

Fairbanks, G. A theory of the speech mechanism as a servosystem. *J. Speech and Hearing Disorders,* **19,** 1954, 133–139.

Mysak, E. D. *Speech pathology and feedback theory.* Springfield, Ill.: Charles C Thomas, 1966. See especially pp. 5–44.

Scientific American, Editors of. *Automatic control.* New York: Simon and Schuster, 1955

Wiener, N. *The human use of human beings* (2d ed.). New York: Doubleday Anchor Books, 1956.

CHAPTER
2

SOUND

"Acoustics"—awe inspiring? For some just the name evokes trepidation. Why? Not so "geology," "marine zoology." Why the mental block over "acoustics"? More scientific than the others? No. More difficult to understand? No. Yes, it's invisible and intangible; geology and zoology deal with matters you can touch. "Acoustics." Evanescent— here now, gone next moment. That's the nature of sound. Maybe that makes you feel uncertain. Maybe just numbers, quantities, bother you. Does this shake your confidence? Don't worry. You don't have to cope

$$I = \frac{1}{T} \int_0^T p v_a \, dt^1$$

[1] A mathematical expression for sound intensity presented for illustrative purposes only.

with expressions like that one—acousticians do—but not you. Simple receptivity to information presented in everyday language, plus a willing suspension of apprehension, can accomplish for you most of what is sought in this chapter: understanding of the origin, transmission, and modulation of sound. All this is done with a bare minimum of equations, a qualitative rather than a quantitative treatment.

PROPAGATION—TRANSMISSION

How, then, does it start? What are the origins of this unseeable event? "EXPLOSION"—that word most completely sums up how sound begins. It is a spreading outward in all directions of a change in the space and pressure relations among the particles (or molecules, if you prefer) that make up the medium, the material, or substance in which the sound is born. Something upsets the normal state of things at a point in the medium and the disturbance thus created expands, spherically. When a stone is dropped in a placid pond, ripples spread outward in ever-expanding perfect circles; as a child puffs air into a toy balloon, that rubber sphere grows with approximate equality along all radii. These homely, familiar occurrences illustrate the pattern of disturbance in a sound wave, except that in the first case the expansion is two-dimensional rather than three.

What upsets the normal state of things? We could devote the rest of this book to a listing of sound sources. Almost any object you can name, if struck sharply, rubbed vigorously, or moved rapidly through the air, can serve as a propagator of the disturbance we are discussing. Two main classes of propagating agents, however, can and should be listed. They are *periodic* and *aperiodic* sources. The former are regular, rhythmic; the latter lack rhythmic repetition. This latter class consists of objects that produce acoustical events better described as *noisy* rather than *tonal*. These events are thumps and clicks, hisses and scratches, sounds, as you will learn, lacking in regularity and sharply reduced in definition. The objects that produce the events are, as you would imagine, such things as falling trees, colliding billiard balls, punctured tires, a hacksaw blade moving through a metal plate, and the like.

Periodic sound, in contrast, is tonal. Its waves are regular and can be accurately defined with respect to dimensions and composition. Vibrating reeds and strings, organ pipes, the lips of the trumpeter, and human vocal cords are among the generators of periodic sounds.

Both classes of sources, remember, have this in common: they introduce change into the sound medium, regularly (periodically) or irregularly (aperiodically), repatterning the spatial relations among the particles of the medium and creating conditions of rising and falling pressures. This they do by impact (the falling tree) or compression, such as the build-up and release of air pressure below the closed and opening vocal cords.

Two properties of sound fields permit the disturbances described above to radiate outward while the field itself retains its constituent parts and maintains its integrity. *Inertia* and *elasticity* are these properties. The tendency of a body at rest to remain at rest or a body in motion to remain in motion in a straight line describes inertia. In our sound field, any individual particle we may settle on for study is to be visualized as moving outward in a straight line from the point and moment of disturbance until acted upon by some force other than the initiating disturbance. Usually the other force is the elasticity of the medium, its tendency to resume its normal or original condition after a change has been introduced.

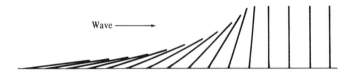

Wave ⟶

Figure 2.1. Toppling dominoes, a progressive disturbance roughly analogous to sound transmission.

Illustrative of the property of inertia is the movement pattern of a pendulum, the arm descends from an extreme right or left position to the lowest point of its arc and rises again, continuing to rise until the force of gravity overcomes inertial movement. At that moment movement is halted momentarily; then the direction of movement is reversed and the pendulum descends again.

In this same illustration gravity is analogous to elasticity, acting to restore a normal or original condition of rest after the pendulum has been placed in motion.

Briefly, in review: an event of impact or compression occurs or is made to occur in a sound field. The disturbance thus created expands spherically, moving outward from point to point in the medium. If you were to consult your dictionary at this point you would learn that the description just given is almost word for word the definition of a wave. This is no coincidence. What we have been describing is a wave, a sound wave. Now, to return to the disturbance and its spherical expansion. Involved in the event are straight-line arrays of particles, almost infinite numbers of them, pointing outward in all directions, three-dimensionally, from the initial point-source. Those particles nearest the disturbance move away from it, and in so doing influence the position of adjacent particles, causing them, too, to move outward. And so it continues as the sphere expands.

If we narrow our attention to one row, one long line of particles, we may compare the event to the successive toppling of dominoes in a row after the first has been upset. There is one important difference, however. Once toppled, the dominoes are down until restored by an outside force, a human hand. In contrast, the displaced particles in the sound field are restored by elasticity to their original positions and then carried on beyond the original positions, back toward the point-source, by inertia. Motion in this direction continues until once again elasticity brings about a reversal of direction. Thus each particle oscillates back and forth, away from and toward the source of sound, creating patterns of spatial relations, successive concentrations of particles (called *condensation*) and deconcentrations (called *rarefaction*).

Figure 2.2. Distribution of particles in a sound field.

What should now be brought to your attention is that the contents of the preceding paragraphs, without a single equation, comprises the necessary conditions for the propagation and transmission of sound. Stated another way, sound consists of alternating conditions of condensation and rarefaction passing through an elastic medium. You will note that no mention has been made of a listener to these events. The presence or absence of a listener we consider to be irrelevant. When there are these alternating condensations and rarefactions, the basic *physical* requirements for sound transmission have been met. The observer and his perceptions constitute a psychophysical refinement of great importance, but one that does not, in our view, establish the presence or absence of sound.

You should realize that the patterning of particles into condensations and rarefactions, previously described and illustrated as a *spatial* phenomenon, is also a *temporal* one. That is, we may conceive of a sound field as something having extent or dimensions. Within this field at any moment in time the particles in the medium may be grouped as in Figure 2.2. Alternatively, we may consider a single point within a sound field—perhaps an observer's ear—and recognize that as time passes in successive moments, the groupings of the particles change from condensation to rarefaction to condensation and so on. Both views, the temporal and the spatial, may be graphed two-dimensionally and hence somewhat more revealingly than in Figure 2.2. As shown in Figure 2.3, condensation may be represented above a base line which represents normal or at-rest conditions, while rarefaction is represented below the line. Figure 2.3 is a sound *pressure* graph, since condensation is equivalent to a condition of positive excess pressure in the medium and rarefaction is equivalent to negative excess pressure.

Particle velocity is also represented in Figure 2.3, with the portion of the curve above the base line conventionally standing for the relative speed of particle movement to the right. Relative velocity leftward is shown by the portion of the curve below the line. These velocities are not to be construed as revealing the rate of movement of sound through the

Figure 2.3. Relation of pressure to particle distribution.

medium, but only the changing instantaneous velocities of the oscillating particles. Over-all velocity of sound, as you doubtless know, is approximately 1,100 feet per second, rising with a rise in the temperature of the medium and descending as the temperature goes down.

Particle velocity and pressure are covariant, or *in phase,* in the direction of travel of the sound wave. Phase, you should know, represents a stage in a cycle and is reported in degrees. Why this should be so is made clear in some of the readings recommended at the end of this chapter, but omitted here in order that greater emphasis may be placed on other topics in acoustics.

Still one more aspect of the unseen particle movement associated with sound transmission may be graphed as in Figure 2.3, this aspect being the degree of *displacement* of the particle to right or left, away from or toward the sound source, from its normal position. Particle displacement, like velocity and pressure, may be considered with respect to either distance or time. However, again for reasons that will not be explored in this chapter, the particle displacement curve is 90° (or one fourth the length or duration of one wave or cycle) *out of phase* with pressure and velocity. This dislocation is illustrated in Figure 2.4.

Briefly to recapitulate the information presented since the last summary statement: a sound wave passing through a sound field creates a disturbance in relations among the particles which comprise the field. This disturbance may be thought of as a space or a time phenomenon and may be considered from the aspect of positive and negative pressures in the field, velocity of particle movement toward and from the source of disturbance, and amount of particle displacement to right and left from the normal position. The first two of these aspects are covariant, or in phase, whereas the last mentioned is 90° out of phase with the others. Most succinctly, the chapter up to this point may be summarized in a definition of sound, a slightly simplified adaptation of the formal definition accepted by the Acoustical Society of America: Sound is an alteration

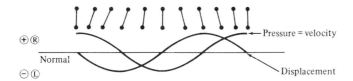

Figure 2.4. Phase relations among pressure, particle velocity, and particle displacement.

(oscillation) in pressure, particle displacement, particle velocity, and so on, propagated in an elastic medium.

It may have occurred to you before this that the graphs in Figures 2.3 and 2.4 are capable of mathematical expression, an even more concise and precise description of an acoustical situation than is rendered by the illustration. This is indeed the case. The kind of sound that has occupied our attention up to now may be specified with great precision in mathematical terms, for it is the simplest of all sounds, the pure tone. This acoustical event corresponds to many similar occurrences elsewhere in nature, all of them falling in the category of simple harmonic motion, or sinusoidal motion. There is nothing magical or mystical about simple harmonic motion. It occurs naturally with sufficient frequency that it has attracted the attention of scientists, has been named, and has been analyzed mathematically. Its particular virtue, so far as we are concerned, is that it constitutes a basic unit of acoustics. In this sense pure tones or sine waves are basic acoustical units. Most meaningful sounds, whatever their complexity, can be broken down or analyzed into simpler components; these simpler components conform to the mathematical definition of simple harmonic motion. In particular, all vowel sounds and many consonants can be so analyzed. What is true of human speech sounds is also true of tones produced by musical instruments; the tone we perceive is really a combination of tones that can be analyzed acoustically for its individual components. Moreover, these same sounds can be synthesized by combinations of pure tones. Later in this chapter, we shall have more to say about sound complexity, quality, or timbre.

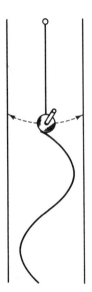

Figure 2.5. Simple harmonic motion traced by a swinging pendulum.

We shall leave the topic now with an operational, illustrative, nonmathematical definition of simple harmonic motion. If we attach a pencil to the ball of a pendulum, start the pendulum swinging, and pull a long sheet of paper past the pencil at a steady rate of speed as shown in Figure 2.5, the path traced by the pendulum-pencil combination is, with very slight error, simple harmonic motion. In verbal terms, simple harmonic motion describes the motion of any body that is displaced from its normal position and then set free, provided that the force needed to effect the displacement is proportional to the amount of displacement.

We said earlier that many speech sounds and musical tones are made up of combinations of pure tones. Each of these individual components, *partials* as they are sometimes called, contributes energy to the complex sound. If we started with one pure tone with a specified frequency and amplitude, and added another, then another and another, we would change the shape of the original sine wave with each successive addition.

The wave-form representations of sounds thus vary as the harmonic constituents of the sounds vary. These waves can be differentiated in other ways. Specifically they vary in amplitude and number per unit of linear distance, as shown in Figure 2.6. These variations, like those associated with the complexity of sound, are extremely important in our story of speech and the bioacoustic bases of communication. In the next several pages, we shall consider in greater detail the various ways in which sounds are differently constituted and perceived.

FREQUENCY—PITCH

As you can see in Figure 2.6, several waves the length of *d* can fit in the space occupied by *c*. Wave *d* is interpretable as representing a higher

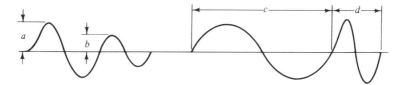

Figure 2.6. Comparison of sound waves by amplitude (*a* versus *b*) and length (*c* versus *d*).

frequency sound than wave *c*. When sound waves vary in number per unit of length of time, or in average length per wave, differences between them are known as differences in *fundamental frequency*. Human perception of this attribute of sound is perception of *pitch*. Fundamental frequency is a simple function of the rate of vibration or oscillation of the sound source. This rate of vibration in turn is impressed on the particles in the medium, which vibrate or oscillate the same number of times per second as the source. If the rate is high, the linear distance occupied by a single wave is short; if the rate is low, the wave spreads over a greater distance. This relation is expressed in one of the simplest of acoustical equations, $\lambda = v/f$, where λ is wavelength in feet (for example, the length of crest plus trough in *a* of Figure 2.6), v is velocity in feet per second, and f is frequency in cycles per second. When the average wave length of a sound is long, the time that elapses between the beginning and ending of a single cycle, termed *period,* also is long. The cycle is a complete back-and-forth oscillation of a particle in the medium (see Figure 2.7), and the time required to complete the oscillation is called the period. Fundamental frequency conventionally is expressed in cycles per second, (cps) or Hertz, abbreviated Hz (cps = Hz). The relation of frequency to period is said to be reciprocal; that is, $f = 1/P$, where f is frequency, 1 is one second, and P is period.

Our interest in frequency is limited to a range with a lower value around 16 to 20 Hz and an upper one between 16,000 and 20,000 Hz. This range encompasses normal human hearing. Values below the

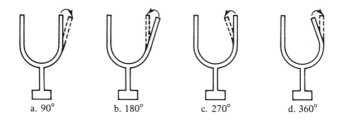

a. 90°   b. 180°   c. 270°   d. 360°

Figure 2.7. Four steps or quarter-cycle stages in the vibration of one prong of a tuning fork. These steps comprise one complete cycle and correspond to a complete oscillation of a particle in the medium.

lower limit are termed *subsonics,* whereas those above the upper limit are called *supersonics.* The sounds of speech are even more limited in range than the values just mentioned. Fundamental vocal cord vibration very rarely extends below about 70 Hz and above 1000 Hz. Overtones and atonal noises in consonant sounds involve frequencies close to the upper limit of hearing, but normal vocal communication requires only about 3200 Hz range to be completely intelligible. Indeed, scientists have succeeded in compressing speech within a much narrower band width and preserving intelligibility by electronic modifications of the original vocal signals.

As we mentioned earlier, pitch is the perceptual correlative of fundamental frequency. Relations between the purely physical (what we can measure) and the perceptual aspect (what we hear) are not simple; pitch does not vary on a one-to-one basis with frequency. Other sound attributes—loudness, quality, and duration—influence our perception of pitch. Because this is true, pitch research frequently is reported in two different kinds of units, one designed to reveal changes in the purely physical character of the phenomenon and the other representing, though with limited precision, human response to such changes. Nonetheless, it is safe to say that as frequency rises, pitch rises also.

For many years voice scientists have sought an ideal system for measuring and reporting human vocal pitch. There has been some objection to the use of a purely physical, cycles per second, scale because what is a perceptible pitch change in Hz at one point in the range may not be perceptible at all at another point.

A truly psychophysical scale of pitch, such as the *mel* scale developed by experimental psychologists, would be very useful. This scale is based on experiments in which observers, or subjects, listened to pairs of tones and reported in fractions or multiples how high or how low one tone seemed to be in comparison with the other. Curiously, this is a judgment which can be made quite consistently by the normal listener. In the mel scale, the relations between the units are such that 2000 mels sounds to the observer twice as high in pitch as 1000 mels. Unfortunately, the mel scale was developed for pure tones and is found to be inapplicable to the complex sounds of speech.

One solution to the problem of scaling vocal pitch has been to utilize an already existing scale, applying the equally tempered musical (ETM) scale to spoken communication. This has the advantage of supplying the voice scientist with a system the units of which are widely known. Each of these units (octaves, tones, semitones), moreover, is a preceptible unit so that no question need arise as to whether a *measured* difference in pitch is also a *perceived* difference. A disadvantage of the ETM scale is that semitone intervals vary in physical and psychophysical magnitude from one part of the musical scale to another. For example, from A to A# in the octave below middle C is one semitone; from G to G# two octaves above middle C also is one semitone. Yet these two semitones are not equal pitch distances in numbers of discriminable stimuli, though the musician may argue that they have equivalence of *esthetic* value or distance.

At any rate, research in this vocal attribute is most frequently reported in Hertz, in units of the ETM scale, or in both. Although conversion from one measuring instrument to the other is easily accomplished mathematically, knowledge of the specific procedures is not required for your general understanding of the topic.

However, the following fundamental facts about the ETM scale should be useful to any student who intends to go further in the field of voice science.

The basic unit comprising the full scale is the octave, which constitutes a difference in frequency between two tones in a ratio of 2 : 1. The octave above the tone A at 440 Hz, for example, has a frequency of 880 Hz.

There are six whole tones in an octave and twelve semitones. The "do-re-mi" octave and the white keys of the piano octave include five whole-tone and two half-tone or semitone intervals.

The tone around which the ETM scale as commonly used in speech research is constructed is the A above middle C at 440 Hz. When this A becomes the key value, the lowest tone in the scale, referred to as "zero frequency level" (0FL), is C_0 at 16.35 Hz.

As must be completely obvious to you by this time, the units in this scale do not have absolute value in cycles per second but only *relative* or *ratio* value above or below any selected point. For example, "re" has no fixed value in Hz but rather is obtained by multiplying "do" by a specific numerical factor.

In a later chapter, we shall have more to say about the pitch attribute of voice. We shall also recommend to you certain techniques for the development of skill in vocal use of pitch. At this point in this chapter, however, we turn our attention to another sound attribute, *intensity*.

INTENSITY—LOUDNESS

Two dimensions of the graphs in Figures 2.3 and 2.4 are required to account for the intensity of a tone. First, the amplitude of particle oscillation, plotted on the vertical axis, is needed. Second, the frequency of vibration, indicated by number of waves per unit of length along the horizontal axis, contributes also. We explain intensity as a "work-done," "energy-expended" concept. Illustrative of the concept is this comparison: a small man with a small wheelbarrow (low amplitude) which he fills, moves, and empties fifteen times in one hour (relatively high frequency) versus the large man with a large wheelbarrow (high amplitude) which he fills and empties only ten times in one hour (relatively low frequency). At the end of an hour, both men have done the same amount of work, moved the same amount of sand or cement, but by different frequency-amplitude combinations. The quantitative acoustician expresses this relation as follows: $I \propto A^2 f^2$. Stated verbally, intensity is proportional to the product of the squares of amplitude and frequency. Intensity is proportional also to the square of pressure (P^2) and the square of particle velocity (V^2).

Sound intensity, as formally defined, involves consideration of the rate of flow of energy through a unit area of the medium, a quantity difficult to measure and frequently awkward to report. This is because the audible range in the basic physical energy units appropriate to this sound attribute is several billion units in extent. Hence it has become a convention to report not sound intensity but sound level, the latter being expressed in ratio units, decibels (dB), rather than the absolute units which appropriately express sound intensity. Sound level may stand for sound *pressure* level or sound *power* level, depending upon the measuring-recording instrument that was used in the collection of data being reported. In any case, the student is encouraged to choose his term accurately since people in the speech field frequently are criticized for injudicious use of "intensity" to mean "sound level" or even "loudness."

Often erroneously described as a sensation unit of loudness, the decibel compares two sound powers or pressures. Usually the lower of these is a value very close to the lowest perceptible sound to human beings (auditory threshold) at 1000 Hz, 0.0002 microbar. The number of dB between this base reference level and the stronger power is revealed by the formula $NdB = 10 \log (P_1/P_0)^2$, where P_1 stands for the stronger value and P_0 stands for the reference value. This equation may also be used to compare any two sounds, the power value of the weaker of the two being substituted for P_0 in the equation. In actual practice, the equation is usually modified slightly to read NdB = 20 times the log of the voltage or current ratios because currents and voltages are revealed by standard instruments as square roots of the corresponding power ratios. Fortunately, it is now rarely necessary to calculate the value of a sound level in decibels; our electronic sound analyzers do the job for us.

As was the case with the frequency-pitch attribute, voice scientists have tried to adapt a subjective scale to the measurement of intensity-loudness phenomena in speech. Such a scale would make it possible for an observer to declare, validly, "A's voice is twice as loud as B's, whereas C's lies halfway between the other two." The advantages for the speech teacher as well as for the voice scientist in a scale of this type are obvious. Unfortunately, the attempts have been fruitless because subjective scaling of complex sounds results in data that are inconsistent and unreliable. Pure tones lend themselves readily to subjective evaluation, and a number of psychophysical scales, of which the *sone* scale probably is the best known, have been derived from experimental data. Variations in the power of the complex sounds of speech, however, typically are reported in decibels.

One of the later chapters will explore further this sound attribute, particularly as the human communicator manipulates it to achieve enhanced vocal flexibility and greater intelligibility. Meanwhile, let us examine another attribute of sound, *quality,* or *timbre.*

WAVE FORM—QUALITY

Frequency, you will recall, has to do with the rate of repetition of identical or almost identical events. Intensity is concerned with frequency, too, but with frequency acting on amplitude or vice versa. Both attributes could be depicted clearly, as in Figure 2.6. Sound quality also, as we shall see, can be graphically represented. Differences in timbre manifest themselves as differences in wave form, variations in the shape of the wave being attributable to the tendency of most sound generators to produce complex tones. These may vary from moment to moment with respect to the combination of pure tones present in them.

It is no accident that acousticians speak of "spectrums" of sound because most sounds, like most visual phenomena, consist of components that vary systematically in wave length. When the components of a tone, or single cycle of a tone, are related mathematically to one another in a particular way, they are called "harmonics." This harmonic relationship is really quite a simple one: components of the tone higher in frequency than the lowest component (fundamental or first harmonic) are integral multiples of the fundamental. For example, a complex tone with a 100 Hz fundamental would have a second harmonic at 200 Hz, a third at 300 Hz, and so on. Each of these harmonics would be present to an extent measurable in terms of its sound level or relative amplitude.

Not all complex sounds, of course, are harmonic. Some are predominantly harmonic with limited inharmonic energy present, and some are predominantly inharmonic. Other sounds (noises) are altogether inharmonic, consisting entirely of elements that are random with respect to frequency, or having all frequencies equally represented (white noise). In these clearly there would be no repetition of wave shape, a necessary condition if sound is to be perceived as tone rather than noise.

As tones increase in complexity with the addition of harmonics, the wave form changes, as shown in Figure 2.8.

Wave form and harmonic spectrum contribute to perceived quality or timbre, as stated earlier. These tonal variations make it possible for us to distinguish tones from wood winds and brass instruments, even when all other acoustic variables are identical. They permit us to identify the voices of friends heard over telephone systems. They also make possible discriminations among different speech sounds, or phonemes, uttered by the same person. When the discrimination involves two different persons producing the same phonetic element, we refer to a difference in voice quality; when it involves two or more phonemes produced by the same speaker, it is a discrimination of phonetic (often vowel) quality. But whether the perception is of vowel or voice quality, the judgment is based upon the number and relative prominence of the harmonics present in the complex tone.

To a certain extent, both determinants of perceived quality (number and relative prominence of harmonics) are physically determined by the original vibrating source. The vocal cords, for example, can vibrate from end to end, producing the fundamental, and in segments, contributing

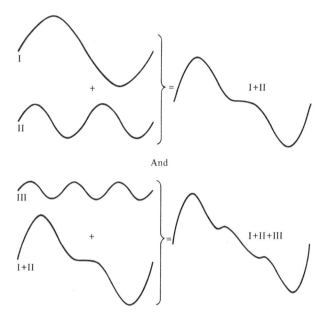

Figure 2.8. What happens to a sine wave (I) when a second harmonic (II) and then a third harmonic (III), each one half the amplitude of the lower one, are added.

higher harmonics or *partials*. However, quality may be modified after an acoustical disturbance has left its source by selective *resonance*. As the wave train passes through tubes or pipes or chambers of various sizes and shapes, the vibration of certain partials in the complex tone may be facilitated by the environment. Tubes and chambers have *natural resonance frequencies* which in a sense enable them to liberate energy associated with comparable frequencies in the complex tone. Resonators do not create energy; rather, they release it or permit it to be expended more rapidly by the wave train.

As a result, a harmonic or a cluster of harmonics of little or moderate prominence in the original tone may achieve dominance as a tone is acted upon after it leaves the source. In the human vocal mechanism tubes and chambers above the vocal cords create resonance effects on cord tone, as will be elaborated somewhat in the next chapter.

When resonators act on vocal cord tone, giving prominence to partials and creating acoustical patterns we have come to identify as specific phonemes, it usually happens that two or three concentrations of energy become detectable by analyzing instruments. These concentrations, once called *centroids* and now generally termed *formants,* are known to be principally responsible for phonemic uniqueness. In Figure 2.9 can be seen

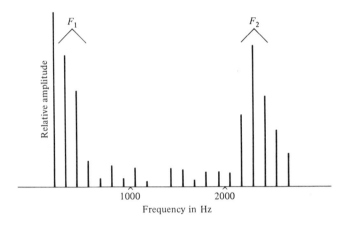

Figure 2.9. Display of the harmonics present in an utterance of the vowel [i], as in "team," with first and second formants identified as F_1 and F_2. The bar on the extreme left is the voice, or fundamental frequency bar. (Adapted from Fletcher, H. *Speech and Hearing in Communication.*)

a typical distribution of energy among harmonics and concentration of energy in formants for a vowel sound. More information about phoneme formants will be found in Chapter 5.

Not only phoneme quality, you will recall, but voice quality as well is based upon or largely determined by the number and relative amplitude of partials in the complex tone. Analyses by voice scientists have been quite successful in associating physiological variations with acoustical variations in the production of different phonemes. The attempts at correlation of different perceived vocal qualities with bioacoustic variation, however, have yielded less reliable results.

As we point out in Chapter 10, the listener can readily identify richness or mellowness of vocal tone and departures from this desirable sound variously labeled nasality, breathiness, thinness, harshness, stridency, and hoarseness. With some of these quality deviations we can associate physiological deviations, as, for example, we frequently find growths on the vocal cords of persons labeled hoarse and failure of the cords to meet in the midline of the larynx in the condition termed breathiness. Minor departures from good quality seem frequently to accompany conditions of excessive tension in vocal musculature. However, the list of correlations is far from complete. In particular, the harmonic concomitants of various perceived qualities require major research effort before authoritative statements can be made. Fortunately, scientists in many university speech laboratories are conducting researches in this area. We return to phoneme quality in the next chapter and voice quality in Chapter 10. Now we turn our attention to the last of the attributes of sound, *duration*.

DURATION

Intellectual grasp of the time attribute of sound is not difficult to achieve. Either an acoustical event occurs or it does not. If it occurs, it does so in time, measurable in units with which the average child becomes familiar at least by the time he starts to school. Yet for all its simplicity, time, the duration attribute, has elements of complexity, and aspects which have yet to be explored experimentally. We know from research done previously how long a sound must persist if it is to be perceived by a listener. We know how perception of pitch and loudness is influenced by presentation of auditory stimuli for very short periods of time. Data have been collected on "normal" reading rate for college students and on average syllable duration in certain types of communication by young adults. Some of this basic information will be brought to your attention in Chapter 7.

Among the things we are beginning to learn about the time attribute, but where the data need supplementation, are the contribution of time to intelligibility of speech, to discriminability of vowels and consonants, to judged effectiveness of speaking and reading aloud, to stress and emphasis. We do not know as precisely as perhaps we should how rate factors interact with articulatory skill, with the effect that one person can communicate with perfect intelligibility at 250 words per minute, whereas another can be understood only about half the time when he speaks that fast.

Probably the most important unknown aspect of time lies within speech feedback, the subject matter area presented in the previous chapter. Investigators have learned that when speech signals are delayed in their return to the ear of the speaker, he suffers some loss of control over vocal output. Exactly why this is true, why the degree of disturbance varies from person to person and group to group, time to time, and environmental condition to environmental condition, why the disturbance varies with the amount of delay, and why there are individual differences in this factor—all these matters are in need of research beyond that already performed and reported.

To summarize once more, descriptions have been presented of variations in physical properties of the acoustic stimulus associated with perceptions and productions of sound by humans. We have discussed the correlation between frequency and pitch, intensity and loudness, wave form and quality. There has been brief mention of scales in the first two of these tonal attributes and a listing of some qualitative terms applied in the third. Finally, the contribution of time factors to sound in general and vocal communication in particular has been touched on. In the remaining paragraphs of this chapter we shall try to bring the acoustical nature of speech into sharp focus as we consider a basic technique for modification of speech feedback control patterns and hence of speech output, directed, selective listening. To accomplish this end we shall encourage the use of the Analytic Speech Profile, a standard speech evaluation form which directs the attention of the listener successively into channels devoted to the attributes of sound and speech discussed in preceding pages.

VOCAL ATTRIBUTES

The Speech Profile, Figure 2.10, will be used in many suggested assignments in and out of class. Accordingly, we suggest that you examine the form in detail so that you may use it most effectively.

To begin with, you will note spaces for the insertion of the names of the listener, the person being listened to (student), and the date. Sometimes your instructor will direct you to preserve the anonymity of the person being listened to by inserting after *Student* "Joe Doakes," "Mary Jukes," or some similar pseudonym. Next, you will see that the Profile is divided into two halves, vertically. On the left side are listed faults of vocal delivery, whereas on the right side are positive attributes. Down the middle are a series of numbered boxes, their values ranging from

ANALYTIC SPEECH PROFILE

Student _____ Date _____

FAULTS	NORMAL							POSITIVE ATTRIBUTES
	−3	−2	−1	0	1	2	3	

Time: ☐ ☐ ☐ ☐ ☐ ☐ ☐ *Time:*
Too fast   Over-all rate
Too slow   Duration of tones
Monotonous   Phrasing
Uncontrolled variability   Variation in syllable duration
Patterned   Variation in pause duration
Hesitancies   Variation in rate of phrases
Repetitions

Loudness: ☐ ☐ ☐ ☐ ☐ ☐ ☐ *Loudness:*
Too loud   Over-all level
Too weak   Syllable stress
Monotonous   Variation in phrase loudness
Uncontrolled variability
Patterned

Pitch: ☐ ☐ ☐ ☐ ☐ ☐ ☐ *Pitch:*
Too high   Near optimum level
Too low   Range
Monotonous   Upward inflections
Uncontrolled variability   Downward inflections
Patterned   Pitch skips

Voice Quality: ☐ ☐ ☐ ☐ ☐ ☐ ☐ *Voice Quality:*
Nasal   Describe: _____
Harsh   _____
Strident   _____
Hoarse   _____
Breathy   _____
Thin

Articulation: ☐ ☐ ☐ ☐ ☐ ☐ ☐ *Articulation:*
Additions   Describe: _____
Omissions   _____
Substitutions   _____
Distortions   _____
General inaccuracy   _____
Oral inactivity   _____
Overly precise   _____

                            −3 −2 −1 0 1 2 3
OVER-ALL EFFECTIVENESS   ☐ ☐ ☐ ☐ ☐ ☐ ☐

Listener _____

Note here any deviant sounds and/or de-   Note here any positive vocal
viant speech attributes not listed above.   characteristics not listed above.

Figure 2.10. Analytic speech profile for use in listening projects.

zero to minus three on the faults side and from zero to plus three on the positive side. The zero box represents normality, whether of campus student speech, the city, the geographical region, the nation, or the English-speaking world is for your instructor to say. Boxes with minus numbers represent increasing degrees of faultiness or deviation from normal for each of the attributes; increasing degrees of skill in the use of the attributes are reflected in the plus boxes. When you evaluate the speech of someone else (or yourself, for that matter), you place an "X" mark in the box which to you reflects the subject's skill in the use of the attribute.

Glancing down the columns on the right and left you will observe, under the headings "Time," "Loudness," "Pitch," "Voice Quality," and "Articulation," descriptive words and phrases which may be checked in partial explanation, at least, of the numerical rating given the subject by the listener. Thus Henry Eustachia, Listener, might evaluate the use of Time by Adolph Mumblia as −3 ("one of the worst I've heard"). Henry would, perhaps, defend this scale value by checking "slow" and "monotonous" as descriptive adjectives under this attribute.

In general, you will see fewer descriptive terms on the positive side of the Profile than on the faulty side. The student is encouraged to supplement the skimpy positive list with descriptive terms of his own to the end that fair, accurate observations may be made on both sides of the ledger.

Centered at the bottom of the Profile is a general nonspecific row of boxes. Here the listener is to put his over-all judgment of the vocal effectiveness of the subject. This rating is not intended to be and should not be an average of the attribute ratings. This direction becomes obvious when you reflect that a person may check out as perfectly normal in all vocal attributes except one, yet that one may be enough to deal the over-all effectiveness a telling blow. One example should suffice. A student born of Swedish parents, educated in Sweden, now studying in this country may very well have normal or superior control of time, loudness, pitch and voice quality, but a considerable number of phoneme substitutions carried over from his primary language. Clearly he would be down-graded on (American) articulation and over-all effectiveness when speaking our language.

The relation of the Profile to the content material of the chapter and the significance of this content material in the development of vocal skills perhaps now are becoming clearer to you. The ability to analyze a phenomenon into its basic components, to visualize the events on microscopic levels that accompany perceived stimuli, should be of value to someone engaged in evaluation and modification of habits of nearly a lifetime. Knowledge and understanding are the power tools of a generation born to apply such tools. We hope that your work in the communications area will not suffer by comparison with your efforts in other fields.

STUDENT PROJECTS

CONTENT ASSIGNMENT

    A. Many of the terms used in this chapter were new to you. Write out definitions for the following in words that have operational significance for you.

1. Condensation	8. Cycle
2. Rarefaction	9. Reciprocal
3. Propagation	10. Psychophysical
4. Transmission	11. Sinusoidal
5. Periodic	12. Decibel
6. Aperiodic	13. Formant
7. Period	14. Harmonic

    B. Represent the following contrasting states of affairs *graphically:*
        1. Amplitude: large vs. small
        2. Frequency: high vs. low
        3. Wave form: pure tone vs. complex tone

LISTENING ASSIGNMENT

You have been introduced to the Analytic Speech Profile. Your structured listening will begin with use of the Profile in describing the speech of five persons. Perhaps your instructor will provide you with copies of the form. Fill it out for the following:

    A. Best student speech you've heard (No name. Label "Good").
    B. Worst student speech you've heard (No name. Label "Poor").
    C. A salesperson in a local shop.
    D. Someone chosen by you (give reason for choice).
    E. Yourself (following the Performance Assignment described below).

PERFORMANCE ASSIGNMENT

Your instructor will designate a time and place for you to appear for your "Before" recording. You should find a paragraph or two, about 150–200 words in length, which you can read easily. Select something from a popular magazine, preferably. Copy or paste that material onto a sheet of notebook paper and hand it in to your instructor. You will be rereading this material in an "After" recording at the end of the semester or quarter.

RECOMMENDED READINGS

Denes, P. B., and Pinson, E. M. *The speech chain*. Bell Telephone Laboratories. Distributed by Williams and Wilkins, Baltimore, Md., 1963, Chaps. 3, 5, 7, and 8.

Fletcher, H. *Speech and hearing in communication*. Princeton, N.J.: Van Nostrand, 1953, Chap. 3.

Gray, G. W., and Wise, C. M. *Bases of speech*. (3d ed.) New York: Harper, 1959, Chap. 2.

Hirsh, I. J. *The measurement of hearing*. New York: McGraw-Hill, 1952, Chap. 2.

Ladefoged, P. *Elements of acoustic phonetics*. Chicago: University of Chicago Press, 1962.

Pierce, J. R., and David, E. D., Jr. *Man's world of sound*. New York: Doubleday, 1958.

Stevens, S. S., and Davis, H. *Hearing*. New York: Wiley, 1938, Chap. 1.

CHAPTER
3

THE
VOCAL
MECHANISM

Most of us are haphazard in our speech habits, partly because we give so little thought to oral communication, and partly because we lack information about the structure and operation of our speech mechanisms. Teachers of speech disagree about how much a student should know about the mechanical speech structure. Advocates of one point of view believe that when the ideas are well enough understood by the speaker, and felt deeply enough by the speaker, he will automatically use his mechanism properly to achieve an effective product. They believe the student need learn little about the mechanism. An extreme opposite point of view might be that purely mechanical planning and control of speech output can be so well done that ideas will be well communicated whether or not the speaker understands them and feels deeply about them. This view is held by very few, if any, leading speech teachers. A middle position, held by your authors, is that knowledge of the nature and capabilities of the speech mechanism will assist the speaker to express his ideas effectively and will assist him in showing his understanding and depth of feeling. Those of us who hold this position are sometimes misunderstood and misquoted as saying that knowledge of the mechanism is *all,* that knowledge of *how* the mechanism works will automatically guarantee its proper use and effective speech. We know that is not the case. But neither are we convinced that most speakers will do their best without knowledge about the nature and functioning of the speech mechanism. We want you to have at least elementary information about your speech equipment so that when reason or feeling dictates a need for a vocal action you will be better prepared to produce it. Most techniques for voice improvement rightly involve programs of self-hearing, but that is not enough. We are convinced that your ability to change your speech output to fit a new auditory pattern will often depend on your understanding and handling accurately the mechanical adjustments of your vocal equipment. For example, it is often necessary, when a person tries to articulate an acoustically sharper, clearer [s], for him to know what the tongue and jaw must do to achieve that end. Elimination of nasality, another example, may depend on the development of consciousness of mechanical use of the soft palate and the structures of the rear wall of the throat.

We are not all exactly alike anatomically, and so, of course, our vocal mechanisms and their operations are not all identical. We should be extremely grateful that such is the case. Individuality, personality, charm—human characteristics—are contributed by our differences. However, there are central tendencies in structural make-up and manner of operation which you must approximate if your speech is to fall within the range of normalcy or acceptability. We shall discuss those central tendencies in this chapter.

Variations from speech structural or operational standards, if extreme, can bring about speech so deviant as to cause communication difficulties. Moderate structural variations can cause vocal unpleasantness, at least. In extreme cases speech correction work or training in special use of the mechanism to compensate for the structural differences often will correct the communication problem or eliminate the unpleasantness. If there are important structural or operational differences among students in your class in voice and phonetics or voice and diction, your instructor will be able to help the students involved to recognize the differences, to evaluate them, and to apply corrective measures if it seems wise. In the mildest instances, certainly, the drills and exercises in this text should be useful. In more extreme cases of speech structure variation your instructor may wish to refer students to a speech correctionist for therapy or for guidance in outlining improvement work.

It is not our purpose here to provide you with a thorough grounding in anatomical structures and physiological processes in the speech mechanisms, but merely to present for you those aspects of the structures and their operation which are most important to the communication process. We believe such information to be helpful in your achieving your best voice and to be urgent for you who are centering your academic studies in the speech field.

Neither do we wish to confuse you by introducing much of the technical language used by the anatomist. We shall give you the names of structures and as much description as seems necessary for clarity. Insofar as possible, however, we shall conduct our discussion in language we believe familiar to those of you who have not had course work in anatomy. As we introduce words that we believe to be unusual or unfamiliar to you, we shall define them briefly.

It is sometimes difficult for students to picture three-dimensional bone and muscle structures from verbal descriptions alone. Standard anatomical charts and models will probably be helpful for classroom drill and discussion.

You will recall from Chapter 1 that the mechanisms used for speaking serve the body in more basic, that is, primarily biological, functions. The speech functions are said to be "overlaid" or secondary to the primary functions. As we discuss the structures involved in communication, we shall point out the relationship of the speech functions to the primary or biological functions.

The biocommunication system operates as a unit, its parts interacting in synchronous and continuous fashion; however, for discussion we find it best to concentrate successively on these major elements: innervation, respiration, phonation, resonance, articulation, and reception.

INNERVATION

The speech act is directed and coordinated by the *central nervous system* (*CNS*) as a small part of the complex and multiple functioning of that system. Both message content and primary control of parts of the mechanism originate in the cerebral cortex or gray matter covering of the brain. Message content, dictated by the immediate communication requirements of the situation, is selected from the stored information collected in past experiences. The precipitating, triggering factor for message initiation may be heard, felt, or remembered, or it may arise from sheer impulse.

The stimuli leading to action are carried along outgoing or efferent nerve fibers to the muscles (or other effectors) on the periphery. Reports of peripheral activity, experiences, and stimuli, on the other hand, are carried to the cortex by ingoing or afferent nerve pathways. The latter give the kind of environmental information from which an action may arise. They also provide reports of results of effector unit (primarily muscle) actions, both kinesthetic (feelings in muscle) and tactile (sensations of touch), making evaluation or monitoring possible in the cortex. In addition to kinesthetic and tactile feedbacks during speech, the CNS gets reports from the hearing apparatus. Those reports add to the information from the muscles and body surfaces and help in evaluation of total muscular and acoustic characteristics of vocal output. Thus a comparison of input ("ideal" message) to output (real message) is effected.

The rapidity of action and coordination of the CNS is amazing. Although it is not immediately relevant to speech, let us consider walking as a striking example. Walking is a bodily action that requires good timing and coordination of a large number of muscle structures. As you would expect, walking involves the leg and foot muscles; but as you may not realize, many other muscles in the arms and the trunk are used to maintain balance and accomplish rhythmical shift of weight as the body moves from one leg to another. Not only does the CNS coordinate all that activity; it also dictates changes, such as faster or slower walking, walking with a springy, eager step, or walking with a slow, casual, strolling step.

The speech act is likewise a complex procedure involving a large number of muscle structures. In this case the adjustments required are finer and more rapid than the somewhat gross muscle adjustments for walking. In saying a simple monosyllable, which lasts about one-fifth second, you must call at least forty pairs of muscles into action, each at just the right instant in just the right manner, so that their coordination is exact; and yet your CNS accomplishes the task accurately. When we recognize that parts of the speech act happen not only sequentially but simultaneously, and that several voluntary acts such as walking and talking can be accomplished at the same time, our amazement at the wonders of the CNS must be multiplied.

One of the most valuable aspects of the operation of the CNS for vocal purposes is that repeated use of a particular neutral pattern will establish it firmly enough that it becomes almost automatic; it becomes a habit. In activities designed to improve speech we begin with a conscious, carefully directed process, controlled through kinesthetic, tactile, and auditory feedbacks; but we work toward establishing near automatic production of the desired process, a habit which can be controlled and directed with a minimum of attention.

RESPIRATION

The lungs are the air sacs of the body, used basically as part of the system for adding fresh oxygen to the blood stream in exchange for the waste carbon dioxide. Also, the lungs provide the reservoir from which the air stream for the voice is derived. The biological function is primary and will, in case of need, supersede the speech function, peremptorily. Recall how you puff and upset your verbal flow after you have just run a long distance and how you sputter in talking when just emerging from an underwater swim; your vocalization is secondary to your body's need for fresh oxygen. Nevertheless, under normal breathing conditions the air in our lungs is available for vocal purposes, and generally we combine the two activities, taking air in for oxygen replenishment and employing it for speech on its way out. These are the inhalation and exhalation processes.

Inhalation

Inhalation for speech is accomplished in two major, simultaneous movements. The diaphragm accomplishes one of them, the chest muscles the other.

The diaphragm is a dome-shaped partition between the thoracic (chest) cavity and the abdominal cavity, with a slight depression in the top of the dome creating a double-humped contour from the front aspect. The diaphragm slopes downward from the front to the back of the body. The central portion is a bean-shaped tendon, its shorter side toward the front. The circumference of the tendon is fringed with muscle fibers which attach to the body cage: sternum (breast bone), lower ribs, and spinal column. In its rest position the diaphragm is arched; and when the fringe of muscle contracts, the arch or double-humped dome is lowered and somewhat flattened. The viscera, the soft body organs in the cavity below the diaphragm, are partly compressed, and usually the front wall of the abdomen bulges. This action results in elongation of the thoracic cavity.

The second major movement in inhalation is the upward and forward lifting of the chest cage, accomplished by a group of muscles. The pectoralis major and minor are pairs of fan-shaped muscles running from the outer, forward aspects of the shoulder structures down and inward on the front of the chest to attach to the upper ribs down to the fifth or sixth. The pectoralis major overlies the pectoralis minor. When the shoulders are set (that is, held firmly in a static position by other muscle structures), contraction of the pectoralis major and minor exerts an upward pull on the upper part of the chest cage.

The serratus posterior superior muscles (a pair) lie on the back of the chest cage. They run down and outward from the upper part of the spinal column to the second to fifth ribs; and when they contract, they exert an upward pull on the chest cage.

The internal and external intercostal muscles help in both inhalation and exhalation. They run from the lower edge of each rib to the upper edge of the next rib below. The fibers of the externals run diagonally downward and toward the center of the body. Fibers of the internals lie beneath the externals and run diagonally in the opposite direction. Contraction of these two sets of muscles tends to close the spaces between the ribs, pulling the chest cage up or down depending on whether the upper or lower part of the cage is set.

Other muscles are sometimes included as muscles of inhalation, but their contributions are thought to be minor. The pectoralis (major and minor), serratus posterior superior, and the intercostals (internal and external) act together to elevate the rib cage. The ribs are curved in such manner that when the entire cage is lifted, the front of the structure moves both upward and forward. This results in enlarging the back-to-front dimension of the inside of the chest cage. As has been explained, the downward-forward movement of the diaphragm results in elongation of the inside of the chest cage on the vertical axis. These two expansions create a pressure differential between the atmosphere outside the body and that inside the lungs. A partial vacuum is created in the lungs and, since there normally is no barrier in the upper breathing tract, throat, mouth, or nose, the outside pressure then pushes air down into the lungs to equalize the pressure. Thus inhalation is accomplished.

At least two other sets of muscles are sometimes used in clavicular breathing or upper chest breathing, an inefficient and highly undesirable process. The scaleni muscles are three (sometimes four) sets of thin, ropelike structures running from the spinal column in the neck down through the sides of the neck to the first and second ribs. The paired sternocleidomastoid muscles run from the under side of the skull down through the neck to insert on the sternum and clavicles (collarbones), the horizontal bones that extend winglike outward from the sternum just above the top rib. When these muscles contract, they lift upward on the upper portion of the chest cage, sometimes causing strain and tension in the phonatory and resonance regions of the throat. Because of that strain, and because upper chest breathing produces a shallow, weak breath, it is considered inefficient and detrimental to good voice.

Exhalation

In exhalation the two major movements just described are reversed. First, the gross abdominal muscles push inward on the viscera, an action that helps push the diaphragm upward, making the chest cavity smaller in its vertical dimension. These paired gross abdominal muscles are the erect, external oblique, internal oblique, and transverse abdominals.

The erect abdominal muscles are broad, ribbonlike muscles that run from the lower part of the front of the chest cage down across the front of the abdomen to the upper portions of the pubic bone, that complex horizontal structure at the base of the abdominal cavity that forms part of the hip joints. The external oblique abdominal muscles run from the lower ribs in a broad sheath downward toward the midline of the body across the front of the abdomen. The internal oblique muscles run in the opposite direction, from the lateral portions of the abdominal framework upward and toward the midline in a broad sheath. The transverse abdominal muscles run straight across the abdomen from the sides to the midline over the entire length of the front abdominal wall.

These four pairs of muscles form the anterior wall of the abdomen and provide the primary inward and upward push on the viscera, consequently on the diaphragm, for exhalation. As the diaphragm is pushed upward, the thoracic cavity is reduced in its vertical dimension, and air pressure within the cavity is increased. The steady strength of an exhaled breath stream in deep, forced breathing for life or for speech depends upon the abdominal muscle group.

The second major movement for exhalation, lowering of the rib cage, is accomplished by gravitational pull and contraction of several muscle pairs. In addition to the erect, internal and external oblique abdominals, at least three other sets of muscles act to depress the rib cage. The two quadratus lumborum muscles lie on the back; they run from the top of the ilium (hip bone) upward and inward in a fan shape to attach to the lowest rib and the spinal column. The pair of serratus inferior muscles runs from the spinal column at the base of the back of the chest cage, upward and outward to attach to the lowest four ribs. The intercostals, which have been described previously, help to pull the ribs downward when the lower part of the chest cage is set by the quadratus lumborum and the serratus posterior inferior. The shape of the ribs tends to cause the front of the chest to move both inward and downward as the rib cage descends. This movement diminishes the back-to-front dimension of the chest cavity. The result of this action, along with the shortening of the cavity brought about by the rise of the diaphragm, is to apply pressure to the air within the lungs, forcing it to flow up and outward. Thus exhalation is achieved.

In summary, the inhalation and exhalation processes occur as illustrated in Figure 3.1 and as described below. Two major movements expand two dimensions of the chest cavity, drawing air into the lungs. The diaphragm moves downward and forward, pressing the viscera, causing the

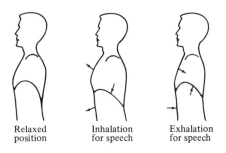

Relaxed
position

Inhalation
for speech

Exhalation
for speech

Figure 3.1. Changes in body outline and thoracic cavity volume from the relaxed position through inhalation and exhalation for speech. The arrows indicate the directions of primary forces during breathing for speech.

abdomen to bulge, and elongating the chest cavity. The chest framework is lifted upward and forward by the pectoralis major and minor, serratus posterior superior, and internal and external intercostal muscles, expanding the chest cavity horizontally. These two expansions of the chest cavity bring about a partial vacuum in the lungs and the greater pressure outside the body forces air in. Then the movements are reversed, compressing the air in the lungs and forcing it outward. The gross abdominal muscles push in on the viscera, which push up on the diaphragm, shortening the chest cavity. With the abdominals, the quadratus lumborum, serratus inferior, and intercostal muscles pull down on the chest cage. These actions assist gravity in lowering the structure and diminishing the horizontal size of the cavity.

The two major exhalation movements serve in different ways to supply breath for speech. The steady strength behind the air stream comes from the constant inward pressure of the gross abdominal muscles. That pressure is controlled and steadied, in the good speaker, by gradual relaxation of the diaphragm. The pulses accompanying speech syllables are provided by the muscles pulling down on the chest cage and probably more by the intercostals than the others in that group. The pulses are overlaid on the steady air stream brought about by the gross abdominal muscle pressure in exhalation. There will be further discussion of breathing for good speech in a later chapter, with suggested activities for improvement of breath strength and control in speech.

PHONATION

Sound is produced by air-stream constriction in the larynx (voice box), much as sound is produced at the stretched mouth of an inflated balloon. This function is secondary to the biological valve functions of the larynx: closing off the air passageway to help prevent entry of food, water, and other foreign materials into the trachea and lungs. The closure of the top of the larynx is somewhat complex, but the vocal folds come together as part of that process. When foreign matter does intrude as far as the vocal folds, they throw out the matter in an explosive action we call a cough. The larynx also serves to prevent the expulsion of air from the lungs when the chest cage must be set. For physical processes that involve muscle pressure on the outside of the body cavities, lifting, for example, it is necessary for the chest framework to be held in a rigid position. The bone structure of the chest and its muscular overlay can best maintain rigidity with a fill of air in the lungs providing internal support. The air taken by inhalation is held in the lungs by muscular contractions in the larynx, which thus help to set the chest cage. The overlaid function of the larynx is to produce sound for speech.

The structure of the larynx, commonly called the Adam's apple, is boxlike, open at the top and bottom, framed by cartilage and covered with muscle and soft tissue structures. The vocal folds themselves are shelves of muscle and soft tissue extending from the sides of the box into the air passage. We shall consider the basic nature of the cartilaginous frame, the musculature, and the soft tissue structures, so that you may better understand the functioning of the larynx in voice production.

There are four primary cartilages. The first is the cricoid, signet ring-shaped, sitting atop the trachea or windpipe. The signet portion is turned toward the back. Further details of its structure are shown in Figure 3.2. It is of hyaline cartilage, which is somewhat flexible, but rigid enough to be broken by a sudden hard blow.

The thyroid cartilage, shown in Figure 3.3, is a larger, butterfly-shaped structure with its wings spread back and around the sides of the cricoid, articulating (connecting) with the cricoid. The thyroid rocks backward and forward around that joint (Figure 3.4). It, too, is of hyaline cartilage. The top, bottom, and back of this cartilage are open.

The last two cartilages that we shall consider are a pair. The arytenoid cartilages, also hyaline, are pyramidal, seated atop the signet of the cricoid. Each is somewhat flat on the back, on the side toward the midline, on

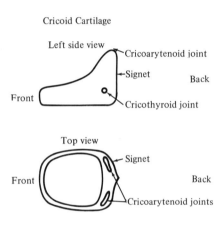

Figure 3.2. Two views of the cricoid cartilage with names of some of the important parts.

the front-sideward slope, and on the bottom. The arytenoids have points at their tops, fronts, and sides. Their joints with the cricoid are complex, making it possible for them to rotate around a vertical axis, to rock forward and backward on a horizontal axis, and to slide together toward the midline, and to slide apart, toward the sides in an outward, downward, and forward motion. This movement was described recently by von Leden and Moore. Further details of the structure and position of the arytenoid cartilages are shown in Figure 3.5.

The vocal folds (Figure 3.6) are ligament, muscle, and soft tissue structures running from the vocal processes and sideward-forward portions of the arytenoids to the inside of the angle of the thyroid. The inside edge of each fold is formed by the thin, strong vocal ligament, to which

Thyroid Cartilage

Left side view

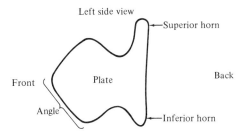

Figure 3.3. Two views of the thyroid cartilage with names of some of the important
parts.

Thyroid-Cricoid joint

Left side views

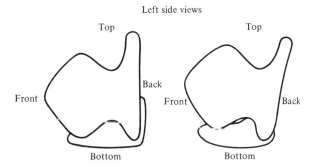

Figure 3.4. The thyroid cartilage rocks downward and
foward and upward and backward on its joint with the
cricoid cartilage at the inferior thyroid horn. In the
schematic drawings both positions are shown: the left
drawing shows the downward and forward position; the
right drawing shows the upward and backward position.

muscle and tissue structures are attached. The sliding and rotating actions of the arytenoids help to close and open the space between the vocal folds, called the glottis. Because of the complex structure of the vocalis muscles, to be described later, it is possible for us to maintain partial closure of the glottis and to achieve complex closure adjustments. Also, the folds may be held together with varying degrees of pressure, involving both the arytenoid actions and muscle adjustments in the folds themselves.

The forward and backward rocking movement of the thyroid on its

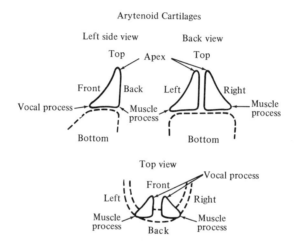

Figure 3.5. Three views of the arytenoid cartilages with names of some of the important parts.

joint with the cricoid and the backward and forward tipping of the arytenoids make possible variations in the length and tension of the vocal folds. As can be seen in Figure 3.7, when the thyroid is down and forward and the arytenoids are rocked back, the folds are elongated. When the thyroid is rocked up and back and the arytenoids are vertical, the cords are shortened.

Five sets of intrinsic (having both end attachments *within* the structure) laryngeal muscles are important in accomplishing the movements that adjust the vocal folds. They are differentiated from the extrinsic muscles of the larynx which have attachments outside the cartilaginous structure. The extrinsics are important in the positioning of the larynx. However, to attain a basic understanding of voice production, the study of the intrinsic laryngeal muscles is more important.

The two cricothyroid muscles have narrow attachments on the sides of the ring of the cricoid and fan up and back to attach to the lower edges of the side plates and inferior horns (short, fingerlike extensions) of the thyroid cartilage. Upon contraction the cricothyroid muscles pull down and forward on the thyroid, acting with extrinsic muscles to cause the thyroid to rock forward in its articulation with the cricoid, helping to elongate, thin, and tense the vocal folds. The opposite action is achieved

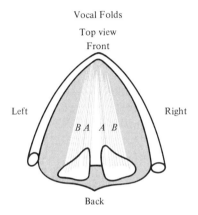

Vocal Folds

Top view

Front

Left   Right

Back

Figure 3.6. The top view of the vocal folds. The white space between the folds is the glottis. The black lines at the edges of the folds indicate the locations of the vocal ligaments. Next to the ligaments are the vocalis muscles (*A*). Next to the vocalis muscles are the thyroarytenoid muscles (*B*).

primarily by the thyroarytenoid muscles to be described later. The drawings in Figure 3.4 illustrate these positions of thyroid and cricoid.

The two lateral cricoarytenoid muscles have broad attachments to the sides of the ring of the cricoid, medial to the cricothyroid muscles and somewhat above the cricothyroid attachments. They have narrow attachments on the forward aspects of the sideward pointed projections— the muscle processes—of the arytenoids. Upon contraction the lateral cricoarytenoid muscles pull the muscle processes forward, causing the arytenoids to rotate on their vertical axes, bringing together the vocal processes (the forward projections of the arytenoids) and helping to close the glottis. The opposite action is accomplished by the posterior ·cricoarytenoid muscles. See Figure 3.7.

The two posterior cricoarytenoid muscles have broad attachments on the back of the signet of the cricoid cartilage and narrow attachments

Arytenoid Cartilage Actions

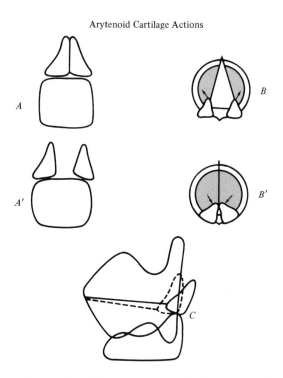

Figure 3.7. The movements of the arytenoid cartilages. Rear views of the arytenoids show them together and apart (*A* and *A'*). The rotating action is shown in the top views (*B* and *B'*). The left side view shows the back and forward tipping motion (*C*); the dotted line indicates the forward position, and the solid arytenoid outline indicates the backward position.

on the back aspects of the muscle processes of the arytenoids. Upon contraction they pull the muscle processes back, rotating the arytenoids on their vertical axes, tipping them backward, parting the vocal processes, and helping to open the glottis. The opposite action is accomplished by the lateral cricoarytenoid muscles. Figure 3.7 illustrates this movement.

The two thyroarytenoid muscles have broad attachments on the vocal processes and sideward-forward surfaces of the arytenoids and much narrower attachments on the interior of the angle of the thyroid. They constitute the basic muscle structure of the vocal folds. Upon contraction they shorten and thicken the vocal folds by rocking the thyroid up and back on its articulation with the cricoid. The action is illustrated in Figure 3.4. The opposite action is accomplished by the cricothyroid muscles described earlier and the extrinsic muscles of the larynx. The thyroarytenoid muscles also squeeze adjacent gland-containing structures to facilitate release of lubricating materials onto the vocal cords.

A part of each thyroarytenoid near the medial edge of the fold forms what is sometimes considered a separate muscle, the vocalis. The vocalis is made up of many fibers having complex attachment patterns. The fibers ·run from the thyroid cartilage to the vocal ligament, from the arytenoid cartilages to the vocal ligament, and in somewhat loop fashion from one point on the ligament to another. The intricacies of this structure of the vocalis make possible the opening or closing of parts of the glottis.

The two arytenoideus muscles attach to the backs of both arytenoid cartilages. The transverse muscle fibers run from one arytenoid to the other straight across the full width of the backs of the arytenoids from the bases to the tops. The oblique fibers crisscross from the lower portion of the back of each arytenoid to the rear of the apex of the other arytenoid, with some fibers continuing into the soft tissue structure above the apex. Upon contraction the transverse and oblique arytenoid muscles slide the arytenoids together on their articulations with the cricoid, helping to close the glottis. When these muscles relax, the arytenoids are returned to an open, rest position. These movements are shown in Figure 3.7.

Three important soft tissue structures form the interior of the larynx. In the lateral walls of the larynx above the true vocal folds there are bulges, or narrow shelves, called *false vocal folds*. The false folds are typically less prominent than the true folds and are not brought into contact with one another during normal phonation. The lining of the larynx above the false folds to the racket-shaped upper margin of the larynx is the aryepiglottic membrane.

Between the false and true folds are indentations in the side walls of the larynx called *ventricles*. They contain, in their upper portions, small duct glands which secrete the sticky mucous material that seems to help lubricate and soothe the vocal folds.

The conical tissue structure that blends the underside of vocal folds with the circular interior of the trachea is called the *elastic cone*. These structures are shown in Figure 3.8.

According to the myoelastic-aerodynamic theory, voice production

in the larynx is accomplished in the following sequence. Muscular adjustments position the thyroid cartilage to control the length and, to some
extent, the thickness and tension of the folds. At the same time the inward
sliding of the arytenoids and the muscular adjustments in the folds themselves accomplish closure of the glottis with the required pressure. The
muscular adjustments within the folds also affect their thickness and tension. During phonation the length of the folds is less than when they

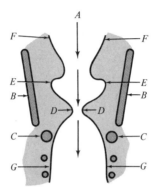

Figure 3.8. The soft tissue
structures of the larynx are
shown on this schematic
drawing of a side-to-side
section of the larynx. *A:*
The air passageway. *B:*
Thyroid cartilage. *C:* Cricoid
cartilage. *D:* True vocal
folds. *E:* Ventricles. *F:*
Aryepiglottic membrane. *G:*
Elastic cone.

are relaxed and open. Air is pushed up from the lungs through the trachea
by the breathing musculature. When the pressure below the folds overcomes the pressure with which they are held together, they open upward
and sideward. With the release of the pressure a sound wave is created
and moves up through the pharynx or throat. The elasticity of the folds
pulls them back to and through their rest position so that they may even
bulge downward into the subglottic space somewhat, though remaining
closed in the downward excursion. As soon as closure is accomplished
once more, air pressure is again built up, and the folds are forced open

in another vibration. The speed with which these vibrations occur determines the frequency of the sound, a basic factor in its pitch.

It should be noted here that another theory of vocal fold vibration,
the neurochronaxic theory, postulates that each vibration is induced by
a nerve impulse, and that each opening and closing of the glottis is accomplished by muscle action. This theory is currently advocated by Husson,
a French writer.

The myoelastic-aerodynamic theory, well supported in a recent article
by van den Berg, holds that the muscle adjustments at given frequencies
are quite constant, and that the combined action of air pressure and elasticity of the folds accomplishes the vibrations. The cartilage position changes
and muscular tension changes that occur almost constantly during vocalization bring about variation in frequency and intensity of the sound being
produced, giving intonations, inflection, and loudness variations to running
speech. Interestingly, as van den Berg notes, von Leden and Moore in
one study and Rubin in another have shown that in the absence of air
pressure beneath the cords, phonation does not occur even though nerve
supply is normal.

A series of articles by Hollien and others describes measurements
of motion pictures and X-ray still pictures of the laryngeal structures
at rest and in operation. From those studies we have gained precise knowledge of the size and manner of operation of the larynx. References will
be made to those studies in the following paragraphs.

The speed of vibration of the folds, and hence the pitch of the sound,
varies with the length, tension, and thickness of the folds. Low pitches
are produced when the folds are short, heavy, and comparatively lax;
they vibrate in a complex, almost undulating manner and as a result
of their thickness and the lack of tension of the vocal ligament and vocal
fold muscles. High pitches are produced (Hollien and Curtis) when the
folds are longer, thinner, and more tense; they vibrate in a comparatively
simple open-and-shut motion. Variations in thyroid position, arytenoid
positions, cord tension, cord thickness, and cord length produce pitch
variations from low to high. There is some evidence of a stair-step series
of cord lengths associated with pitch variation (Hollien and Moore). According to Hollien, larger larynxes produce lower voices, and smaller
larynxes, higher voices. Also, as the pitch of the vocal cord tone rises,
there is a tendency for the vocal folds to be progressively elevated (Hollien
and Curtis). Apparently it is normal for the larynx to rise with pitch,
but we must note here that this action carried to the extreme can lead
to an excessively elevated and tense larynx with a consequent "pinched"
sound and perhaps seriously distorted pitch and quality.

The cartilaginous, muscular, and membranous make-up of the individual larynx will help determine the pitch range and presumably the pitch levels most easily produced and most used. This leads to the concept of a "natural" or "optimum" pitch level or range. Like any other mechanism the vocal system probably will operate more efficiently under some conditions than others, that is, more efficiently at some pitch and loudness levels. We can identify inadequate laryngeal functioning at very low pitches and very high pitches as well as very low and very high loudness levels. However, no evidence is available that describes in any more specific way the "optimum" range of the larynx.

Loudness of the voice is strongly influenced by variations in the pressure with which the cords are closed. Firmer closure helps produce more sudden and apparently more forceful opening and closing of the glottis and greater loudness of sound. For loud sounds the folds seem to be closed a greater part of the vibration cycle than for less loud sounds.

The preceding discussions of pitch and loudness production in the larynx are oversimplified. The two are closely interrelated. Rubin says that they are so interdependent as to be almost indivisible. Harris and Weiss showed experimentally that when loudness is increased there is an involuntary rise in fundamental frequency averaging 34 percent and when loudness is decreased the fundamental is involuntarily lowered. Lieberman described the falling fundamental frequency at the end of a sentence, or other breath-group, as the result of both lowered subglottic breath pressure and the absence of increase in laryngeal tension to maintain the fundamental frequency. Apparently the balance between the vocal cord tensions and subglottic air pressure functions to effect both the speed and vigor of fold vibration. Because this is the case, voice improvement work will often include both pitch and loudness in the same drills.

The tone produced by the vocal cords is complex in the sense that it has not only a fundamental component but also a more or less complex structure of overtones because of the complicated nature of the cord vibration. The nature of the complex tone, that is, the number and strengths of harmonics (partials) present, depends on the structure of the individual's vocal cords, the exact nature of the muscle, cartilage, and soft tissue; it also depends on adjustments in the larynx at the moment of sound production. Apparently the nature of the vocal cord tone can be changed very swiftly as a person speaks. As an example, Wendahl showed that listeners could identify as little as one vibration per second variation in the fundamental of an electronically produced 100 Hz tone as "rough," a part of the disturbance in harshness. It is reasonable to suspect, that the "roughness" produced in some harsh voices is caused by very small and rapid variations in the fundamental of cord tone. The complexity of the vocal cord tone can be the source of speech problems as well as blessings.

The innervation of this intricate vocal process is achieved by a branch of the tenth, or vagus, nerve. That branch, the laryngeal nerve, is further divided into the inferior or recurrent portion, primarily concerned with muscular action, and the superior portion, concerned partly with sensory feedback and partly with muscular action.

We must add a word about the falsetto voice, as that phenomenon is often fascinating to students. Recent high-speed photography by Rubin and Hirt disclosed the thyroarytenoid muscle mass to be important in the shift or break between normal and falsetto phonation. Apparently, the cords are incapable of greater tension and length when producing their highest pitch. A sudden relaxation for the shift to falsetto results in movement of the thyroarytenoid muscle mass sideward away from the cord edges, creating very thin vibrating edges. Rubin and Hirt describe an "open chink" mechanism. The folds are not completely brought together when falsetto voice is produced in this manner. Apparently, tension adjustments in the cord edges change the pitch level. In some of their subjects "open chink" was not seen, but they found the sideward massing of the thyroarytenoid to be characteristic of falsetto voice production. In the very high falsetto sometimes an open chink with a progressive cord damping from back to front accompanies rising pitch, with the highest tone being produced by a pinpoint opening at the front of the cords. Research seems to indicate that there is considerable individual variation in the manner of falsetto voice production.

RESONANCE

Rising from the larynx into the chambers of the throat, mouth, and nose, the complex vocal cord tone is subjected to changes by resonance, that is, building up or damping of parts of the tone. You will recall from Chapter 2 that selective amplification occurs in cavities of such sizes and shapes as to reinforce certain frequencies. Damping of some parts of a complex sound occurs through absorption of sound by soft surfaces and irregular spaces or cavities not tuned to those frequencies.

Everyone is somewhat familiar with resonance systems in musical instruments. The box of a guitar is an example of a comparatively simple resonance chamber. The French horn, on the other hand, with its turns and unusual cavities, has a more complex resonance system.

Examples of resonance and damping are not difficult to find. Recall the resonant, hollow sound of an empty house; the hard, exposed surfaces reflect and build up sound. A heavily draped and carpeted room, however, has a hushed, quiet, dead sound because of absorptions by the soft surfaces. There is resonance in a soft-drink bottle when you blow across the mouth to make a tone. Afer you remove some of the liquid its tuning is changed because a larger air chamber is involved, and the tone to which it is resonant changes also.

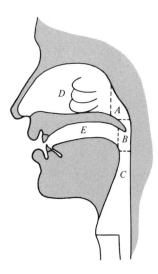

Figure 3.9. The resonators. In this schematic drawing areas labeled A, B and C are the nasopharynx, the oropharynx, and the laryngopharynx. The three make up the long tube of the pharynx. D indicates the nasal cavity, and E the oral cavity.

The human vocal resonance system is made up of irregularly shaped cavities, with a variety of hard and soft surfaces linked together in a complex manner.

The pharynx (see Figure 3.9) stands vertically behind the nose, mouth, and larynx. The pharynx is a long, tubelike resonator with soft side and rear walls which can be moved somewhat toward the center and back to rest position by muscular action. The front of the tube is irregular, made of soft tissue and muscular structures of varying shapes. The upper portions of the pharynx open into the oral and nasal cavities. The presence of adenoidal tissue and the size of such tissue compared to the size of the opening from the oral to nasal pharynx are important factors in the resonance functions of the pharynx. Sometimes adenoidal tissue obstructs the opening into the naspoharynx and nose, thereby distorting speech resonance.

The two nasal cavities lie in front of the top quarter of the pharynx. The nasal cavities are open, front and back, and are divided by a vertical bone and cartilage wall. Toward the back, the side walls are hard, with thin tissue coverings subject to swelling that can cause resonance distortion. Toward the front, the side walls are soft, with tissue and cartilage making up the structures. The presence of turbinates, bony protrusions, three on each side, makes the rear portions of the cavities irregular and narrow. Aside from changes produced by swelling or filling with discharge material, the nasal cavities are not variable resonators. It is possible, however, to shut them off partly or entirely from the resonance system through use of the mobile soft palate.

The oral cavity is the most variable of the resonance chambers. The lower jaw is moved downward to various extents to help adjust the size and shape of the oral cavity. The tongue moves to a great variety of positions to help alter the size and shape of the cavity. The lips determine the size and shape of the front opening of the oral resonator and help adjust its length. The hard, arched roof of the mouth probably acts as a reflector of sound, whereas the soft cheeks, lips, and tongue doubtless absorb sound. In size and shape and in sound-reflecting or absorbing surfaces the oral cavity is the most variable of the speech resonance chambers.

In speech the resonators act in two important ways. First, the vowels are formed by adjustments in the resonance characteristics of the oral cavity and oropharynx. The raising and lowering of the jaw effect changes in over-all oral opening, the location of the hump of the tongue divides the cavity into resonance areas, and the position and shaping of the lips control the outward opening and length of the cavity in front of the tongue hump. These adjustments create the resonance conditions for the vowels which are to be discussed further in Chapter 5. Second, voice quality is partly determined by the sizes, shapes, coupling, and tensions in the resonance system. This matter of resonance and quality will be discussed more thoroughly in Chapter 10.

Biologically, the resonators serve as tubes through which air is carried from the outside into the body, to the larynx, and on into the lungs.

The oral cavity and the pharynx are also used in chewing and swallowing food. The lower portion of the pharynx opens into the upper end of the esophagus, or food-carrying tube, as well as into the larynx and the air-carrying structures. Resonance of speech sounds is a secondary function of the nasal, oral, and pharyngeal cavities.

ARTICULATION

The production of speech sounds by alteration of the free flow of the expired air stream is called *articulation.* It is accomplished by seven articulators. Although this process is to be considered in detail in Chapter 6, we shall discuss articulation briefly here to make clear the position it takes in the total speech process.

The structures used in articulation are biologically important in breathing and eating. Their speech functions are secondary.

The opening or closing of the *vocal folds* for production of voice or for silent expulsion of the air stream is the first articulation adjustment. The only difference between some pairs of sounds lies in the voicing. When we alter the air stream to produce a voiced sound or to permit silent escape of air, we make a true articulator adjustment. Also, we sometimes make an aspirate or a breathy noise at the larynx which is characteristic of one speech sound, [h], in American English.

The opening or closing of the velopharyngeal structure is also an articulation adjustment. The *soft palate,* or velum, a muscle and tissue backward extension of the hard palate, can be moved upward and backward and can be stretched. These movements help to close the opening into the upper pharynx and nasal cavities, the nasal port. Further, the side and back walls of the pharynx are moved forward and inward to meet the soft palate in accomplishing velopharyngeal closure. Just above the level of the velum on the back wall of the pharynx, when that wall is moved forward, a small horizontal hump is formed, called Passavant's pad or cushion. The velum is raised against or near that pad to accomplish or to approximate closure with the rear wall of the pharynx.

In American speech we close or nearly close the nasal port for all vowel and consonant sounds except the nasal consonants. For the latter the nasal port is open, permitting nasal resonance, which is their distinctive feature.

The *lower jaw* may be moved downward in varying degrees toward its widest opening, providing a basic determinant of oral shape and size. Movement of the lower jaw assists also in adjustment of tongue position for the vowels and certain of the consonants.

The *tongue* position is not entirely controlled by lowering of the jaw. In spite of the limitations imposed on tongue movement by its attachment to the lower jaw, it is still the most mobile and versatile of the articulators. Because of a network of intrinsic muscles running lengthwise, crosswise, and vertically, as well as multiple extrinsic muscular attachments, the tongue can be humped, curled, grooved, pointed, flattened, and so on. It is easily brought into contact with or close to other oral structures—lips,

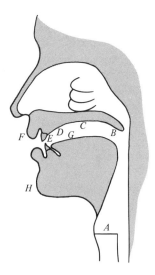

Figure 3.10. The articulators. *A:* Vocal folds. *B:* Soft palate. *C:* Hard palate. *D:* Alveolar ridge, part of the hard palate. *E:* Teeth. *F:* Lips. *G:* Tongue. *H:* Lower jaw.

teeth, hard palate, and soft palate—to achieve alterations in the free flow of the expired breath stream.

The *hard palate* and *teeth* provide rigid, immobile surfaces against which the tongue and lips move in making the constrictions and stoppages that help produce some of the speech sounds.

Finally, the *lips* provide the last possible point of alteration of the breath stream as it leaves the oral cavity. They can be, in varying degrees, rounded and protruded, narrowed and retracted, or folded back to touch the teeth or tongue. Figure 3.10 shows the articulators.

It is important for you to keep in mind that the adjustments made by the articulators are made rapidly and in complex sequences. Many small and intricate muscle structures are involved even in short, simple articulation movements. For speech processes to be carried out with the utmost efficiency, the articulation movements should not be stiff, difficult, and forced, but relaxed, smooth, and easy. That is the end toward which articulation improvement activities described in Chapter 6 are directed.

AUDITION

The fifth process involved in communication between human beings is hearing—audition. Sounds produced by the processes described above are carried through the conducting medium, usually air, to the ear of

Figure 3.11. Schematic drawing of the ear. *A:* The pinna or outer ear. *B:* The external auditory canal. *C:* The middle ear space containing the chain of small bones. *D:* The Eustachian tube leading down to the nasopharynx. *E:* The cochlea or inner ear. *F:* The auditory nerve.

the listener, where a complex system of reception is set in motion. Also, the ear of the speaker functions to receive his own speech as part of his self-monitoring, as has been pointed out.

The pinna, or external ear, has only little value as a sound concentrator or localizer. The outer canal, or meatus, conducts the air-borne sound to the eardrum at its inner end. That membrane is set into vibration at the same frequency as the communicated sound. Changes in amplitude of the incident sound are reflected in changes in the amplitude of vibration of the drumhead. In the *middle ear,* behind the drum, the sound, as mechanical vibration, is carried across an air space by a chain of three tiny bones, the ossicles. At the inner end of that chain the sound goes into the inner ear; it is introduced into a closed fluid system contained in the cochlea, a coiled space enclosed in bone. The cochlea contains the basilar membrane, which vibrates selectively along its length to frequencies introduced into the fluid surrounding it. Vibrations of that membrane and its superstructure, the Organ of Corti, stimulate tiny endings of nerves which conduct the message to the brain. The manner of reception of the various dimensions of the sound is complex and not thoroughly understood. The *eighth cranial* nerve, or auditory nerve, provides a major trunk or pathway to the brain.

Summary

The entire human communication system achieves an amazing and wonderful operation. The activity involved in communication of the single syllable "top" is exhausting when considered in sequence. First, the need to communicate the syllable arises in the brain, from the circumstances reported by its peripheral information centers and its stored memories. The efferent nerve fibers carry impulses to set in motion the following events. The diaphragm is lowered and the chest cage is lifted, drawing in air. Then the abdomen is pulled inward and the diaphragm is relaxed progressively. At the same time the chest is pulled downward. These movements, employing for the most part different muscle groups from those used for inhalation, force air out of the lungs through the larynx. (The vocal cords are held open but ready for closure after the first sound, the voiceless [t], is exploded. For the vowel sound, they will be drawn together by actions of the intrinsic muscles of the larynx, to just the required length, tension, and thickness and with just the required firmness of closure to produce the desired frequency and intensity. The air stream, silent at first, then voiced, will rise through the pharynx.) The soft palate and walls of the pharynx are pulled into place to close off the nasal opening. The tongue tip and edges rise to close against the hard palate or the upper teeth all around the inside of the upper jaw as the lower jaw is held in a slightly open position. The voiceless air stream is blocked in the mouth behind the tongue. To explode the [t] and move to the next sound, the lower jaw is dropped open and the tongue is relaxed and lowered quickly. The tongue moves to the low, back-humped position for the vowel, just as the now voiced air stream comes through the oral cavity. After a brief part of a second, the voice is stopped by the opening and relaxing of the vocal folds, and a silent air stream is again sent through

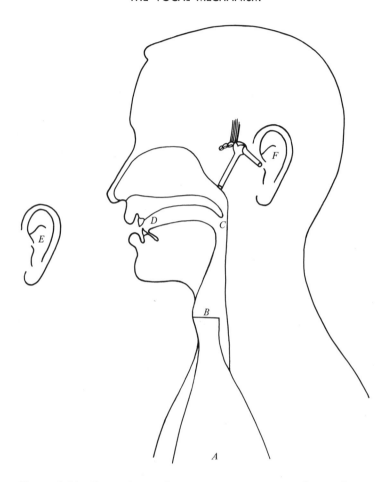

Figure 3.12. The entire oral communication system. *A:* The lungs provide the air supply. *B:* Sound is formed at the vocal folds. *C:* The sound is resonated through the throat and cavities of the head. *D:* Articulation is achieved mostly in the oral cavity. *E:* The ear of the listener receives the sound. *F:* The ear of the speaker returns auditory feedback to the brain.

the pharynx and oral cavity. The lips now must be brought together and the lower jaw must be brought up to an almost closed position; the tongue is relaxed in the bottom of the mouth. After a brief stoppage of air behind the lips, the lower jaw must be dropped slightly and the lips opened quickly to permit the formation of a plosive puff of air, [p]. The structures must then relax and return to their rest positions. During this process the nervous system has been constantly sending kinesthetic, tactile, and auditory messages to the brain, reporting on the progress of the activities, watching for and guarding against erroneous interpretation and erroneous production of the original intent, constantly comparing the result with the mental picture of the desired syllable.

Can anyone contemplate this highly condensed summary of a short, simple speech activity, "top," multiply it by the number of times such sequences are necessary to produce a mere ten-minute conversation, and not be awed by the ingenuity and efficiency of our communication mechanisms?

You will work to expand your understanding and use of this communication system in the remainder of this course. Do not lose sight of the place in the total vocal pattern of the small part of that pattern on which you are working at a particular time. Your understanding of the *parts* of the vocal process will enhance your understanding and use of the entire mechanism; but, you must not become so involved in controlling the *parts* that you forget that your goal is integration of the parts into a smooth, efficient, total speech-producing operation.

STUDENT PROJECTS

CONTENT ASSIGNMENT

A. Define each of these terms:

cortex	ilium	falsetto
kinesthetic	trachea	resonate
sternum	larynx	velum
diaphragm	set (chest cage)	pinna
clavicle	glottis	meatus
pubic bone	ventricles	cochlea
viscera	cartilage	Organ of Corti

B. Sketch each of the cartilages of the larynx and label all the parts you can.

C. 1. Reproduce Figure 3.9 and designate the resonance cavities on it with colored pencils.

   2. List the articulators and label them on the sketch you made for question C. 1.

D. Do a schematic drawing of the outer, middle, and inner ears. Label and name the parts.

E. Write as indicated:

1. List the six phases of the human oral communication process and tell briefly what happens in each.
2. List the breathing muscles described in the text, their attachments, and their effects when they contract.
3. List the muscles of the larynx, their attachments, and their actions.
4. Define articulation.
5. Describe the body movements that accomplish inhalation and exhalation.
6. How is voice produced in the larynx?
7. How does laryngeal adjustment help produce changes in voice loudness and pitch?
8. How are vowels formed? Would you say they are resonance or articulation phenomena, or both?
9. How are the velum and adenoidal tissue alike in their effect on resonance?
10. How is the diaphragm used in breathing for speech?
11. What is wrong with "upper chest" breathing for speech?
12. How is falsetto voice produced?
13. How do the myoelastic-aerodynamic and the neurochronaxic theories of phonation differ?
14. Which consonant sounds require nasal resonance for their distinctive features?
15. Describe the actions of all the speech structures in producing a short word, "pan" for example.

RECOMMENDED READINGS

Berg, J. van den. Myoelastic-aerodynamic theory of voice production. *J. Speech and Hearing Research,* **1,** 1958, 227–243.

———, Physiological basis of language. *Logos.* **4,** 1961, 56–66.

Bloomer, H. A roentgenographic study of the mechanics of respiration. *Speech Monogr.,* **3,** 1936, 118–124.

Dedo, H., and Dunker, E. Husson's theory. *Arch. of Otolaryngology,* **85,** 1967, 503–513.

Faaborg-Anderson, K. , Yanagihara, N., and Leden, H. von. Vocal pitch and intensity regulation. *Arch. of Otolaryngology,* **85,** 1967, 448–454.

Gray, G. W., and Wise, C. M. *Bases of speech.* (Rev. ed.) New York: Harper, 1959, Chap. 3.

Harris, C. and Weiss, M. Effects of speaking conditions on pitch. *J. Acoustical Society of America,* **36,** 1964, 933–936.

Hollien, H. Some laryngeal correlates of vocal pitch. *J. Speech and Hearing Research,* **3,** 1960, 52–58.

————, Vocal pitch variation related to changes in vocal fold length. *J. Speech and Hearing Research,* **3,** 1960, 150–156.

————, and Curtis, J. F. A laminagraphic study of vocal pitch. *J. Speech and Hearing Research,* **3,** 1960, 361–371.

————, Elevation and tilting of the vocal folds as a function of vocal pitch. *Folia Phoniatrica,* **14,** 1962, 23–36.

————, and Moore, G. P. Measurements of the vocal folds during changes in pitch. *J. Speech and Hearing Research,* **3,** 1960, 157–165.

Hoshiko, M. Sequence of action of breathing muscles during speech. *J. Speech and Hearing Research,* **3,** 1960, 291–297.

Husson, R. *Physiologie de la Phonation.* Paris: Masson et Cie., 1962.

Leden, H. von. The mechanism of phonation. *Arch. of Otolaryngology,* **74,** 1961, 660–676.

———— and Moore, G. P. Mechanics of the cricoarytenoid joint. *Asha,* **3,** No. 2, 1961, 59–61.

Lieberman, P. *Intonation, Perception and Language.* M.I.T. Research Monograph No. 38. Cambridge, Mass.: M.I.T. Press, 1967.

Rubin, H. Experimental studies on vocal pitch and intensity in phonation. *Laryngoscope,* **73,** 1963, 973–1015.

————. The neurochronaxic theory of voice production–a refutation. *A.M.A. Arch. of Otolaryngology,* **71,** 1960, 913–920.

————, and Hirt, C. The falsetto. A high-speed cinematographic study. *Laryngoscope,* **70,** 1960, 1305–1324.

Stetson, R., and Hudgins, C. V. Functions of the breathing movements in the mechanism of speech. *Arch. Neerlandaises de Phonétique Expérimentale,* **5,** 1930, 1–30.

Temple, W. J. The mechanism of human speech. In O'Neill, J. M. (ed.) *Foundations of speech.* Englewood Cliffs, N.J.: Prentice-Hall, 1946, Chap. 6.

Tiffin, J., Saetveit, J., and Snidecor, J. C. An approach to the analysis of vibration of the vocal cords. *Quart. J. Speech,* **24,** 1938, 1–11.

Wendahl, R. Laryngeal analog synthesis of harsh voice quality. *Folia Phoniatrica,* **15,** 1963, 241–250.

CHAPTER
4

THE
BREATH
STREAM

Convinced that speaking isn't simple? Looks it—but it's not. Not if done well. So now we talk about breathing. Routine—breathing. But we can help you do it better—for speech anyway.

It's different from breathing just to live. Sure, same mechanisms and basically the same body movements. Change the old carbon dioxide for new oxygen. But when the mechanism takes on a second function, speech, the system changes and the job grows rougher.

First, there is a time difference. The ratio of inhalation time to exhalation time is about one-to-one in relaxed life breathing. In breathing for speech the ratio averages about one-to-seven. That is, you take breath in more quickly and sustain the exhalation longer when speaking than when breathing passively.

There is also a control difference. In most circumstances respiration is involuntary, unconsciously controlled. It goes on night and day without your having to give thought to raising and lowering the rib cage or to moving the diaphragm and the gross abdominal muscles. If an emergency arises and you need to alter the process to take in more oxygen, or to space your inhalations differently, you can assume conscious control of the breathing process. Swimming is an example of activities requiring spacing of inhalations. You can use the same control in speaking situations. You can adjust the rate, depth, and spacing of inhalations and rate and manner of exhalations to the needs of the speech materials at hand as long as your body's continuous need for fresh oxygen is satisfied. Of course, when the need is difficult to satisfy, as in speech just after a long race, it becomes necessary for you to break your sentences into appropriate short groups which will allow you both to breathe and to talk. When there is no unusual breathing demand, your phrasing can be much longer and can be adjusted to the meaning of the material. Although it sounds simple, establishing good speech breathing habits requires concentration and practice from some people.

Two definitions will be especially helpful in our discussion of the nature of good speech breathing. *Vital capacity* is the amount of air that can be expired from the lungs after the fullest possible inhalation; it averages about 3700 c.c. in adult males, somewhat less in females. *Tidal air* is that quantity moved in and out during silent, life breathing; it averages 500 c.c. in adult males (about a pint) and somewhat less in females. There are numerous other technical terms used with respect to breathing, but these are the two with which we shall be most concerned.

SOME COMMON MISCONCEPTIONS

In the heyday of the Greek orators, and ever since, there has been concern about the breathing process and its contribution to the final vocal effect. Unfortunately, many misconceptions have developed that have led to faulty procedures by some students in their efforts to improve speech habits. We shall discuss some of them briefly here in relation to research findings that shed light on their validity. Most of the investigations mentioned in the next three paragraphs were done at Louisiana State University under the direction of Giles W. Gray.

It was once believed that the person with the largest vital capacity, who could take and hold the largest amount of air, was certain to have an advantage in producing good speech. However, Barnes found no significant relationship between vital capacity and ability in oral reading, and Wiksell found no relationship between vital capacity and intensity of isolated vowels.

It once seemed reasonable to believe that the person who habitually took large inhalations, regardless of his actual capacity, would surely be a good speaker. In experimental work by Sallee, depth of inhalation was found to bear no relation to audibility; Idol found no measurable aspect of casual breathing or breathing for phonation, including depth of inhalation, to be related to a group of voice characteristics necessary for effective speech. Recently Hoshiko and Blockcolsky found that most of their subjects did breathe more deeply when anticipating phonation of a vowel or a sentence than they breathed for life purposes only. This is not in conflict with the findings of Sallee and Idol since Hoshiko and Blockcolsky did not concern themselves with evaluation of the speech output of their subjects as did the other two researchers. Hoshiko and Blockcolsky's work does cause us some concern about a speaker's ability to control his intake so as to breathe a bit more deeply for speech than for life. This concern for control will be reflected in exercises later in this chapter. Their research does not support the idea initially expressed in this paragraph, that deeper breathing will result in better speech.

In past years, much work was done to help students to breathe with expansion in a particular part of the torso. Some teachers held abdominal breathing to be best, some medial, some thoracic; others recommended a combination of breathing movements. In experiments testing efficiency of chest breathing (measured just below the armpits), medial breathing (measured just below the lowest ribs), and abdominal breathing (measured at midabdomen), the following conclusions were reached. There is no loudness advantage in one of the types of breathing (Wiksell); there is no audibility advantage in one of the types of breathing (Sallee); there are no relationships between a number of attributes of good speech and area of body expansion in breathing (Gray).

GOOD BREATHING FOR SPEECH

All the conclusions just discussed are negative. What positive information can we give you?

First, let us call your attention to the research of Stetson and Hudgins. With pneumatic devices they observed the timing patterns of abdominal and thoracic movements during speech. For each syllable in slow speech, below two syllables per second, they found definite movement in both areas, with the abdominal movement preceding the thoracic pulse. At rates faster than two syllables per second they found the abdominal pressure to continue over spans of several syllables with a chest pulse still present for each syllable.

Hoshiko, using electromyographic techniques, found results somewhat at variance with Stetson's description of the roles of individual muscles in initiating and terminating syllables. However, he confirmed Stetson's findings with respect to general patterns of respiration, including the absence of abdominal pulses in connected speech.

From these studies it is possible to conclude that both abdominal and thoracic pressures are needed for speech and that the gross, comparatively continuous pressures for strong speech exhalations come from the abdominal muscles, with syllabic pulses being supplied by the chest and abdominal muscles acting together.

Although the chest muscles are difficult to bring under conscious control, it is quite possible to learn to depend on abdominal strength for exhalation in speech. This is sometimes misleadingly referred to as "diaphragmatic support of tone." It is true that when the diaphragm is in the lowered position, having contracted its fringe of muscle and flattened its dome shape, relaxation of the diaphragm muscle fibers and the natural elasticity of the structure will cause it to move upward, assuming the dome-shaped position. Clearly, however, the role of the diaphragm in this aspect of exhalation is passive, not active. As reported in the preceding chapter, the strength for exhalation is supplied by the pressure of the gross abdominal muscles on the viscera, which in turn push upward on the diaphragm, and by the movements of the internal and external intercostals and other muscles which pull downward on the chest cage. The term "diaphragmatic breathing" is accurately applied only to the inhalation phase of respiration for speech. One might more accurately refer to the normal process of breathing for speech as "abdominal breathing" since that area is influenced both by the downward movement of the diaphragm and by the inward pressure for exhalation by the gross abdominal muscles.

The diaphragm is used in exhalation in a passive manner. Its gradual relaxation helps to control the force of the abdominal muscles preventing sudden and wasteful expulsion of air. Through use of a fluoroscopic technique Huyck and Allen compared diaphragmatic movements during speech in good and poor speakers. They found that poor speakers have jerky, irregular upward movements of the diaphragm in exhalation, whereas good speakers have slow, steady movements of the diaphragm. Regardless of your habitual body expansion pattern in breathing, you are well advised, first, to develop the ability to use the gross abdominal muscles to give your expired breath stream strength and, second, to learn to keep that movement regular and smooth by steady abdominal pressure and controlled relaxation of the diaphragm.

Our third positive suggestion arises from the observation that many speakers fail to make maximum use of expiration because they exhale part of the air supply before beginning to talk. That part of the exhalation does no work; it claims time and energy for its in-and-out movement and contributes nothing to the speech process. In the recent study previously cited, Hoshiko and Blockcolsky reported that prespeech tidal volume in their subjects was just above 50 percent of vital capacity whereas the volume of air in the lungs at the moment of initiation of phonation was about 44 percent. This emphasizes our statement that speakers fail to utilize their inhaled air efficiently. You should develop the habitual use of all your inhaled air by beginning speech at the top of your inhalation, so to speak, thereby increasing the amount of speech possible on a breath and making fewer inhalations do the job. Note that no recommendation for increased depth of inhalation is made. Our experience has been that fewer than one student in twenty must rise at dawn, face an open window, and engage in the "one-two, one-two, one-two" type of exercise recommended by some authorities. If it is found in the work you do in the speech laboratory that you have a genuine need for physical education of your respiratory musculature, you may depend on your instructor to make this fact known to you and to advise you accordingly.

There is general agreement among researchers and textbook writers that upper chest or clavicular breathing is inefficient and undesirable for speech. Hence our fourth suggestion is that you avoid development of such breathing habits. In the clavicular type of breathing, the scaleni and sternocleidomastoid muscles which run downward from the under side of the skull and the neck vertebrae through the neck, pull up on the upper ribs, elevating the upper portion of the chest cage as described in Chapter 3. Typically the movement is too slight to supply an adequate amount of air, and the speaker rapidly runs out of power; nor is there enough strength behind the expired breath stream for the average speech task. In addition, the tensing of the neck muscles is likely to cause similar tensions in the phonatory and resonance areas, resulting in inefficient and often unpleasant voice production. Awareness of the dangers of such breathing techniques should help the student avoid those complications. But if clavicular breathing is present, we recommend that you eradicate it. Kinesthetic feedback—awareness of muscle movement—will be useful in these efforts.

In summary, good breathing for speech requires, primarily, use of the abdomen for the strength of exhalation, control, and coordination of the abdominal and chest movements, plus efficient speech use of all the inspired air. Notice we do not say that the greatest *amount* of movement must be in the abdominal area; we are speaking of the strength of pressure. You can feel equally assured of an adequate breath supply if the lower chest region provides the greatest amount of expansion-contraction in your breathing cycle. These good speech breathing movements and coordinations do not always come easily. You must develop the ability to judge your respiration needs for speech and to adjust, habitually, your inhalations and steady, coordinated exhalations to fit those needs.

You must learn to group words and phrases naturally and meaningfully, to let your breathing be controlled automatically by speech needs. At first it may be anything but automatic; in fact, you may need to force your control of breathing to fit speech pauses. However, as you practice you should find controlled respiration becoming easier and more natural.

In considering length of phrases to use, you might be guided, especially in the practice drills later on in this chapter, by the findings of Snidecor. Five superior readers recorded two readings and did an impromptu speech for analysis. Snidecor found that they averaged 12.5 words per breath in reading and 10.6 words per breath in impromptu speaking. In both reading and speaking the subjects grouped phrase lengths at about 7 to 9 words per breath and about 14 words per breath. Snidecor concluded that 7 to 14 words per group, with occasional larger groups, should be recommended to students. One of his subjects went as high as 28 words per breath.

Extensive and detailed study of grouping of grammatical units and placing of pauses for the best effect in speech is left to other courses, those in interpretive reading and public speaking. However, you won't be taught absolute rules in such classes, because there are many factors that influence phrasing. For example, the word-grouping you do in speaking probably will not duplicate your grouping in reading aloud. In examining the spoken and read performances of the same materials by superior speakers, Snidecor found that phrase limits appeared at different places in the identically worded materials. In the readings, phrases tended to be longer than in the speeches. Individual choice also is one of the important factors in placement of pauses, lending personality to speech performances. Rules governing grouping—placement of pauses—are by no means absolute.

Nevertheless, we can give you a few tips that may be helpful:

1. Periods and semicolons almost always indicate natural places for pauses; commas sometimes do but not always; a pair of commas may merely indicate a parenthetic idea requiring pitch, loudness, or rate changes without breath pauses.

2. Syntactical units usually belong together. For example, the subject and its modifiers, phrases, and clauses usually should not be split up by pauses.

3. Periods of silence for emphasis or to indicate doubt or emotion will provide time for inhalations.

4. As we reported, Snidecor found phrase lengths grouped at 7 to 9 words and at 14 words per phrase. Phrases of from 7 to 14 words would seem best for practice.

You will learn other guiding principles in other classes, but perhaps these will suffice for now.

DEVELOPING BREATHING SKILLS IN THE SPEECH LABORATORY

Instrumentation

Two common laboratory instruments used in measuring and recording factors of breathing will be of interest and perhaps of use to you in improving breathing habits. If such instruments are available, doubtless your instructor will demonstrate and explain their uses. If they are not available, you may be able to improvise similar equipment by ingenious use of whatever is at hand. At the very least, careful observations of breathing movements will acquaint you with your own and your classmates' patterns of respiration.

The *wet spirometer* is used to measure air volumes. It resembles one bucket turned upside down in another, the lower being partially filled with water. The subject breathes air through a tube into the enclosed space beneath the overturned bucket, causing it to rise, with the assistance of a counterweight system. Measurements in cubic centimeters are indicated by a pointer on a linear scale. This device was used in many of the studies previously cited on depth of breathing for various types of speech compared with depth of breathing for life.

The *pneumograph* is an instrument that responds to bodily expansion and contraction during breathing. Expansible tubes—parts of closed air systems—are fastened around the chest, midtrunk, and abdomen. As the body expands in breathing, the air pressure is changed in the tubes by their expansion and contraction. Each is connected to a small bellows that controls the position of a recording pen or stylus. These elements comprise a *polygraph recording system* by which graphic representations of body movements are made.

Activities for improving breathing for speech

The following exercises are designed to develop control, efficiency, and adaptability of breathing for speech.

1. If you have a wet spirometer available, you may find it interesting to measure your vital capacity. It holds little importance in terms of your speech ability, except that, as previously noted, extreme lack of air volume could cause speech difficulties. Inhale as deeply as possible and exhale all the air you can into the input tube of the spirometer. The volume of air indicated on the spirometer scale is your vital capacity. Repeat, twice more. Compare the average of your readings with the average vital capacity measurements of your classmates. Consult your instructor if your capacity is very low.

2. It may also be interesting to you to observe your areas of trunk expansion as you breathe silently and for speech. If you have a pneumo-graph-polygraph, use it to measure and compare expansions in the three areas. If this instrument is not available, stand sidewise before a long mirror and observe bodily movements during silent and speech breathing. You may need a partner to help by observing for you and recording observations.

3. To concentrate your attention on the use of abdominal muscles for strong, controlled exhalation, place your right hand on your abdomen, or just below your breast bone, your left hand on your chest; say "ah!" in a quick staccato fashion about ten times, pressing in steadily with your right hand. Repeat the exercise, letting the abdominal muscles alone do the pushing inward and letting your right hand merely follow and feel the inward movement.

4. The following procedure will help you build abdominal muscle control. Take a deep breath and produce a series of vowel sounds, "ah," or "o," or "ae," three seconds long separated by three second intervals, on a single breath. When you are holding between phonations, keep the air stream in control with the breathing muscles, not by closing the glottal valve or the mouth. Holding loudness as constant as possible see if you can increase the number of vowel phonations you can achieve per breath over five trials. Your instructor may want to record and compare class members' individual numbers of phonations for five trials, averages for five trials and the average increase in the class from trial one to trial five.

5. Say a series of slow syllables—"ha, ha, ha . . ."—starting and stopping them by starting and stopping the inward movement of the abdominal muscles and downward movement of the rib cage. Be careful not to use the laryngeal valve to start and stop the air stream—use the abdominal muscles. Repetition of this exercise will concentrate your attention on controlled pressure from the abdominal area.

6. Produce a firm "ah" sound after taking a full breath, maintaining

it as long as you can sustain clear tone. Record the time. Repeat four times, emphasizing a slow, steady pressure from the abdomen; record the time. Perhaps your instructor will put the times of all the class members on the chalkboard, so that you can compare your breath control with that of your classmates. Of course, phonation efficiency is also involved here; you may need work on that later. If you repeat this drill frequently, striving to attain longer and longer production of the vowel, you will increase control of the muscles of exhalation.

7. After you have enough control of exhalation to prolong an "ah" to about twenty-five seconds or more, practice estimating depth of breath and controlling expiration. Set yourself a time goal; for example, begin with ten seconds. Take a breath deep enough to make an "ah" at medium loudness for that length of time. The object is to have your breath supply and the time run out at exactly the same time. You may need to adjust the way you make the "ah" to release more or less air as you approach the time limit. Notice how the loudness of your tone will almost automatically change; notice also that pitch will often shift as you change the rate and strength of air flow. Try this control exercise for each five-second interval from ten to your longest timed "ah," ten seconds, fifteen seconds, twenty seconds, and so on.

8. The control of exhalation must be coupled with adjustment of breathing to speech needs. As we pointed out earlier, you must learn to group phrases and words naturally and meaningfully; let your breathing for speech be controlled by phrasing. Following is a short paragraph with slanted lines indicating what we believe to be natural grouping for meaning. Read it aloud, taking breaths only at those lines.

The average college student,/ although presumed to be primarily devoted to academic matters,/ is beset by a variety of tempting, sometimes enchanting, alternatives./ The social life of an energetic, young adult holds great promise;/ clubs and special-interest groups lure many;/ unassigned reading often seems more enticing than that required;/ and it is considered downright disloyal, by some students, to miss major sporting events./ Sometimes it seems a wonder/ that books get any attention at all;/ but they do.

To indicate the nature of awkward phrasing read it again as indicated below:

The average college student, although presumed/ to be primarily interested in/ academic matters, is beset by a variety of/ tempting, sometimes enchanting, alternatives. The social life of an energetic, young adult/ holds great promise; clubs and special/-interest groups lure many; unassigned reading often seems/ more enticing than that required; and it is considered/ downright disloyal, by some students, to miss major sporting events. Sometimes it seems/ a wonder that books get any attention at all; but they do.

Notice that in this case the awkward sound was achieved by intentionally awkward grouping. It is also possible to phrase awkwardly without intent because of breathing needs. You must adjust your breathing control to the demands of proper grouping in the material at hand rather than let the breathing dictate awkward phrasing.

Phrase the following passage for the best results in communicating its meaning:

No college student, no matter how devoted to his academic pursuits, can afford to ignore the significant social, economic, and political movements of his day. Strong movements are usually born of vital and demanding needs. Sometimes the first signs of change are not the best guides to permanent solutions, but insofar as they point to problems and needs, signs of change must be recognized and dealt with by serious citizens. The tendency of the scholar to isolate himself from the real events of his time has been recognized since medieval days; however, today's scholar must be aware that wisdom is a human trait that can exist only in human environments. The false security of isolation and blindness to new ideas and movements must be exchanged for the creative development of reasoned answers to real problems, answers developed by wise people.

9. Probably it would be helpful for you to observe your own phrasing in impromptu speaking. Let a classmate pick a subject at random, and you tape-record a one- to two-minute completely unprepared discussion of the topic. Play it back and observe the phrasing. How many obviously poorly placed pauses can you find? How many well-placed pauses? Exchange tapes with your classmates and give your ear practice identifying both good and poor phrasing. Did you do as well as the other students whose tapes you heard? Better? Did you hear a perfectly phrased speech? We suspect you did not.

Count the number of words you used in each breath group; find the average and compare it to the average used by Snidecor's superior speakers as reported on page 67.

10. Now write a six- to eight-sentence comment on the topic you used in the last activity. Mark it carefully with slanted lines for phrasing.

Record it and compare it on playback with the impromptu delivery. Are you convinced you can improve your phrasing with effort?

11. From a book of speeches or a magazine of current speeches, copy a 75- to 100-word passage and mark it with black slant lines for proper phrasing, then with red for awkward phrasing. For the "good example" recall the suggestions we gave you earlier on grouping. Watch punctuation, syntactical units, and emphatic silences for hints; keep most of your phrases about 7 to 14 words long. Practice reading it with both good and poor phrasing and remember to begin speaking at the top of your inhalation. Breathe only during marked pauses. You are not attempting here to determine what is or is not the best phrasing in speech. Instead, you are learning to adjust breathing to the demands of speech materials as phrased; as we have said, in other speech classes many of you will work long and hard to learn the characteristics of grouping and phrasing for effective delivery. By that time, your breath control must be so habitually good that it is a secondary concern.

12. Following is a typical piece of news such as you probably hear daily on radio and television. Mark it for meaningful phrasing and practice it aloud. You will probably find some unexpectedly awkward phrasing. Correct the marking. Read it again, remembering to give it vitality and interest.

State legislators called a recess after today's second meeting of the special session and left the capitol until next Tuesday afternoon. Lawmakers left behind them little hope for an early solution to the reapportionment problem. Other measures on the governor's call for the session appear to be in for tough sledding, too. Democrats introduced the first proposed map for redistricting at today's meeting. It's a plan they called a bi-partisan agreement. It would combine two Democratic districts in Centerville and throw a Republican and Democrat into one district upstate. Republicans have other ideas, however. In a move that apparently scuttles the possibility of a quick agreement, the GOP set up a sixteen-man committee to draw up their proposal for apportioning the congressional delegation. Rebelling house Republicans decided to set up the committee yesterday at a caucus and triggered cancellation of a scheduled top-level Democrat-Republican meeting later in the day at which the whole problem was to be aired.[1]

[1] From a newscast on WCIA, Champaign, Illinois, by permission from Midwest Television, Inc.

Try rephrasing the material into extraordinarily long word groups. Are you able to adjust your breathing to such demands? If not, practice reading it that way until you can command breath supply for the needs of the material. Remember to start speaking at the top of your breath intake.

Count the number of words you used in each breath group, find the average and compare it to the average used in reading by Snidecor's superior speakers as reported on page 67. Your groups should be longer than those you used in speaking in exercise 9.

13. Read the following paragraph from a typical newspaper story. Notice the long phrases, the long sentences. The material was written to be read silently. Reading such material aloud gives you an opportunity to practice control for long word groups. Read it, first, purposely expiring about half your breath just after inhalation before beginning each phrase. Notice the struggle near the end of the phrase. You probably will have difficulty with pitch and loudness control and perhaps will feel great strain as you force your voice to the end of your breath.

James P. Wellington, district director of internal revenue reminded taxpayers this morning that midnight tomorrow is the deadline for filing federal income tax returns./

April fifteen fell on Saturday this year giving taxpayers two extra days in which to prepare returns./ However, by twelve-oh-one A.M. Tuesday all reports must be filed./

Assistance in filing returns may be obtained between eight-thirty A.M. and four-thirty P.M. tomorrow by calling PO seven-eight-four-one-three and asking for taxpayers' assistance/ or by going to the Taxpayers' Assistance Office in the downtown Marketing Building at fourteen-twelve West Lincoln Street.

The deadline for filing the new state income tax returns was last night at twelve o'clock; however, late returns may be filed in the next two weeks with minimum penalties.

Now read it again, being careful to begin phonation at the top of your breath. Conserve power; do not waste air by making a breathy or unnecessarily loud voice. Can you detect a difference in the greater ease with which you complete phrases and the continued efficiency of voice to the ends of phrases? Repeat the contrasting performances.

In the *Student Projects* at the end of this chapter you will find a description of a performance task which requires putting to use the skills you have been studying. If your class undertakes the performance, record your judgments. Perhaps your instructor will make his written judgment and those of your fellow students available to you. From these you would learn how others appraise your ability to relate respiratory function to communication requirements.

STUDENT PROJECTS

CONTENTS ASSIGNMENT

Write answers to the following questions about the text:
 1. How does breathing for speech differ from life breathing?
 2. What are three disproved but commonly held misconceptions regarding breathing for speech?
 3. What are three positive suggestions for developing good breathing for speech?
 4. What is the one highly undesirable type of breathing for speech? Why?
 5. Define "vital capacity" and "tidal air."
 6. How do abdominal and thoracic muscles cooperate in exhalation for speech?
 7. Where does the greatest strength of exhalation for speech come from?
 8. List four hints for good phrasing for speech.
 9. Which of the instruments discussed measure body movement and which measure air volumes?
 10. What is wrong with the term "diaphragmatic support" of vocal tone?
 11. Why did the findings of Hoshiko and Blockcolsky relate to the earlier Sallee and Idol findings?
 12. Can one say that very deep breathing will produce better speech?
 13. What is the relationship between depth of breathing for speech and for life?
 14. Must the "top of your inhalation" for speech correspond with the largest possible inhalation you can achieve?

15. Where is the inhalation level for speech likely to fall compared to the level totally achievable (vital capacity)?
16. What breathing skills can be improved that will help efficiency of breathing for speech?
17. How are the purposes of exercises one through seven related to the purposes of exercises eight through thirteen?
18. Identify Gray, Idol, Hoshiko and Blockcolsky, Huyck and Allen.
19. If a student found himself continually running out of air during a speech performance, which drills would you suggest he review and practice frequently?
20. Describe the action of the diaphragm in breathing for speech.

PERFORMANCE ASSIGNMENTS

A. Select a one- to two-minute speech by a single character from a modern play of your choice. Mark it for meaningful and expressive phrasing. Practice it carefully, giving special attention to good breath control, and read it before the class. Hand your instructor a brief description of your material; include author, title, and a summary of the contents. A student can learn by careful listening. Each student may evaluate the performances of all the other students with respect to breath use, breath strength, breath control, and phrasing. An exchange of evaluations or a discussion of class evaluations after each performance would be useful.

B. If possible, repeat the speech performed in the assignment above by changing radically the interpretation you give it. Speed it up or slow it down, make it more or less intense, change the mood, change the pitch and loudness of your voice. Mark your material with red slash marks to indicate the *new* pauses, the *new* natural breath groups. Notice that your ability to change the way you use your breathing mechanism (and the rest of the vocal apparatus) will help you adapt to the new interpretation. Perhaps your instructor will have time for each class member to do this performance as well as the first for the listening, evaluation, and discussion experience of the class. If not, perhaps there will be time for three or four members to do the performance with two different versions of the same speech to emphasize how breath control varies when vocal interpretation varies.

RECOMMENDED READINGS

Barnes, J. Vital capacity and ability in oral reading. *Quart. J. Speech Educ.*, **12,** 1926, 176–182.

Gray, G. W. Regional predominance in respiration in relation to certain aspects of voice. *Louisiana State University Studies,* No. 27. Baton Rouge: Louisiana State University Press, 1936, 59–78.

———, (ed.) *Studies in experimental phonetics: Louisiana State University Studies,* No. 27. Baton Rouge: Louisiana State University Press, 1936.

———, and Wise, C. M. *The bases of speech.* (Rev. ed.) New York: Harper, 1959.

Hoshiko, M. Sequence of action of breathing muscles during speech. *J. Speech and Hearing Research,* **3,** 1960, 291–297.

Hoshiko, M., and Blockcolsky, V. Respirometric study of lung function during utterance of varying speech material. *Speech Monogr.,* **34,** 1967, 74–79.

Huyck, E., and Allen, K. Diaphragmatic action of good and poor speaking voices. *Speech Monogr.,* **4,** 1937, 101–109.

Idol, H. A statistical study of respiration in relation to speech characteristics. In *Louisiana State University Studies,* No. 27. Baton Rouge: Louisiana State University Press, 1936, 79–98.

Sallee, W. H. An objective study of respiration in relation to audibility in connected speech. In *Louisiana State University Studies,* No. 27. Baton Rouge: Louisiana State University Press, 1936, 52–58.

Snidecor, J. C. An objective study of phrasing in impromptu speaking and oral reading. *Speech Monogr.,* **11,** 1944, 97–104.

———. Temporal aspects of breathing in superior reading and speaking performances. *Speech Monogr.,* **22,** 1955, 284–289.

Stetson, R. H. Speech movements in action. *Transactions of the American Laryngological Association,* **55,** 1933, 29–41.

———, and Hudgins, C. V. Functions of the breathing movements in the mechanism of speech. *Arch. Neerlandaises de Phonétique Expérimentale,* **5,** 1930, 1–30.

Temple, W. J. The mechanism of human speech. In O'Neill, J. M. (Ed.) *Foundations of speech.* Englewood Cliffs, N.J.: Prentice-Hall, 1946.

Wiksell, W. A. An experimental analysis of respiration in relation to the intensity of vocal tones in speech. In *Louisiana State University Studies,* No. 27. Baton Rouge: Louisiana State University Press, 1936, 37–51.

CHAPTER
5

SPEECH
SOUNDS
AND
SYMBOLS

English spelling doesn't do it. Misses the sounds—or it puts in sounds where they don't belong. Ever spell a word "just because it sounds that way?" And you missed it because the letters came in from left field in a language change years back and nowadays the letters and the sounds don't agree? Sure. Ever mispronounce a word because the spelling misled you? Sure. Anything but exact and consistent, writing our language. But, the hard way, we all learn and eventually spell and talk with acceptable accuracy.

But suppose you need precise representation of speech sounds—no chance of misunderstanding—English spelling won't do; there are too many variations in the uses of the letters and their combinations. For example, the symbol "g" might be sounded as in "go," "image," "mirage," or "tough," or be silent as in "though." The letter "c" might be sounded as in "cat," "cease," "suspicion," and so on. Ridiculous as it may seem, "cioegh" could be a spelling for "sheaf" if "ci" were sounded as "sh" as in "species," "oe" as "ee" as in "subpoena" and "gh" as "f" as in "cough." The strange spelling might even be "sheep" if the "gh" were sounded "p" as in "hiccough." This illustrates, of course, that although we can take many cues to pronunciation from letter combinations, we cannot make a conclusive decision about the pronunciation of a single letter away from its spelling environment.

Yet, in some endeavors, especially in certain divisions within the field of speech, it is necessary to speak of and to work with individual *sounds* alone, away from spelling or sound environment; and it is necessary to be able to symbolize the sounds exactly and accurately. Since it is not feasible to use the English alphabet for such purposes, it is necessary to have other symbols, each of which *always represents the same sound, and only that one sound.*

Why not use diacritical marks, a system with which many of you are familiar and which has been used successfully for many years in dictionary pronunciation guides? Without doubt for that purpose the system is quite adequate. However, the fact that the same acoustic event, the individual speech sound, can be represented in two or three different ways militates against use of that system for dynamic representation of vocal signals. The sound usually spelled "uh" in comic strips is one for which there are several equivalent representations achieved by attaching diacritical symbols to conventional letters. For this reason and because the competitive system we will describe can be used more rapidly in the transcription of speech, we recommend the International Phonetic Alphabet to you.

THE INTERNATIONAL PHONETIC ALPHABET (I.P.A.)

The I.P.A. is used, as its name implies, internationally, by linguists, phoneticians, language teachers, and speech teachers. Its primary advantage is that it has a set of *symbols, one symbol per sound and one sound per symbol.* And, though it does not eliminate the element of human judgment, it greatly increases the possibility of representing speech sounds accurately.

In actuality, each symbol of the I.P.A. represents a *phoneme* or family of sounds sufficiently alike to be represented by a single symbol. *Allophones*—variations within a phoneme—result from influences of surrounding phonetic elements, individual and regional articulation differences, and accidental minor misarticulations. However, if any variation of a sound does not enter another phoneme or become unrecognizable, it can be represented by the symbol for that phoneme. For example, research shows us clearly that all the "t" sounds represented by the phonetic symbol [t] are by no means identical. They vary somewhat in tongue positioning, comparative duration of implosion and explosion, strength of explosion, and so on; but these allophones all belong, in our language, to the same sound family and can be clearly represented in broad transcription by the symbol [t]. In this connection we might note research by Moses and others. They introduced artificial palates dusted with white

Selections from

INTERNATIONAL PHONETIC ALPHABET (I.P.A.)

Consonants

[p] — *p*ut
[b] — *b*ack
[t] — *t*o
[d] — *d*og
[k] — *c*at
[g] — *g*um
[m] — *m*ouse
[n] — *n*ow
[ŋ] — passi*ng*
[f] — *f*ast
[v] — *v*im
[θ] — *th*ink
[ð] — *th*en
[s] — *s*ee
[z] — *z*oo
[ʃ] — *sh*am
[ʒ] — vi*si*on
[tʃ] — *ch*ip
[dʒ] — *j*ump
[hw] — *wh*en
[w] — *w*alk
[j] — *y*es
[r] — *r*ed
[l] — *l*et
[h] — *h*at

Vowels

[i] — b*ee*t
[ɪ] — h*i*t
[e] — *a*pe
[ɛ] — r*e*d
[æ] — c*a*t
[a] — h*a*lf [haf]
[ɑ] — f*a*ther
[ɒ] — h*o*t [hɒt]
[ɔ] — l*aw*
[o] — g*oa*t
[ʊ] — f*oo*t
[u] — m*oo*n
[ʌ] — m*u*ddle
[ɝ] — p*er*son
[ɜ] — b*ir*d [bɜd]
[ɚ] — moth*er*
[ə] — sof*a*

Diphthongs

[aɪ] — *i*ce
[ɔɪ] — b*oy*
[aʊ] — h*ou*se
[oʊ] — t*oe* (see text on [o])
[eɪ] — m*ay* (see text on [e])

Substandard Consonant

[ʔ] — bo*tt*le [bɑʔl̩]

powder into the mouths of their subjects, then carefully removed the artificial palates and examined them after each consonant production. The technique is known as palatography. Results of these studies showed that variations occur among speakers in tongue-palate contacts and that variations occur in the same speaker's tongue-palate contacts from production to production of the same sound. The sounds produced by such variations, however, all belong to the same phoneme.

Of course, there are numerous symbols in the I.P.A. for sounds that occur in other languages but are not used in American English. The German "ch" as in "ich," for example, is symbolized [ç]; however, we do not use that sound in American English. Hence, in this book we shall not be concerned with the symbol. If our primary purpose in this text were to help you learn the proper pronunciation of another language, the matter would be different. In such circumstances you might find it very helpful to learn phonetic symbols for all the new and unfamiliar sounds. However, as we explain at greater length below, we wish to provide you with a tool that you will find immediately useful, so we shall concern ourselves only with the symbols for the sounds of American English.

Nor shall we expect you to acquire skill or knowledge comprehensive enough to permit you to undertake "fine" phonetic transcription, the very exact, narrow transcription that uses superscripts to indicate colorings or other slight variations observable in allophones. In more advanced speech work you may find it necessary to become adept at fine transcription; but for our present purposes use of the phonemic symbols in broad transcription will suffice.

USES OF PHONETICS

A knowledge of phonetics is important and very useful in a number of ways in the study of speech. In fact, it is probably among the most basic skills used by students and teachers of speech.

For students of public address or platform speaking it is important to self-evaluation and improvement that they be able to hear and analyze their sound usages. Elimination of substandardisms, unusual dialect variations, mispronunciations, and poor articulation will depend in large part on the speaker's ability to hear accurately the sounds he uses and to make the necessary adjustments to correct or modify the output. Symbolic representations of the correct and incorrect sounds are helpful.

In radio and television training it is urgent that pronunciation standards, current usages, new words, foreign words, and technical phrases be understood and mastered. Here, too, elimination of poor articulation, substandardisms, dialect variations, and mispronunciations may depend greatly on the speaker's knowledge of phonetics and his ability in self-analysis.

In acting for the legitimate theater and in interpretative reading the occasional need to speak in dialect and the constant requirement that subtle control be exerted in phonetic aspects of speech are apparent. Mere emotional understanding of a desired artistic effect is not enough; the phonetic sensitivity and bioacoustic know-how are indispensable.

Finally, in speech pathology phonetics is a basic tool. To recognize sound errors, to describe them accurately, and to design and carry out corrective procedures, the clinician must have superior and discriminating phonetic sensitivity as well as the ability to handle the phonetic alphabet swiftly and exactly.

Whatever your major interest in the speech field, you can be sure that your accuracy and speed in phonetic transcription will help to determine your ultimate success.

Skill in phonetics will also be useful to students of the English language in analyzing and understanding the changes and adjustments that have taken place and are constantly occurring in our language. As was pointed out, students of other languages probably will find it necessary to add symbols to the alphabet they learn from this text. A solid knowledge of sounds, however, and a sensitive ear provide a good start in learning another language. You can doubtless think of numerous applications of phonetics. The point is, the skill is useful in many other areas of learning as well as in speech.

The sounds will be introduced as consonants, vowels, and diphthongs. Each sound will be thoroughly described. It is assumed that you will learn to write the symbol of each sound upon hearing it produced and, conversely, to produce the sound upon sight of the symbol. The ability to write swiftly and accurately in phonetics or to read swiftly and accurately from phonetics depends primarily on your having the symbols thoroughly memorized. If you have difficulty establishing the sound-symbol relationship in your mind, it may be helpful to select for each symbol a key word containing the sound and to memorize the symbols and words together.

CONSONANTS

The consonants are the dividing units in connected speech; they often separate the vowels and sometimes influence the beginnings and endings of the vowels, modulating the flow of sound. It is interesting to note that vowels so influenced by initiating and terminating consonants are more easily recognized than vowels produced and heard in isolation. A consonant is produced when the articulators alter the free flow of the expired breath stream. The alterations occur as the speaker blocks, constricts, or directs the air stream, producing noise. When the consonant is voiceless, there is noise alone, as in [s] and [f]. When the consonant is voiced, the noise is combined with periodic or musical sound from the larynx, as in [z] and [v].

Some consonants appear in pairs basically alike except for this voicing; these are called cognates. Probably it will be helpful for you to learn immediately to associate the pairs.

Students sometimes have difficulty recognizing the difference between voiced and voiceless sounds. This characteristic of consonants is phonemically significant and hence important to the accurate use of phonetics. Errors in sound production sometimes are attributable to this error of perception. A good interpretative reader or actor may want to use voicing differences selectively to achieve dialectal effects. The voiced or voiceless characteristic of each consonant will be discussed in the following pages. However, here are a few examples. Produce each word and continue the final sound. Put your finger tips on your larynx to feel the vocal vibration when you produce these continuants: [m] as in "room," [l] as in "all," [v] as in "give." The first two, [m] and [l], have no voiceless equivalents in our language. However, [f] as in "life" is produced as [v] except that it is unvoiced, that is, without vocal fold vibration. Produce [v] then [f]; hold each sound for several seconds. Notice the [v] has an underlying vocal "hum" which [f] has not. Some other such pairs are: [s] as in "miss" and [z] as in "buzz," [t] as in "hat" and [d] as in "head." Notice that the latter pair are not continuants; you cannot hold and prolong them. Repeat the word pair and note the voicing difference on the final sounds, "hat" and "head." Here are some words that are just alike phonetically except for the voicing of one consonant. Such words are said to be "homophonous"; that is, they are alike in their place of formation. Other characteristics than voicing of sounds can be varied to produce homophonous words but these examples involve voicing differences only:

sing	— zing	find	— vined
fussy	— fuzzy	calf	— calve
bus	— buzz	pad	— bad
face	— phase	pallid	— ballad
tore	— door	flappy	— flabby
tell	— dell	rapid	— rabid
petal	— pedal	rope	— robe

sorted — sordid	nap — nab
fat — fad	carry — Gary
root — rude	cage — gauge
face — vase	flocking — flogging
flack — flag	sack — sag

Vowels and diphthongs are all voiced. Unvoicing of vowels and diphthongs as in whispered speech does not change their recognizable characteristics. Voicing of vowels and diphthongs is then not a variable phonemic characteristic.

Continuant sounds are those which can be made and maintained in a single articulator position; they do not depend on explosion, or glide movement for their characteristics. Fricative and nasal consonants are continuants, whereas plosives and glides are not. These classes of consonants are described in detail a little later.

Distinctive features

Each of the consonant sounds is presented in this text in terms of three descriptive elements: (1) the place of production of the sound, that is, the locus of blockage, constriction, or diverted air stream; (2) the type of sound, that is, the acoustical nature of the sound, whether fricative, plosive, and so on; (3) the voicing of the sound, that is, whether or not vocal cord tone is present. This organization of the information about consonants is rather standard in books designed for beginning students in phonetics. In your studying you should emphasize these three aspects of consonant production.

However, there is a system of comparatively recent development to which you should be introduced. Jakobson and Halle discussed it at length in a 1956 publication.[1] This analytic method describes all the speech sounds of English through use of a series of binary (either-this-or-that) choices called "distinctive features." Some of those either-or descriptions are the same as the descriptions you will find on following pages: for example, "vocalic" (vowel-like) versus "consonantal," "nasal" versus "nonnasal," "continuant" versus "interrupted," "voiced" versus "voiceless," and "tense" versus "lax."

---

[1] Much work is being done on the exact acoustical nature of speech sounds, their effects on each other in connected speech, and their irreducible distinctive characteristics. Research workers at Haskins Laboratories in New York City and the Massachusetts Institute of Technology are among the leaders in this work. Several of their reports are listed in your suggested readings.

Other pairs of terms of the distinctive features classification system you will not find used in our detailed discussion of the individual consonant sounds. The latter are primarily derived from acoustical analyses of the sounds but are related to the articulation processes involved. The following binary choice distinctive features, listed by Jakobson and Halle, are presented by name but are not defined here. These pairs are distinguished by acoustical variations in timbre, frequently imperceptible to the novice: "strident" versus "mellow," "compact" versus "diffuse," "grave" versus "acute," "flat" versus "plain," and "sharp" versus "plain."

Let us restress the fact that distinctions between most of the pairs of these last terms must be made instrumentally; the analysis cannot be done by ear.

A revision of this classification system was published by Chomsky and Halle in 1968. While retaining many of the concepts of Jakobson and Halle, the newer work related more closely to the place-type-voicing system that we recommend to you.

It seems unnecessary for you, at this point, to learn to describe the English sounds in terms of their distinctive features. However, these concepts may emphasize for you the complex nature of the phonetic events that we shall describe in terms of place of articulation, type of sound, and voicing. Moreover, the increasing use of distinctive features analysis makes it desirable that you have at least a nodding acquaintance with the concepts as groundwork for study and research you may undertake later.

You must keep one more idea in mind as you read the descriptions of the sounds. We have set down a description of a typical place and manner of articulation of each sound. Speakers will vary somewhat in exact positions and movements for the same sound; even the same speaker will vary on one sound from one production to the next. Speech involves moving the articulators rapidly through many positions to produce the series of sounds accurately enough that their distinctive characteristics are recognized by the listener. We do not maintain that our description presents the only way to make the sounds accurately, nor do we hold the exact *positions* to be of absolute importance; speech is made, after all, with movements.

Here are the descriptions of the consonants.

Plosives

These noncontinuant sounds, three voiced paired with three unvoiced, are produced in two phases, the implosion or air-stream blocking phase and the explosion or release phase. The place of the blockage in the oral cavity apparently gives the sound of the explosion its acoustical characteristics, that is, determines the frequency band where greatest energy concentration is found in a wide-spectrum noise.

These sounds are also produced in concluding positions or in combination with other consonants without the explosion phase, depending for their recognition partly on the context and partly on their influences on the acoustical characteristics of neighboring sounds. We shall discuss these variations further later in this chapter.

[p] AND [b].   These labial plosive cognates, the first voiceless and the second voiced, are produced by an implosion or damming of the air behind closed lips. The nasal port is closed, the jaw is slightly lowered, and the tongue probably is in movement toward its position for the following sound. Tongue position is not critical for this pair of sounds. When the lips are opened, a burst of air is released, making an aspirate noise. The noise is overlaid on voicing for the [b]. These sounds are used in the following words: "*p*ut" [pʊt], "o*p*en" [opən], "li*p*" [lɪp], and "*b*ack" [bæk], "a*b*out" [əbaʊt], "ca*b*" [kæb]. (In some of the consonant descriptions to follow, it will be necessary for illustrative purposes to use the phonemes with vowels not yet described. If this is a source of confusion for you, look ahead to the next section, which covers the vowels.)

[t] AND [d].   These cognates, the voiceless [t] and the voiced [d]—the alveolar plosives—are produced by implosion of air behind a closure involving the raised tongue tip and sides, the alveolar ridge, and the upper dental arch and gum ridge all around the mouth. The nasal port is closed, the jaw is lowered somewhat, and the lips are relaxed and open or in movement to the position for the following sound. A burst of air is released, making an aspirate noise. This noise is overlaid on voicing for the [d].

These sounds are used in the following words: "*t*o" [tʊ], "au*t*o" [ɔto], "cu*t*" [kʌt], and "*d*og" [dɔg], "ra*d*io" [redɪo], "pa*d*" [pæd]. Numerous possible spellings for [t] will be presented later as an example of the confusion you may encounter in phonetic transcription if you try to depend on spelling for cues.

[k] AND [g].   These cognates, the voiceless [k] and the voiced [g]—the velar plosives—are produced by an implosion of air behind the closure effected by the humping of the back of the tongue against the back of the hard palate (or part of the soft palate) and the side structures of the mouth. Thus closure of the entire posterior portion of the oral cavity is accomplished. The soft palate is up, closing the nasal port; and the lower jaw is dropped slightly. The lips are either relaxed and open or in movement toward the next sound. When the backward hump of the tongue is lowered,

a burst of air is released, making an aspirate noise, overlaid on voicing for the [g].

These sounds are used in the following words: "*c*at" [kæt], "ba*k*er" [bekɚ], "hoo*k*" [hʊk], and "*g*um" [gʌm], "wa*g*on" [wægən], "le*g*" [lɛg].

Nasals

These three voiced continuants are the only English sounds for which the nasal port must be open; one of their distinguishing features is nasal resonance. Their distinguishable differences, however, are produced by articulator positions in the nonnasal area, shaping the oral resonance cavity and producing characteristic effects on neighboring phonetic elements.

[m]. Articulator positions for this voiced, labial, nasal, continuant consonant are similar to those for the [p] and [b] plosives. The lips are closed; the jaw is lowered slightly; the tongue is relaxed on the floor of the mouth or moving to the position for the next sound; and the vocal cords are adducted, producing voice as the air stream is forced through them. The nasal port is *open,* permitting the sound to pass through the nasal cavities.

The [m] is heard in these words: "*m*ouse" [maʊs], "a*m*ount" [əmaʊnt], and "su*m*" [sʌm].

Because of its sonorous, resonant nature, the [m] sometimes takes the place of a vowel element in a syllable, that is, it becomes syllabic. In such cases its syllabic function is indicated by a dot beneath the symbol: for example, "chasm" [kæzm̩] and the substandard [kæpm̩] for "captain."

[n] This voiced, alveolar, nasal, continuant consonant is produced by articulator positions similar to those for the [t] and [d]. The tongue is raised for a closure between its tip and sides and the alveolar ridge and the upper dental arch and gum ridge all around the mouth. The jaw is lowered slightly; the lips are relaxed and open or in movement to the position for the following sound. The nasal port is *open,* permitting emission of sound through the nasal resonance cavities. The vocal cords are adducted, producing sound as the air stream is forced through them. Apparently the shorter length of the oral resonance cavity for this postdental nasal produces a significant acoustical variation from the labial consonant [m]. Examples of use of the [n]: "*n*ow" [naʊ], "mi*nn*ow" [mɪno], and "pa*n*" [pæn].

Like the [m], this sound sometimes acts as the vowel element in a syllable; that is, it becomes syllabic. The fact is noted by a dot beneath the symbol; for example, "kitten" [kɪtn̩], "patent" [pætn̩t], "button" [bʌtn̩].

[ŋ]. Articulator positions for this voiced, nasal, velar, continuant consonant are similar to those for the [k] and [g]. The back of the tongue is humped against the back of the hard palate or part of the soft palate and the side structures of the oral cavity, accomplishing complete closure; the lower jaw is dropped slightly; the lips are either relaxed and open or in movement toward their position for the next sound. The soft palate is *lowered,* permitting emission of sound through the nasal resonance chambers. The vocal cords are adducted, producing voice as the air stream is forced between them. Apparently the resonance situation created by the omission of the oral cavity from the resonance chain produces for this sound a characteristic acoustic pattern which differentiates the [ŋ] from the [m] and [n]. The [ŋ] is not used in English to initiate words; examples of its use are "si*ng*er" [sɪŋɚ] and "passi*ng*" [pæsɪŋ].

Fricatives

As their name implies, these phonemes rely for their characteristic sounds on friction noises made as the air stream is forced between approximated articulators. They are continuant sounds which, except for the [h], occur in voiced-voiceless pairs.

[f] AND [v]. To produce these cognates, the voiceless [f] and the voiced [v]—the labiodental continuant fricatives—the lower lip is brought up and back slightly to touch the upper teeth in the area of the incisors. The nasal port is closed, the tongue is relaxed or in movement toward the next phoneme position, the jaw is lowered slightly, and the air stream is forced through the labiodental constriction. These adjustments produce a diffuse friction noise, [f]; the noise is overlaid on voicing for the [v]. Examples of their use are "*f*act" [fækt], "o*ff*er" [ɔfɚ], "cu*ff*" [kʌf], and "*v*im" [vɪm], "o*v*en" [ʌvən], "lo*v*e" [lʌv].

[θ] AND [ð]. These cognates, the voiceless [θ] and the voiced [ð]—the linguadental continuant fricatives—are produced by raising the tip or blade of the tongue to touch the upper incisors. The sides of the tongue touch the upper dental arch and gum ridge all around the mouth to form closure, the nasal port is closed, the lower jaw is dropped slightly, and the lips are relaxed open or moving toward their next position. The air stream is forced through the linguadental constriction to make a diffuse friction noise that is overlaid on voicing for the [ð]. Examples of their use are "*th*ink" [θɪŋk], "ba*th*room" [bæθrum], "pa*th*" [pæθ], and "*th*en" [ðɛn], "brea*th*ing" [briðɪŋ], "smoo*th*" [smuð].

[s] AND [z]. These cognates, the voiceless [s] and the voiced [z]—the postdental continuant fricatives—are also called sibilants because of their hissing sounds. They are produced by the grooved tongue, pressed against the hard palate or upper gum ridge at the sides, directing a narrow stream

of air past the alveolar ridge and down over the cutting edges of the lower incisors. A friction noise results. This is one manner of production; you may find that you use a different one. Many tongue positions will do the job. For example, the tongue tip can be elevated, straight forward, or pointed downward· behind the lower incisors. The nasal port is closed, the lower jaw is dropped slightly, and the lips are relaxed and open or moving to their next position. The friction noise is generally high-pitched, although there is some sound spread through the spectrum; it is overlaid on voicing for the [z]. These sounds are used in "see" [si], "a*ss*ume" [əsum], "pa*ss*" [pæs], and "*z*oo" [zu], "buz*z*er" [bʌzɚ], "fuz*z*" [fʌz].

[ʃ] AND [ʒ]. The [ʃ] is voiceless, and the [ʒ] is voiced. Also called sibilants, these postdental (or linguapalatal), continuant fricatives are produced by air forced through a wide constriction between the tip or blade of the tongue and the alveolar ridge, then over the cutting edge of the teeth. The tongue closes against the upper teeth or gum ridge on the sides, the nasal port is closed, the jaw is lowered slightly, and the lips are open and protruded slightly. The [ʃ] sound is mostly high-pitched noise, though not as high as [s], with some energy in lower frequencies especially when stressed; it is generally stronger and has less widely spread energy than the [s]. For the [ʒ] the friction noise is overlaid on voicing. The sounds are used in these words: "*sh*am" [ʃæm], "fa*sh*ion" [fæʃən], "wa*sh*" [wɑʃ]; and since the [ʒ] doesn't initiate words in English, there are only two examples here. "Vi*s*ion" [vɪʒən] and "mira*g*e" [mɪrɑʒ] exemplify its appearance in medial and final positions.

[h]. This voiceless, glottal continuant has no cognate. It is made by air rushing over the vocal cords, which may be partially adducted. The nasal port is closed, and the lips, tongue, and jaw are in or moving toward their positions for the vowel which is to follow. The aspirate noise has a spread of acoustical energy through the spectrum, with some possible concentrations determined by the vowel shape of the oral cavity. It is used in these words: "*h*ouse" [haʊs] and "a*h*ead" [əhɛd]. It is not used as a final consonant in English.

Affricates

[tʃ] AND [dʒ]. These two cognates, the first voiceless and the second voiced, combine the implosion and explosion of the plosives, [t] and [d], with the friction noise of the sibilants, [ʃ] and [ʒ]. Each is imploded as in the appropriate plosive sound, then exploded into the fricative sound. The initial articulator positions are as for the [t] and [d]. The tongue is raised so that the tip and sides touch the alveolar ridge and the upper dental arch and gum ridge all around the mouth. The nasal port is closed, the jaw is lowered somewhat, and the lips are protruded for the [ʃ] or [ʒ] which is to follow. When the tongue is dropped from the palate, it takes the position for the fricatives [ʃ] and [ʒ], making a wide, shallow opening between the tongue tip or blade and the alveolar ridge but maintaining contact with the upper teeth or gum ridge on the sides. The exploded burst of air is directed through that constriction and over the cutting edge of the teeth. The resultant sound has a silent implosion period followed, first, by a high-frequency noise burst across most of the acoustic range, then concentrating in the higher frequencies. For the [dʒ] this is overlaid on voicing. The sounds are used in these words: "*ch*ip" [tʃɪp], "wat*ch*ing" [wɑtʃɪŋ], "mu*ch*" [mʌtʃ], and "*j*ump" [dʒʌmp], "ba*dg*er" [bædʒɚ], "ed*ge*" [ɛdʒ].

Glides

Each of the four glide sounds depends for its characteristics on the moving or gliding motion of one or more articulators. The glides begin with positions and with acoustical features similar to vowel and semivowel sounds but glide rapidly (both physiologically and acoustically) to the following phonetic element.

[hw] OR [ʍ] (both symbols are widely used) AND [w]. These cognate glides—the first of which is voiceless, the second voiced—begin with the articulators in approximately the position for the vowel [ʊ], a sound to be described in the next section. It is the sound of the "oo" in "foot." The soft palate is raised; the tongue is humped up and back, making a narrow opening with the rear portion of the hard palate; the front of the tongue lies on the floor of the mouth; the jaw is lowered slightly; and the lips are protruded and well-rounded. As the consonant is produced, the lips, jaw, and tongue glide into their positions for the next sound. The [hw] is made with no voice; the noise produced is like that of the [h] being forced through the oral cavity shaped for [ʊ]. The [w] is voiced and the sound is an [ʊ] gliding to the next sound. For both sounds the [ʊ] position is held for only a very brief time. Undoubtedly the influences of the articulator glides on the following sounds help in the recognition of the glides. These sounds occur only initially and medially in words; for example, "*wh*en" [hwɛn] and "buck*wh*eat" [bʌkhwit], "*w*alk" [wɔk], and "Mid*w*est" [mɪdwɛst].

[j]. This voiced, palatal glide is made between the moving hump of the tongue and the hard palate. It begins with the articulators in approximately the position for [ɪ], the vowel in "hit," to be described in the next section. The lips are retracted slightly and opened; the tongue is humped

forward toward the alveolar ridge, making a narrow opening with the palate; the jaw is almost closed; the nasal port is closed; and there is voice from the larynx. As the sound is produced the lower jaw is dropped; the lips are moved to their position for the next sound; the tongue is moved downward from front to back, making a gliding motion near the palate and moving into position for the following sound. The position for the [ɪ] vowel is present for a very brief time only. The movement to the next vowel is an important characteristic of this consonant. The sound appears only in the middle and at the beginnings of words in English: "yes" [jɛs], "onion" [ʌnjən].

[r]. There is considerable disagreement about the nature of this consonant element. In some classification systems it is listed only as a semivowel. However, since we shall discuss the vowel forms of this sound elsewhere, and since its consonant characteristics are more like the glide consonants than the semivowel, we shall place it here.

This voiced, palatal glide can be produced from at least two beginning positions. For both the soft palate is up and there is voicing. The sound may begin with the middle of the tongue humped up and back toward the hard palate, dividing the oral cavity into two resonance areas. This is called the *nonretroflex* position. Also, the [r] may begin with the tongue tip turned up and back approaching the hard palate behind the alveolar ridge, again dividing the oral cavity into two resonance areas. This is called the *retroflex* position. Either of these positions will suffice for production of the corresponding [ɝ] vowel. However, for the consonant glide, this position is held for a very short time only, with the tongue, jaw, and lips gliding into their positions for the following phonetic element. Apparently the movement from the approximated [ɝ] position and the influence the [r] has on the following vowel are factors crucial to the recognition of this consonant glide. The evidence, however, still is not complete, especially regarding [r] influence on contiguous vowels. Curtis and Hardy found, in controlled observations of misarticulations of the [r] consonant and vowel forms, that the physiologic similarity in their production and perhaps their auditory similarity may not be as strong as they are held to be by many writers. There is no doubt, however, of the acoustical behavior of the glide [r]. Potter, Kopp, and Green show on sound spectrograms that the [r] begins, acoustically, in a manner similar to the onset of the vowel sound [ɝ]. The glide sound is used in these words: "red" [rɛd], "around" [əraʊnd], and "car" [kɑr].

There is some disagreement about the nature of the final [r] sound in such words as "car," "ear," "far," "pear," "implore," and "despair." Some phoneticians hold that final sound to be vowel-like and write it as [ɚ]: [kɑɚ], [ɪɚ], [fɑɚ], [pɛɚ], [ɪmplɔɚ], [dɪspɛɚ]. We shall hold that when the

[r] element does not act as the vowel in the syllable, the [r] consonant symbol, representing an off-glide, will suffice: [kɑr], [ɪr], [fɑr], [pɛr], [ɪmplɔr], [dɪspɛr]. Perhaps your instructor will want you to follow another convention in this matter; if so he will explain the reasoning behind his preference.

Semivowel

The semivowel is related to the glides in that there is movement involved in its consonant function. The semivowel also depends heavily on its sonorous, resonant nature for recognition.

As was explained above, the [r] is often considered a semivowel. However, since we shall present the vowel functions and symbols of that sound in the vowel section, and since its function as a consonant more closely resembles the glides, it is listed only among the glides.

[l].   There is, then, only the lateral alveolar, voiced, continuant semivowel [l]. The sound is produced in a resonance situation set up by elevation of the tip or blade of the tongue to the alveolar ridge. The sides of the tongue remain lowered to permit passage of sound around the raised front portion. The soft palate is up, the jaw is lowered moderately, the lips are open and relaxed. A voiced breath stream is directed through the oral cavity. The result is a vowellike sound. From the position described, the tongue, jaw, and lips move into the position for the following sound. The movements form a definite glide.

Not only the glide, but the initial nature of the [l] sound will sometimes be influenced by its phonetic environment. For example, if the portion of the tongue back of the blade is humped toward the palate, especially in the final position and before consonants, a "dark [l]" is formed. This "dark [l]" can be heard in the typical production of the word "mi*l*k." The "clear [l]" is usually heard preceding vowels, as in these words: "*l*et" [lɛt] and "a*ll*ow" [əlaʊ].

Since this is a semivowel sound, it is reasonable to find that at times it takes the place of a vowel element in a syllable just as [m] and [n] do. The same convention is followed as that described for use with syllabic [m] and [n]. A dot appearing under the symbol indicates its syllabic nature: for example, "bottle" [bɑtḷ], "whittling" [hwɪtḷɪŋ], and "little" [lɪtḷ].

Substandard plosive

All the consonants previously described are used in acceptable pronunciation of General American English words. There is one substandard, unacceptable sound that should be introduced because of its usefulness in

CLASSIFICATION OF SOUND

PLACE OF ARTICULATION	PLOSIVE		FRICATIVE		NASAL		GLIDE		SEMIVOWEL		AFFRICATE	
	Voiceless	*Voiced*	*Voiceless*	*Voiced*	*Voiceless*	*Voiced*	*Voiceless*	*Voiced*	*Voiceless*	*Voiced*	*Voiceless*	*Voiced*
LABIAL	p	b				m	hw (ʍ)	w				
LABIODENTAL			f	v								
LINGUADENTAL			θ	ð								
ALVEOLAR	t	d				n				l		
POSTDENTAL			s, ʃ	z, ʒ							tʃ	dʒ
PALATAL								j, r				
VELAR	k	g				ŋ						
GLOTTAL	ʔ		h									

Figure 5.1. Consonant Chart. American-English sounds are identified by acoustical classification, place of articulation, and voicing.

describing an error or substitution that sometimes occurs. You may as well hear about it now and be prepared with the symbol when you find you need it.

[ʔ]. The glottal plosive is formed by closing the vocal folds tightly and opening them suddenly; this causes a sharp release of sound or air. It is a frequent misarticulation of the oral plosives, voiced and voiceless. Mispronunciations of these words sometimes contan the glottal stop plosive: "bottlc" [bɑʔl̩], "metal" [mɛʔl̩], and "walking" [wɔʔɪŋ].

Summary of consonants

We have described individually and in appropriate pairs the plosive, nasal, fricative, affricate, glide and semivowel consonant sounds of American English, plus one substandard plosive. Each was described as to voicing and articulatory adjustments for production. In many cases the nature of the acoustic pattern for the sound was described. This may seem to you to be a large mass of material, difficult to organize and master. All the consonants are shown in summary in Figure 5.1, the consonant chart. Careful study of the chart, together with study of the descriptions of the sounds, should help you to set the consonants in order in your mind. Also, you will find useful practice materials in *Student Projects* at the end of this chapter.

VOWELS

The vowels and diphthongs are continuant sounds. They are sonorous, resonant in nature, and consequently carry most of the quality, the musical characteristic, of speech. Vowels are formed by resonance cavities acting on the vocal cord tone to produce several frequency areas of sound concentration (formants), the lower two of which determine the recognizable characteristics of the individual vowels. For the [r]-colored vowels the third format is also important (see Figure 5.2). The nasal port is usually closed; however, individuals differ in this aspect of vowel production. Some speakers leave an opening into the nasal cavities which gives a nasal coloring to their vowel sounds in running speech. Generally, however, we think of the English vowels as nonnasalized sounds.

The terms "front," "central," and "back" are used to refer to the front-to-rear position of the hump of the tongue in the mouth during the production of the vowels; and "high," "mid," and "low" are used to refer to the degree of elevation of the hump of the tongue. Figure 5.3, the vowel diagram, indicates the approximate position of the hump of the tongue for the production of each vowel.

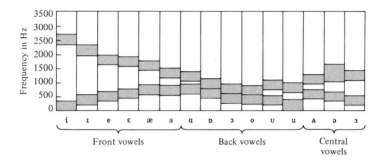

Figure 5.2. Vowel formants. Typical locations are shown of the first two formants of English vowels as produced by adult American males (adapted from *Visible Speech*, by R. Potter, G. Kopp and H. Green, Copyright, 1947, by D. Van Nostrand Co., Inc., by permission of Van Nostrand Reinhold Company.

The terms "tense" and "lax" traditionally have been used to refer to relative amounts of tension in the tongue muscles during production of the vowel sounds. Obviously the tongue cannot be held in a humped position away from its neutral position without some tension as compared with a lower, more central position. There are observable variations in amounts of tension present during the production of different vowels, and the terms "tense" and "lax" have long been used to designate those variations. In a review of pertinent research Jakobson and Halle concluded that tense

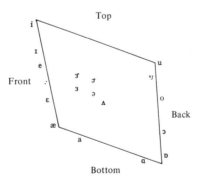

Figure 5.3. Vowel diagram. The locations of the vowel symbols on the diagram represent the locations in the mouth of the high point of the tongue in vowel production.

vowels have significantly more air pressure behind the sound source, the vocal cords, than do their lax counterparts. They stressed also that tense phonemes are produced with the structures in positions of greater deviation from a neutral or central position than their companion lax phonemes. For example, the tense [i] is produced with the tongue farther forward than for the lax [ɪ], the tense [e] is produced with the tongue farther forward than for the lax [ɛ], and the tense [u] is produced with the tongue farther back than for the lax [ʊ].

The tense vowels in American English are: [i], [e], [ɔ], [o], [u], and [ɝ]. The lax vowels are: [ɪ], [ɛ], [æ], [a], [ʊ], and [ʌ].

Perhaps you will notice at this point that the acoustical information in Figure 5.2 and the physiological information in Figure 5.3 appear to be directly related. The front, back, and central vowels are grouped together on each chart and the front and back vowels follow one another in the same order on each chart. Delattre examined extensive data on these relationships; his conclusions may be summarized this way:

FORMANT 1 — as the over-all opening of the oral tract grows larger, the frequency of formant 1 rises;

FORMANT 2 — as the front-to-back dimension of the front mouth cavity grows longer through lip rounding and tongue retraction, formant 2 frequency descends;

FORMANT 3 — as the velum descends in nasalizing, formant 3 frequency rises, whereas the frequency descends when the tongue tip rises to effect r-coloring.

Following are descriptions of the individual vowels. In learning to write the vowel symbols, you should refer to the handwritten forms of the symbols used in Figure 5.3; attempts to imitate the printed vowel symbols may lead you to inaccuracies.

Front vowels

Note that the positions of the front vowel symbols down the left of the vowel diagram (Figure 5.3) indicate a gradually lowered and retracted tongue hump. Typically this is accompanied by a gradual reduction in lip retraction and an increase in jaw depression. These result in wider over-all mouth opening, hence a gradual rise in the first formant, according to Delattre. A progressive lengthening of the front resonance cavity also results, effecting a gradual lowering of the second formant. The front vowels are [i], [ɪ], [e], [ɛ], [æ], and the front-central [a].

[i], as in "beet," is a high, front, tense vowel. The lower jaw is up, approaching closure with the upper jaw; the lip opening is narrow with the corners retracted; the tongue is humped high and forward to produce a broad, shallow opening near the alveolar ridge. There are two resonance areas, one behind the hump of the tongue and one in front of it; they are connected by the shallow opening. The first formant is very low because of the small over-all mouth opening. The second formant is higher than it is for any other vowel because of the very short front resonance cavity. The [i] is heard in these words: "beat" [bit], "evil" [ivəl], "see" [si], and "steep" [stip].

[ɪ], as in "hit," is a high, front, lax vowel. The lower jaw is elevated almost as high as for [i]. The hump of the tongue is lowered and backed slightly from the [i] position, dividing the oral cavity into two resonance chambers connected by the comparatively shallow, wide opening between the hump of the tongue and the hard palate. The first formant is low but slightly higher than it is for [i], because of a wider mouth opening. The second formant is lower than it is for [i]. The [ɪ] is heard in these words: "hit" [hɪt], "in" [ɪn], "middle" [mɪdl̩], "funny" [fʌnɪ], and "pity" [pɪtɪ]. You may find it hard to accept [ɪ] as the transcription of "y" in such words as "funny," "pity," "happy," and the like, but research reveals that it is [ɪ], rather than [i], that normally occurs in this unstressed syllable.

[e], as in "ape," is a middle, front, tense vowel. The jaw is moved downward a little less than half the distance to its widest opening for [ɑ]; the tongue hump is at a middle height toward the front of the mouth but back somewhat from the [ɪ] position. The lips are open and may be retracted slightly at the corners. Again the opening between the tongue hump and the hard palate joins two oral resonance cavities, one behind and the other in front of the high point of the tongue. The first formant is slightly above that for [ɪ], since the mouth opening is wider, but still quite low. The second formant is lower than that for [ɪ] since the front resonance cavity is longer. This vowel is often combined with [ɪ] in the diphthong [eɪ]. (A diphthong, as will be explained in greater detail later, is a vowel-like phoneme made up of a glide combination of two vowels.) It is sometimes used, however, in the nondiphthongized or pure vowel form as in "ape" [ep] and "take" [tek]. For broad transcription purposes, differentiation between the [e] and [eɪ] probably is not important. You may wish to use one or the other consistently, not attempting to decide whether the sound being transcribed is or is not diphthongized.

Peterson and Coxe examined the [e] pure vowel and diphthong forms on spectrograms. They concluded that there is a "fully distinct" vowel [e], and further, that the diphthong form, though generally written [eɪ], is more likely to be [ɛɪ] or [ɛe]. The pure vowel occurs most often when the sound is unstressed, and diphthongization occurs when certain kinds of stress lead to lengthening of the vowel or raising of the tongue or rounding of the lips. We conclude that in broad transcription it may be wisest to use the [e] arbitrarily for both pure and diphthong forms, recognizing the probability that diphthongization is actually occurring at least part of the time.

If your instructor wishes you to identify the diphthongized and non-diphthongized forms in transcription, he will tell you which forms he prefers you to use.

[ɛ], as in "red," is a middle, front, lax vowel. The lower jaw is moved downward a little more than half of its total excursion; the lips are open and relaxed; the hump of the tongue is at a low-middle height, back somewhat from the [e] position, still toward the front of the mouth. The cavity in front of the tongue hump is longer than that for [e]; hence there is a lower second formant. The first formant is slightly higher than that for [e]. The sound is heard in these words: "red" [rɛd], "excell" [ɛksɛl], and "bet" [bɛt]. Other possible spellings of the [ɛ] vowel will be presented later in this chapter.

[æ], as in "cat," is a low, front, lax vowel. The jaw is lowered almost to its widest opening; the tongue is humped slightly toward the front of the mouth but not as far forward as for [ɛ]; the lips are open and relaxed. Because of the width of the mouth opening, the first formant is above that for [ɛ], approaching the highest first formant frequency found in [ɑ]. The second formant is lower than that for [ɛ], since the front cavity is longer. This vowel is heard in "cat" [kæt], "back" [bæk], "actor" [æktɚ], and "paddle" [pædl].

Two vowels not widely used in American English might be presented here for general interest and because one of them is used in diphthong forms you will study later. The first, [a], is a low, front, central, lax vowel typically heard in the British or Eastern American pronunciation of "dance" [dans], "half" [haf], and "bath" [baθ]. To the ear of someone who speaks the General American dialect it sounds somewhat like a combination of [æ] and [ɑ]. The jaw is opened quite wide, which produces a high first formant, almost as high as for [ɑ]. The hump of the tongue is very low in the mouth and just behind the position taken for [æ], making a slightly lower second formant than that for [æ] but not quite so low as that for [ɑ]. We hear it as the first element in two diphthongs: [aɪ], as in "ice" [aɪs], and [aʊ], as in "house" [haʊs].

The second vowel not commonly heard in American English is [ɒ], as in the British pronunciation of "hot" [hɒt], "rob" [rɒb], and "top" [tɒp]. This vowel is a low, lax, rounded, back vowel. The jaw is open almost to its widest vowel position, the first formant being just a little below that for the [ɑ]. The tongue hump is low and just back of its normal position for [ɑ] which, together with the slight lip rounding and protrusion, results in a slightly longer front resonance cavity and a slightly lower second formant. The [ɒ] is occasionally heard as the first element of a variation of the [aɪ] diphthong, [ɒɪ].

Back vowels

Note that the positions of the back vowel symbols, up the right side of the diagram (Figure 5.3), indicate a gradually raised and advanced tongue hump. Typically, this is accompanied by a gradual rounding and protrusion of the lips and raising of the jaw. The over-all mouth opening is progressively smaller, so the first formant is lowered progressively. The upward movement of the tongue hump and the protrusion of the lips result in a longer front resonance cavity and progressively lower second formant. The back vowels are [ɑ], [ɒ], [ɔ], [o], [ʊ], and [u].

[ɑ], as in "father," is a low, lax, unrounded, back vowel. The jaw is at its widest vowel opening and the tongue hump at its lowest position for this sound. The lips are open and relaxed. The tongue hump is low and far back, producing a longer front resonance cavity than that for any front vowel. The first formant is higher for this vowel than for any other, since the widest over-all mouth opening is used. The sound is heard in "father" [fɑðɚ], "odd" [ad], "top" [tɑp], and "crop" [krɑp].

[ɔ], as in "law," is a low, back, rounded, tense vowel. The jaw is just above its widest opening, for [ɑ], producing a first formant slightly below that for [ɑ]. The hump of the tongue is a little higher than it is for [ɑ] but back a little farther and the lips are rounded and protruded slightly. The long front resonance cavity produces a second formant below that for [ɑ]. The sound is heard in "raw" [rɔ], "awful" [ɔfəl], and "caught" [kɔt]. Some authorities insist that [ɔ] is the vowel sound that precedes [r] in such words as "horse" [hɔrs] and "for" [fɔr].

[o], as in "goat," is a middle, back, rounded tense vowel. The jaw is at a position about halfway to its widest vowel position. The hump of the tongue is far back, slightly forward of its position for [ɔ], and at about a middle height. The lips are moderately rounded and protruded. Because of the over-all mouth opening, the first formant is lower than that for [ɑ] or [ɔ] and about the same as that for [e], which requires a similar mouth opening. The first formant appears below that for [ɔ]. Because of the lengthening of the front resonance cavity, the second formant is also lower

than that for [ɔ]. This vowel is often combined with [ʊ] to form the diphthong [oʊ]. Also, it is sometimes used in the nondiphthongized or pure vowel form, as in "goat" [got], and "rope" [rop]. For broad transcription purposes differentiation between the [o] and [oʊ] probably is not important. You may wish to use one or the other consistently, not attempting to decide whether the sound being transcribed is or is not diphthongized.

In the work by Peterson and Coxe previously cited, the [o] was examined in pure vowel and diphthongized forms on spectrograms. They concluded that the pure vowel occurs most often when the sound is not stressed and the diphthongized form occurs when it is given certain kinds of stress, resulting in lengthening of the vowel, or when the tongue is raised after the [o] or the lips rounded after the [o].

We conclude that it may be wisest arbitrarily to use the [o] in all cases in broad transcription, recognizing that diphthongization probably is occurring part of the time. Your instructor may wish you to identify the diphthongized and nondiphthongized forms in transcription; if so he will tell you which forms he prefers you to use.

[ʊ], as in "foot," is a high, back, rounded, lax vowel. The jaw is almost closed, just short of the highest position used for [u] and [i], producing a lower first formant than that for [o]. The tongue hump is quite high, though not as high as for [u], forward of that for [o] and, breaking the pattern, also forward of its position for [u]. The lips are well rounded and protruded. The resultant long front resonance cavity produces a low second formant but slightly higher than that for [ɔ] or [o]. The sound is heard in "foot" [fʊt], "good" [gʊd], and "pull" [pʊl].

[u], as in "moon," is a high, back, rounded, tense vowel. The jaw is almost closed, producing a very low first formant. The tongue hump is high, almost as high as it is for [i], and far back; it is farther back than it is for [ʊ], but not so far back as it is for [o]. The lips are well rounded and protruded, but not so far as they are for [ʊ]. The long front resonance cavity produces a low second formant, lower than that for [ʊ] and about the same as for [o]. The sound is heard in "moon" [mun], "tooth" [tuθ], and "true" [tru].

Central vowels

Five vowel sounds are made with the raised portion of the tongue somewhere in the central part of the oral cavity, apparently depending strongly on phonetic environment for their exact positioning. They are [ʌ], [ɝ], [ɚ], [ə], and [ɜ].

[ʌ], as in "muddle," is used only in stressed syllables, in unstressed form becoming [ə]. It is a mid-central, lax, unrounded vowel, probably made toward the back of the oral cavity. It is heard in "*mu*ddle" [mʌdl̩], "*du*st" [dʌst], and "*u*p" [ʌp].

[ɝ], as in "p*er*son," is used only in stressed syllables, in unstressed syllables becoming [ɚ]. It is a midcentral, tense, r-colored vowel. This is the stressed vowel form of the phoneme introduced among the consonants as the glide [r]. It may be produced by raising the middle portion of the tongue toward the hard palate or by curling the tip of the tongue up and back in the "retroflex" position. According to Delattre, this movement appears to effect the lowering of the third formant frequency, lending the r-coloring to the vowel. It is heard in "p*ur*se" [pɝs], "f*ir*st" [fɝst], and "occ*ur*" [əkɝ], as these words are produced in the General American dialect areas of the United States. In portions of the East and South it becomes the non-r-colored central vowel, [ɜ].

[ɚ], as in "moth*er*," is the unstressed form of the [ɝ] vowel and the unstressed vowel form of the consonant [r] phoneme. It is a midcentral, lax, r-colored vowel, produced in about the same way as the [ɝ]. It is heard in "moth*er*" [mʌðɚ], "p*er*tain" [pɚten], and "mann*er*" [mænɚ], as those words are spoken in the General American dialect area. In dialect regions where the [ɜ] is the stressed form, the [ə] is used in unstressed positions. As mentioned earlier, some phoneticians prefer [ɚ] to [r] in diphthongal forms with other vowels, as in "far" [fɑɚ] and "near" [nɪɚ].

[ə], as in "sofa," is called the "schwa."[2] It is the unstressed form of the [ʌ]; it is a midcentral, lax, non-r-colored vowel. Many of the vowels when unstressed in speech take on this unstressed neutral sound, for example, the first "o" in "c*o*ntrol" [kəntrol]. Since unstressed syllables occur often, the "schwa" is a very frequently used sound; this symbol is an important one.

[ɜ], as in "b*ir*d" [bɜd] when it is pronounced by someone from the Eastern American dialect region or a speaker of standard British, is a midcentral, tense, non-r-colored vowel, appearing only in stressed syllables. Unstressed, the [ɜ] becomes the schwa, [ə]. The [ɜ] is not used in the General American dialect.

Diphthongs

These are vowel-like sounds made by gliding two vowels together, producing a combination that takes on some of the characteristics of a single phoneme. The most common diphthongs are [aɪ], [ɔɪ], and [aʊ]. ([eɪ] and

---

[2] From the Hebrew *shewa*, a symbol used under a consonant to indicate that the letter is without its own vowel. Literally, *shewa* means "empty," or "worthless."

[oʊ] are often included as diphthongs. Their omission in this section of the chapter is explained earlier, in the sections on [e] and [o]).

[aɪ], as in "*ice*," in some areas takes the form [ɑɪ], or even [ɒɪ]. However, in General American speech [aɪ] is most prevalent. The [aɪ] is heard in "*ice*" [aɪs], "*fly*" [flaɪ], and "*night*" [naɪt].

[ɔɪ], as in "*boy*," is heard in "*choice*" [tʃɔɪs], "*alloy*" [ælɔɪ], and "*oil*" [ɔɪl].

[aʊ], as in "*house*," is sometimes [ɑʊ] throughout the eastern and northern United States, and sometimes even [æʊ] in the South; but [aʊ] is most frequently heard in the western and middle United States. [aʊ] is heard in "*about*" [əbaʊt], "*our*" [aʊr], and "*cow*" [kaʊ].

Summary of vowels and diphthongs

Phonetic symbols for the front vowels, back vowels, central vowels, and diphthongs have been presented and related to the vowel diagram (Fig. 5.3) and the acoustical chart (Fig. 5.1). Careful study of those figures, plus practice in writing and sounding the symbols, should help you to become acquainted with these musical speech sounds. *Student Projects* at the end of the chapter will provide useful practice materials.

PHONETICS AND SPELLING

In order to identify the speech sounds for you as quickly as possible and to help you become acquainted with the entire phonetic alphabet as simply as possible, we did not point out the numerous spellings by which each of the speech sounds is sometimes represented. Recall that one advantage of the I.P.A. over ordinary English spelling is that confusion is eliminated in sound transcription. Following are some of the spelling variations for the [t] and [ɛ], included as evidence for our earlier assertion that orthography is a fallible guide to pronunciation. Similar evidence could be presented with other phonemes in starring roles.

[t] —	t — take	[ɛ] —	e — bet
	tt — better		ea — spread
	te — crate		ai — said
	ed — missed		ie — friend
	th — Thomas		ay — says
	ct — indict		a — any
	ght — eight		u — bury
	pt — ptomaine		ae — aesthetic
			eo — leopard

Whereas the preceding paragraph revealed multiple spellings associated with individual phonemes (as acoustical events), the purpose of the present paragraph is to remind you that the appearance of a letter does not necessarily mean that the sound usually associated with it will be pronounced: for example, the "t" in Christmas" [krɪsməs], the "b" in "comb" [kom], the "p" in "psychology" [saɪkɑlədʒɪ], the "k" in "knee" [ni], the "s" in "aisle" [aɪl], and the "w" in "answer" [ænsɚ]. Nor can we be sure, as was pointed out earlier, that a letter, when sounded, will always be sounded in the same way. This illustrates the important idea that when writing in phonetics you must tune your ear to the sounds being produced and not be misled by the spelling.

WRITING IN PHONETICS

As in any symbolic system, certain coventional usages make for efficiency in phonetic transcription. Become familiar with a few simple rules and use them habitually. This will save you time in the future.

1. Writings in phonetic symbols appear within brackets (square parentheses), thus alerting the reader to the symbol system in use: for example, "One may say [aɪðɚ] or [iðɚ]."

2. Accent marks may be used to indicate stress in words: above the line before a syllable for primary stress, below the line before the syllable for secondary stress. Although they are not always necessary, and often omitted entirely, these accent marks are helpful when stress placement must be made clear: for example, "intensify" [ɪnˈtɛnsɪˌfaɪ].

3. When a consonant sound becomes vowel-like, forming the vowel element for a syllable, a dot is placed beneath it. This situation occurs with the [n̩], [l̩], and [m̩]: for example, "cotton" [kɑtn̩], "cattle" [kætl̩], or the substandard [opm̩] for "open."

4. In accurate representations of dialects particularly it is sometimes helpful to indicate prolongation of a vowel sound. The use of two dots immediately after the symbol conventionally indicates such prolongation: for example, [ɑ:], [æ:], [ɛ:]. The Eastern American dialect pronunciation of the word "car" might be represented [kɑ:], indicating that the [r] is not present and that the [ɑ] is held somewhat longer than usual.

5. In phonetic transcription no capitalization or punctuation other than the period is used. "But," you ask, "what of [ɪ] and [ʊ]? Aren't they capital letters?" No, indeed. These are symbols standing for certain sounds. They are made in exactly the same way whether they come at the beginning or at the end of a sentence, at the beginning of a proper noun or in the middle of an adverb.

A student who expects to learn the phonetic alphabet thoroughly and to be able to transcribe speech into phonetics must memorize the symbols and the sounds they represent. The task is not so difficult as it may seem at first glance. Many of the symbols and their sounds are taken directly from their most common usages in English spelling. The unfamiliar symbols may require a bit more drill and practice. It is sometimes helpful to associate a key word with a new symbol, thus having a demonstration of the sound at tongue-tip. With enough use the key word will be replaced by an automatic association of symbol and sound. A list of key words for all sounds may be drawn from the discussions of the individual sounds earlier in this chapter.

You need not be perfect in recall of sound-symbol combinations to begin practice in phonetic transcription. In fact, practice will help to fix the alphabet in your mind. At the end of the chapter are lists of practice words selected to stress difficult sounds and give practice on sounds that frequently confuse students. You will also find a performance assignment of fifty short, comparatively simple words to be written in phonetics and fifty to be transcribed from phonetics. Another assignment lists longer, more difficult words for the same kind of practice. Transcribe your own pronunciation of each word. If you wish to determine the acceptability of your pronunciation, we recommend that you use one of the phonetic dictionaries in the suggested readings at the end of this chapter.

For most students rapid and accurate use of the phonetic alphabet requires concentration and practice. Further practice is easily available with the pronouncing dictionary. A student may write his own word list in phonetics and check his accuracy by the dictionary. Students working in pairs sometimes dictate words to each other from the dictionary, thus getting practice both in reading and in writing the symbols. We have known students who practiced phonetic transcription by taking notes in the I.P.A. symbols in other classes. Although that is excellent practice in transcription, the I.P.A. is not a shorthand system. In fact, some symbols (the "x" in "extra" [ɛkstrə] is one) require more pencil strokes in the I.P.A. than standard spelling requires.

GRADATION AND ASSIMILATION

Transcription of connected speech is more difficult than transcription of words alone. This is not only because of the greater quantity and speed of delivery. Added to the difficulty is the modification undergone by many speech sounds when they occur in certain phonetic contexts or under special conditions of delivery. Some of these modifications and the reasons for them will be discussed in this section. First it should be noted that the changes in pronunciation to be discussed under the headings of gradation and assimilation are normal and acceptable. Efforts to avoid them, to be too perfect, often will result in distorted, pedantic speech.

Vowel gradation, which comes about as a result of movement of the tongue hump downward and sometimes toward the middle of the oral cavity, often occurs when a vowel is unstressed. For example, the [aɪ] in "coincide" [koɪnsaɪd] becomes a schwa when that syllable is unstressed in "coincident" [koɪnsədɛnt]; the [i] in "city" [sɪti], as the word may be pronounced alone, becomes [ɪ] in connected speech, [sɪtɪ]; the [ɑ] in "solve" [sɑlv] becomes a schwa in "solution" [səluʃən].

In rapid, connected speech, vowels in auxiliary verbs and connective words are sometimes graded downward as a result of their unstressing. For example, [hæd] may become [həd] in "I knew he had gone." [aɪ nu i həd gɔn.] [wɑz] may become [wəz] in "It was black and white." [ɪt wəz blæk ənd hwaɪt.]

In transcribing connected speech, the listener must be able to identify the exact vowel value quickly; if he attempts to isolate and repeat the individual words and to write them from his pronunciation, he will probably miss the vowel gradation influence, and an inaccurate transcription will result.

Assimilation is the process by which a sound comes to resemble a neighboring sound, physiologically and acoustically. Since the spoken language is the principal medium through which change in the written language is accomplished, this process is very important.

The assimilation is said to be progressive or regressive, depending on the direction in the word of the influence that produces the change. If a sound affects the one following it, the change is said to be progressive. If a sound affects the one preceding it, the change is said to be regressive.

Assimilation is also described according to the nature of the change effected. When the place of production of a sound in the articulation mechanism is altered, the process is called "place assimilation." When the effect is to change the voicing of the assimilated sound, the process is called "voicing assimilation."

Following are examples of place assimilation which have become part of our language: "conquer" from [kɑnkɚ] to [kɑŋkɚ], regressive assimilation, [n] becoming [ŋ] responsive to the influence of the velar [k]; "grandpa" from [grænpɑ] to [græmpɑ], the last step being regressive assimilation, alveolar [n] yielding to labial [m] under the influence of labial [p].

Following are examples of voicing assimilation which have become part of our langauge. The plural [s] has changed to [ż] after a voiced consonant as in "birds" [bɜˑdz], and "cards" [kɑrdz], progressive assimilation in both cases. Past tense endings have changed from [d] to [t] after voiceless consonants as in "walked" [wɔkt], and "snapped" [snæpt], progressive assimilation. "Attic" becomes [ædɪk] in some people's speech, reflecting change of the voiceless [t] to the voiced [d] under influence of vowels (voiced, of course) on either side, a combination of progressive and regressive assimilation.

From this voicing assimilation process, one typical pronunciation problem in English arises. The plural ending "s" or "es," as noted above, takes on the voicing of the consonant which it follows. "Cabs," for example, might erroneously be pronounced [kæbs]; because of the voiced "b" before the plural, it should be [kæbz]. A similar word, however, has a voiceless consonant before the plural ending and should therefore be pronounced with a voiceless postdental sibilant: "caps" should be [kæps] not [kæpz]. Some students, unfortunately, do not have accurate auditory perception of the voicing of the plurals and fail to recognize the voicing distinction. The result is frequent errors in voicing.

Certain acoustical phenomena of connected speech are neither gradation nor assimilation, as we have defined them. Yet the events that occur result from essentially the same process that accounts for gradation and assimilation: facilitation, the tendency of the organism to accomplish a specific task with the smallest possible expenditure of energy, moving the parts (articulators) through the least possible distance. Thus consonants often are blended together or even omitted from connected speech. This occurs in single words: for example, the [k] and [t] in "asked" are combined so that the explosion of the [k] and the implosion of the [t] are lost. Nevertheless, the two sounds are identifiable and must be written as two sounds.

Blending or combining of consonants also occurs between words in running speech, perhaps more often than in words alone. For example, "pick cotton" in connected speech becomes [pɪkɑtn] in actual sound; but conventionally it is transcribed [pɪk kɑtn]. "With thin excuses" sounds like [wɪθɪn ɪkskjusəz] but is conventionally transcribed [wɪθ θɪn ɪkskjusəz].

Consonants sometimes are dropped entirely from connected speech. For example, the "h" in "his" disappears in rapid production of the sentence, "It was his own fault." [ɪt wəz ɪz on fɔlt.]

When your handling of the phonetic alphabet has become proficient and you are writing single words with fluency, begin transcribing connected speech. A performance assignment at the end of the chapter gives you practice in working from phonetics and in transcribing connected speech into phonetic symbols.

PRONUNCIATION STANDARDS

If languages could be planned in advance and forms and usages set up in an entirely logical way, our learning and teaching tasks would be considerably simpler. However, languages are dynamic; they live and grow through use. They are constantly in processes of changing, growing, adapting to new times. Pronunciation changes are part of that process.

Between the period of general use of an old and accepted pronunciation and the adoption of a gradually evolved new pronunciation, there is an in-between time when both pronunciations are acceptable. Currently the following English words, among others, are in this twilight period in American usage. The pronunciations given here are listed in the 1960 Funk and Wagnalls' Standard Dictionary as disputed pronunciations; each one given is acceptable to some authorities:

> adult [ə'dʌlt], ['ædəlt]
> advertisement [æd'vɝtɪzmənt], [ædvɚ'taɪzmənt]
> amen [emɛn], [ɑmɛn]
> camellia [kəmiljə], [kəmɛljə]
> either [iðɚ], [aɪðɚ]
> envelope [ɛnvəlop], [ɑnvəlop]
> fertile[fɝtl], [fɝtaɪl]
> humor [hjumɚ], [jumɚ]
> leisure [liʒɚ], [lɛʒɚ]
> neither [niðɚ], [naɪθɚ]
> oblique [oblik], [oblaɪk]
> patronize [pætrənaɪz], [petrənaɪz]
> quinine [kwɪnaɪn], [kwaɪnaɪn], [kwɪnin]
> tomato [təmeto], [təmɑto]

Ordinarily, in such cases, individual choice or local usage determines selection of pronunciation. It is probably wise to be consistent in your pronunciation of a given word and words similar to it, and perhaps it is wise to be consistent in being conservative or progressive in pronunciation usage in general.

For the average person the following self-guidance principles may be helpful in deciding on pronunciation: It is generally best not to initiate a new pronunciation. Best also to think twice before pioneering someone else's new pronunciation in your community. On the other hand, it is perhaps wise to avoid being excessively pedantic or old-fashioned about pronunciations that are being replaced. Your occupation, your community, and your own tastes will help you in making such decisions. Above all, however, consistency in pronunciation of comparable groups of words is urgent; for example, you must be consistent with the secondary accent group, "stationary," "cemetery," "secretary," and the like. These words may be correctly pronounced with a strong secondary accent [ˈsteʃənˌɛrɪ], [ˈsɛməˌtɛrɪ] [ˈsɛkrəˌtɛrɪ] or without a secondary accent, which eliminates a syllable; [ˈsteʃənrɪ], [ˈsɛmətrɪ], and [ˈsɛkrətrɪ]. Either way is correct; such factors as individual preference, community prejudice, and the consensus within your occupational or professional group will be decisive in your adoption of one stress pattern or the other. The same caution applies to [iðɚ], [aɪðɚ], and [niðɚ], [naɪðɚ]. Apply consistently some guiding principle to your selections among pronunciations that are optional.

Of course, there is only one correct pronunciation for most English words. It behooves the ambitious student of speech to build as much knowledge of the acceptable pronunciations and as much confidence in his own pronunciations as he can manage.

MAJOR AMERICAN DIALECTS

A knowledge of phonetics and phonetic change processes can heighten a student's recognition and appreciation of the interesting dialect variations within his own nation. Notice the word "dialect" is used to mean a regional variation of the language, accomplished with phonetic and melodic changes. It is a more acceptable term in this meaning than "accent," a commonly used variation. "Accent" is more properly used to refer to stressed speech elements. Usually these are syllables, but they may be words or even phrases.

Acceptable American speech can be divided into three large regional dialects which can be differentiated on the basis of inflectional patterns and timing as well as by sound usages. The General American dialect is spoken by the greatest number of people in the United States. It is used, generally in the West, the Southwest, and the Midwest as far south as the Mason Dixon line and as far east as the Appalachian Mountains. This is the form of American English most heard currently on radio, television, and in nondialect movies. It is characterized by pronunciation of the vowel and consonant "r" sounds, rather than substitution of [ə] for [ɚ], [ɜ] for [ɝ], and omission of [r] in some contexts, as occurs in the other dialects. The General American dialect is also characterized by lack of the Southern British vowels and secondary stress influences heard in Eastern and Southern American speech.

The Eastern American dialect is used in the New England states, with the exception of the New York City area, in which are found a great variety of dialects, typical of various areas of our country. Following are eight sound and stress charactᵔristics from among the many listed by authorities on regional speech, characteristics that help to make Eastern American speech different from General American:

1. The "broad a" [a] is used, though not as extensively as some people believe; it appears especially before the "s," "lf," "gh," and "th" endings.
2. There is a tendency for [ɑ] to become [ɔ] in words with [w]; examples are "want" [wɔnt], "watch" [wɔtʃ], and "water" [wɔtɚ].
3. There is a tendency for [ɛ] to become [æ] in "air," "are," "arry" words; examples are "chair" [tʃæ:], "care" [kæ:], and "marry" [mærɪ].
4. There is a tendency for [ɔ] to become [ɑ] in "og" words; examples are "log" [lɑg] and "fog" [fɑg].
5. Unstressed suffixes tend to contain [ɪ]; examples are "salad" [sælɪd], "roses" [rozɪz], and "biggest" [bɪgɪst].
6. The [ɜ] is used in "ear," "er," "ir," words; examples are "heard" [hɜd], "firm" [fɜm], and "term" [tɜm].
7. Although the dialect seems to be changing in this feature, preconsonantal and final "r" are often silent; examples are "cart" [kɑ:t], "for" [fɔ:], "car" [kɑ:], and "park" [pɑ:k].
8. The secondary stress in "ery," "ary," "ory" words may be dropped; examples are "cemetery" ['sɛmətrɪ], "stationary" [steʃənrɪ], and "dictionary" ['dɪkʃənrɪ].

There are other differences, especially in vowel usage, too detailed for attention here.

The third major dialect is Southern American speech, closely related to the Eastern dialect in many aspects. It is used in the southern states as far west as Arkansas and Louisiana and part of Texas. The first seven characteristics of the Eastern American dialect listed above are also part of this dialect. In addition, the following three variations should be considered:

1. There is a tendency to use [ə] for final "r," as in "core" [koə], "fire" [faɪə], and "pair" [pɛə].
2. The "drawl" or prolongation, diphthongization, and triphthongi-

zation are considered substandard variations; examples are "pop" [pɑəp], "baby" [beɪəbɪ], and "bless" [blɛjəs].
3. The omission of the second half of a diphthong is also considered substandard; examples are "ice" [as], "fine" [fan], and "oil" [ɔl].

There are many subordinate dialect variations in the United States, some of them with acceptable dialect forms, but most of them characterized by substandardisms: for example, southern mountain speech, east Texas speech, and speech of certain metropolitan areas. *Brooklynese* is among the latter and the term intends no reflection on the city but is merely a label for a type of dialect found in parts of many large cities, for example, Philadelphia, Chicago, St. Louis, Jersey City. Another such term is *Hoosier* speech, referring not only to the speech of Indiana residents but to the speech of many people throughout the Ohio River basin.

Probably you should speak the dialect most acceptable to educated, cultured people of your community, usually one of the three major American dialects.

STUDENT PROJECTS

CONTENT ASSIGNMENT

A. List the twenty-six consonants discussed in your text under the following headings. Be careful to write the symbols correctly. Encircle each voiced consonant: plosives, fricatives, glides, nasals, semivowels, affricates.
B. Draw the vowel diagram, putting the seventeen vowel symbols in their proper positions on it. List the diphthongs.
C. Define "formant."
D. For practice write the appropriate symbol in each case:

Initial Consonant	Final Consonant	Middle Consonant
cow	map	singer
show	porch	cousin
when	rang	oven
jump	trees	Roger

Initial Consonant	*Final Consonant*	*Middle Consonant* (*Cont.*)
photo	laugh	vision
cheek	wash	package
seed	horse	leather
cease	mirage	cupboard
rain	bath	away
youth	bathe	arrow
these	fix	medium
thin	arc	hello

E. For practice write the proper symbol for the *italicized* vowel or diphthong in each word.

p*a*th	s*e*lls	ent*er*
c*au*tion	pr*ai*se	*ear*th
fl*oa*t	s*a*tin	sof*a*
s*ee*p	pr*ea*ch	*a*bout
l*o*t	b*ea*n	Ca*e*sar
n*ur*se	cr*o*ss	clich*e*
S*ue*	pr*i*me	p*o*nd
g*oo*d	sn*ou*t	p*e*rtain
s*oi*l	p*aw*n	j*u*st
pl*o*t	p*u*ll	t*oi*l
fl*i*nt	b*u*dge	br*ea*k
pl*ay*	print	s*o*lid

F. For practice with voiced and unvoiced consonants transcribe into phonetics the word lists on pages 82 and 83.

G. *Practice Words for Vowels Frequently Confused in Transcription*
Transcribe the following pairs of words into phonetic symbols; give special attention to the vowel sounds.

(1) [a]   [æ]   (2) [i]   [ɪ]

bond	— band	seat	— sit
sock	— sack	beet	— bit
rock	— rack	heat	— hit
lob	— lab	meat	— mit
mod	— mad	greed	— grid
flop	— flap	deep	— dip
gob	— gab	sheep	— ship
blond	— bland	shield	— shilled
pond	— panned	scream	— scrim

(1) [a]   [æ]

cop — cap
sodden — sadden
flock — flack
mock — Mack
clock — clack
bottle — battle

(2) [i]   [ɪ]   (*Cont.*)

feet — fit
cheap — chip
ream — rim
heal — hill
feel — fill
reaches — riches

(3) [ɪ]   [ɛ]

bit — bet
mit — met
sit — set
lit — set
knit — net
tin — ten
bin — been
Jim — gem
rid — red
did — dead
sill — sell
fill — fell
bid — bed
Dick — deck
rick — wreck

(4) [e]   [æ]

bake — back
slake — slack
take — tack
make — Mack
bade — bad
rate — rat
bait — bat
steak — stack
nape — nap
fade — fad
save — salve
stain — Stan
brain — bran
pale — pal
hail — Hal

(5) [ɪ]   [ɛ]   [e]

bit — bet — bait
mit — met — mate
sit — set — sate
lit — let — late
bin — been — bane
rid — red — rain
sill — sell — sale
fill — fell — fail
bid — bed — bade
rick — wreck — rake
pin — pen — pain

(6) [ɪ]   [ɛ]   [æ]

bit — bet — bat
mit — met — mat
sit — set — sat
knit — net — gnat
tin — ten — tan
bin — been — ban
Jim — gem — jam
did — dead — Dad
sill — sell — Sal
bid — bed — bad
rick — wreck — rack
pin — pen — pan

(7) [ɔ]   [o]

tossed — toast
bossed — boast

(8) [ɑ]   [o]

tot — tote
got — goat

(7) [ɔ]   [o]   (8) [ɑ]   [o]   (*Cont.*)

mossed	— most	rot	— wrote
gauze	— goes	sock	— soak
taws	— toes	doll	— dole
bawl	— bowl	Moll	— mole
pshaw	— show	Ron	— roan
hall	— hole	pop	— pope
fawn	— phone	rod	— rode
Paul	— pole	mod	— mode
daunt	— don't	Todd	— toad
pawn	— pone	nod	— node
awes	— owes	fond	— phoned
law	— low	hod	— hoed
fall	— foal	hop	— hope

(9) [ɔ]   [or]   (10) [ɑr]   [or]

cord	— cored	park	— pork
fought	— fort	far	— four
caught	— court	tar	— tore
dawn	— adorn	car	— core
fawn	— fourth	mar	— more
sawer	— sower	bar	— bore
pawer	— pour	are	— ore
salt	— sore	gar	— gore
		tarred	— toward
		lard	— lord
		hard	— hoard
		star	— store
		par	— pour

(11) [ɔ]   [ɑ]   [o]

taught	— tot	— tote
law	— la	— low
wrought	— rot	— wrote
mall	— Moll	— mole
Maude	— mod	— mode
naught	— not	— note
fawned	— fond	— phoned
Salk	— sock	— soak

(21) [ʊ]   [ɝ]   (22) [u]   [ʊ]   [ɝ]   [ʌ]

      stood — stirred   cooed — could — curd   — cud
      hood — heard   tooth — took — Turk   — tuck
      good — gird   stewed — stood — stirred — stud
      took — Turk   who'd — hood — heard — Hud
      could — curd
      look — lurk

(23) Which vowel appears in each   (24) Which vowel appears in
     of these, [ʌ] or [ʊ]?   each of these, [u] or [ʊ]?

      pluck   push   soon   lose
      full   crutch   book   soup
      jump   lull   boot   brook
      putter   stood   foot   fruit
      hood   crook   moon   good
                                             rook   grew
                                             glue   hook
                                             rule

(25) Which vowel appears in each   (26) Which vowel appears in each
     of the following, [ɛ] or [ɪ]?   of the following, [ɔ] or [o]?

      said   very   cross   brawl
      net   build   groan   more
      pit   yen   croak   hoarse
      Henry   simple   for   toss
      medal   chest   horse   gross
      blip   blessed   blown   lost
      stead   kid   note   pour
      flippant prism   pall   cold
      blend   mister   call   gore
      credit   blimp   cord   most

(27) Which vowel appears in each   (28) Which vowel appears in each
     of the following, [ɑ] or [ɔ]?   of the following, [e] or [ɛ]?

      bark   north   break   fled
      salt   pot   bread   nail
      garden   balk   plane   flake
      warn   large   bled   Helen
      paunch   north   drain   pencil

H. Transcribe these for practice with front vowels:

intense	entertain	potash	mystic
pelting	French	Rockette	prefect
varnish	painted	vacation	brackish
treasure	festive	prestige	freezing
fatal	happy	integrate	backless

1. The pleasant background was hidden by fences and gates.
2. Weather warnings can't take the place of weather watches.
3. Hacks attempt to appeal to readers' bad taste.
4. Religion leads many people to contentment.
5. Sarah breaks glasses frequently by flipping them.
6. Never say never, say maybe.
7. Guess the amount of gas my heap takes every day.
8. Pressure prints the final picture on the back of the paper.
9. Maintain a steady head and a stiff back.
10. He came in whenever the band played rock.

I. Transcribe these for practice with back vowels:

puddle	induction	broken	quadroon
importune	tunic	prosper	Saugatuk
caustic	proof	lucrative	lunar
solemn	pronounce	cartoon	football
produce	trawler	palsy	awful

1. The tune proved louder and more bouncy than John wanted.
2. Shovel the snow and be glad there is no more.
3. Funny shows are not casually found.
4. Foolishness took a toll of his hours.
5. Walking and talking could be enjoyable for all of us.
6. Sore toes make jumping harder.
7. Toss the ball to Sue then to Walter.
8. I hope it costs more than the old one.
9. The tufted bird is a cardinal.
10. Pardon comes swiftly to those who are sorry.

J. *Practice Words for Consonants Frequently Confused in Transcription*

(1) Spelling sometimes helps, but not always. These are pronounced and transcribed as one would expect from the spelling:

[dʒ]	[g]	[dʒ]	[g]	[g]	[dʒ]
Joe	— go	jail	— gale	bag	— budge
jay	— gay	jest	— guest	bug	— badge

[dʒ]	[g]	[dʒ]	[g]	[g]	[dʒ]
(*Cont.*)					
jet	— get	Jerry — Gary		rig	— ridge
jar	— gar	juice — goose		egg	— edge
just	— gust	job — gob		leg	— ledge
				brig	— bridge

(2) These initial consonants are spelled differently and pronounced the same:

[dʒ]	[dʒ]
Jim	— gym
jerk	— germ
Jeanne	— gene
jeep	— gee

(3) These are all spelled with "g" or "gg" and pronounced with [g]:

ragged
digging
aghast
logger
wagon
biggest
ago
frigate
baggy
ragged

(4) These are all spelled with "g" or "dg" and pronounced with [dʒ]:

rigid
digest
pages
region
frigid
budget
aged
regeant
edge
badger

(5) These are all spelled with "j" or "dj" and pronounced with [dʒ]:

majestic	rejoice	adjoin	injustice
adjust	enjoy	injury	
rejuvenate	perjury	pajamas	

(6) Transcribe these for practice in recognizing [dʒ] or [g]:

pageant	rigging	trigger	stage
adjoin	pudgy	engine	flog
agate	gallop	genius	rigorous
digress	gymnasium	logistics	vigilant
journey	ginger	gypsy	pledge
jump	ledger	lodge	project
gauge	gesture	gelatin	jealous

(6) Transcribe these for practice in recognizing [dʒ] or [g]:   (*Cont.*)

sargeant	grotesque	giving	interrogate
register	passage	magic	intelligent
haggard	gantry	telegraph	flagrant
rogue	George	colleague	tragic

(7) [dʒ]   [dz]   (8) [dʒ]   [j]   [dʒ]   [j]

rage	— raids	jell	— yell	jay	— yea
siege	— seeds	jam	— yam	jet	— yet
age	— aids	jaw	— yaw	Jew	— yew
		jeer	— year	joke	— yoke
		Jello	— yellow	jowl	— yowl
		Jack	— yak	jot	— yacht

(9) The [j] is often confused with [dʒ] because of spelling. These are all for practice with the [j] sound:

youth	yard	your
yes	yearling	Yankee
yesterday	yeast	yearn
yawn	yarn	yarrow
yodel	yokel	York
yank	yule	yelp

onion	emulate	confuse
million	view	deluge
milieu	beauty	ambulance
banyon	butane	bilious
bayou	cute	ebullience
muscular	dude	celluloid
senior	imbue	bugle

(10)   [j]   not [j]   (11)   [j]   not [j]

deluge	dilute		pure	purchase
emulate	emulsify		salutation	salute
accurate	accouter		evacuate	vicuna
astute	toot		volume	voluminous
butte	boot		cure	curl
punitive	punish		uranium	urban
immune	immovable		huge	hug
			humility	humble

(12) Transcribe the following with care to spot the [dʒ], the [j], or perhaps neither:

badger	digest	drugged	pads
measure	sages	Don Juan	entourage
joist	educate	adjutant	courage
gymnasium	huge	jeep	ledgible
digress	purge	banjo	imagine

(13) Transcribe these taking care to spot and include the [j] when it is there:

ameliorate	injustice	fragile
luminous	utility	formula
mute	urn	finish
voyage	useless	eyesore
manufacture	Tulsa	eureka
lunar	Tucson	etymology
lawyer	truck	dooryard
bayonet	truly	partial
stallion	tallyho	fission
exultation	figure	bacteria
ampule	marjoram	ballistic
gallant	junior	askew
granulate	Juanita	aqua
illustrate	Jungfrau	acquaint
individual	jugular	diary
indulge	Yugoslavia	daring
Daniel	educate	effectual
multiply	mummy	Muriel
punctuate	sulfur	murder
tuna	rendition	future

(14) According to the pronouncing dictionary[3] these may be pronounced with or without a [j]; transcribe each both ways:

news	stupid	tumor
tune	suit	Tudor
tuber	tulip	

(15) Practice words for the [tʃ]:

chalk	etching	botch
chum	inches	leech

[3] Kenyon, J. and Knott, T. *Pronouncing Dictionary of American English.* G. & C. Merriam Co., Springfield, Mass., 1944.

(15) Practice words for the [tʃ]: (*Cont.*)

churn	launching	punch
chop	purchase	such
child	flinching	match

(16)

[tʃ]	[ʃ]	[tʃ]	[ʃ]	[tʃ]	[ʃ]
choose —	shoes	watcher —	washer	batch —	bash
chip —	ship	matches —	mashes	much —	mush
cheap —	sheep	Fitch's —	fishes	hatch —	hash
cheek —	sheik	latching —	lashing	catch —	cash
chide —	shied	hatching —	hashing	hutch —	hush

(17)

[tʃ]	[ts]	[tʃ]	[ts] (cont'd)
catch —	cats	rich —	Ritz
batch —	bats	hitch —	hits
notch —	knots	patch —	pats
blotch —	blots	match —	mats
ouch —	outs	witch —	wits

(18) Transcribe these words taking care to put the [tʃ] in the proper places:

child	actual	perch
cello	acting	hoax
character	picture	patch
char	satchel	stomach
chance	searching	flinch

(19) The final "ed" is often misleading; it may be pronounced [t] or [d] or [əd].

[t]	[d]	[əd]
passed	housed	painted
crossed	pleased	plated
briefed	loved	fitted
cashed	rammed	patted
blocked	ringed	wilted
racked	bruised	inflated
sneaked	glazed	grounded
hacked	purged	minded
reached	hummed	herded
branched	banned	crusted

(20) Transcribe these giving care to the correct symbols for the final "ed":

lacked	purred	dragged
braved	blasted	stripped
plodded	hounded	brushed
stirred	planned	batted
flared	seated	howled
winced	crashed	stranded
hanged	pounded	bowled

(21) Various spellings of the [k] sound sometimes trouble students. In the following words the sound appears in various spellings and sometimes is not present though the letter "k" is used:

kin	walker	book
kangaroo	winking	leak
cap	sacreligeous	frantic
cool	saccule	fantastic
college	across	plastic
cattle	active	comic
cross	accuse	hectic
clap	saccharine	Arctic
chloroform	echo	stomach
cheat	ratchet	hatch
chair	richer	flinch
know	acknowledge	pack
knee	picnic	hook
knack	racket	bleak
extra	exhale	maximum
box	flux	hex

(22) Practice for the [s] sound; notice the different spellings:

soup	passing	miss
seven	household	press
salad	lesson	douse
statue	risk	purse
scrap	awesome	cats
cell	raceway	dance
certain	placement	pounce
circus	cancer	brace
cease	encircle	enhance
cipher	incessant	place
scissors	examine	Rex
sciatica	proximity	fix

(22) Practice for the [s] sound; notice the different spellings: (*Cont.*)

scene	hexagon	mix
scintillate	mixing	matrix
science	Mexico	annex

[s]	[sk]	[sk]	[sk]
scissors	scream	scheme	skip
science	scope	school	skirt
scene	scorch	schooner	skat
sciatica	scooter	schedule	skate
scintillate	score	schizoid	skill

(23)

[s]	[ʃ]	[s]	[ʃ]	[s]	[ʃ]
mass	— mash	crust	— crushed	sow	— show
plus	— plush	fasten	— fashion	said	— shed
bass	— bash	messing	— meshing	seep	— sheep
brass	— brash	leased	— leashed	sallow	— shallow

(24)

[s]	[z]	[s]	[z]	[s]	[z]
see	— zee	faces	— phases	loss	— laws
sip	— zip	bussing	— buzzing	hiss	— his
Sue	— zoo	placing	— blazing	cross	— craws
seal	— zeal	recent	— reason	purse	— purrs
sink	— zinc	caustic	— causes	France	— Franz

(25) Final "s" or "es" may be pronounced [s] or [z]:

[s]	[z]
cats	plows
pumps	hams
jacks	figs
flints	bleeds
muffs	burns
mocks	panels
sheets	wreathes
strips	prods
laughs	guys
parts	wishes
notes	houses
dates	places
kites	masses
hopes	praises
rakes	benches

(26) Transcribe these words being careful to transcribe correctly the [s] and other sounds with which it may be confused:

socks	physics
blots	suitable
corns	ensue
paddles	verses
askew	interpretation
passenger	cease
position	seize
passengers	holds
phases	coats
hazy	codes
breezes	misery
scissors	miser
visible	fasten

(27)

[s]		[θ]	[s]		[θ]	[s]		[θ]
sing	—	thing	placing	—	plaything	pass	—	path
song	—	thong	mystical	—	mythical	miss	—	myth
sump	—	thump	dressy	—	breathy	face	—	faith
some	—	thumb				force	—	fourth
sank	—	thank				mouse	—	mouth

(28)

[θ]	[ð]	[θ]		[ð]
think	then	breath	—	breathe
thought	this	wreath	—	wreathe
thorough	those	lath	—	lathe
thousand	that	bath	—	bathe
thick	than	cloth	—	clothe
pathway	wither	mouth	—	mouthe
mythical	heather			
pathology	bother			
wrathful	fathom			
mathematics	rhythm			
with	scathe			
Kenneth	writhe			
wealth	lithe			
sloth	mouthe			
mirth	scythe			

(29) Practice differentiating between [θ] and [ð] in these words:

thin	dearth	third	breather
thump	the	bathroom	thimble
them	plethora	scathing	Hathaway
birth	weather	thirst	southern
tooth	bothering	breathy	north

K. (1) The letter "x" does not represent a sound used in American speech. Words spelled with "x" and those in which that sound is heard instead are transcribed as they are sounded, usually [ks]:

hex	treks
axe	hacks
knox	knocks
ox	socks
lax	lacks

(2) The letter "q" is not a phonetic symbol in American speech; the sound of "q" is transcribed, usually [kw]:

quick	aqua
quill	acquaint
quilt	inquest
quip	acquire
quiet	loquacious

L. Short Words for Phonetic Transcription practice:

1. [taɪm]	1. pop
2. [lɔs]	2. cat
3. [ʃɔl]	3. side
4. [trɪm]	4. pick
5. [wɑnt]	5. vase
6. [hæf]	6. fish
7. [pliz]	7. goat
8. [aɪʂ]	8. mile
9. [θʌm]	9. chose
10. [ðɛn]	10. thump
11. [tʃaɪmz]	11. short
12. [hɔɪst]	12. press
13. [vudu]	13. fling
14. [fɝ·vɚ·]	14. burst
15. [vɪʒən]	15. turn

L. Short Words for Phonetic Transcription practice: (*Cont.*)

16. [sæləd]	16. toil
17. [lɪnt]	17. book
18. [ples]	18. tale
19. [rɪtən]	19. wash
20. [raɪtɪŋ]	20. paper
21. [kɝt]	21. trees
22. [portɚ]	22. stove
23. [tɝmz]	23. young
24. [trɪmz]	24. jump
25. [ɔɪlɪ]	25. page
26. [hɛvən]	26. anger
27. [dʒʌmbl̩]	27. daughter
28. [tɛkst]	28. earth
29. [ɝlɪəst]	29. become
30. [hæpən]	30. laugh
31. [kæptɪv]	31. stood
32. [frɔg]	32. rooms
33. [əlon]	33. taxi
34. [prɑgrɛs]	34. pressing
35. [sup]	35. action
36. [prunz]	36. enter
37. [taɪpt]	37. postage
38. [fæntəsɪ]	38. creeper
39. [laʊdɚ]	39. puddle
40. [əmʌŋ]	40. zebra
41. [sikɚ]	41. atone
42. [fækts]	42. outside
43. [trɛʒɚ]	43. choices
44. [tɛləfon]	44. parrot
45. [kraʊd]	45. control
46. [stɔntʃ]	46. possess
47. [ɪntɚ]	47. gallop
48. [pleket]	48. pester
49. [sɔɪld]	49. thankful
50. [rivaɪv]	50. million

M. Polysyllable Words for Phonetic Transcription Practice:

1. [risɛsɪv]	1. beautiful
2. [pɛrədɑks]	2. tragic
3. [ɪntrɛpɪd]	3. exchequer

M. Polysyllable Words for Phonetic Transcription Practice: (*Cont.*)

4. [pɔɪzənəs]
5. [fæntæstɪk]
6. [lokəmotɪv]
7. [ʃipɪʃlɪ]
8. [prikɜ˞sə˞]
9. [sælɪvet]
10. [junəfaɪd]
11. [dʒʌstəfəkeʃən]
12. [stupɪdətɪ]
13. [rizənəbl̩]
14. [æloket]
15. [fɪləbʌstə˞]
16. [ɛndʒɔɪmənt]
17. [hɛzətənt]
18. [ɪntə˞lopə˞]
19. [præktɪkælətɪ]
20. [stɑrveʃən]
21. [blɪstə˞ɪŋ]
22. [dɛdɪket]
23. [rəpɪdətɪ]
24. [plæstɪk]
25. [rilɪdʒəs]
26. [ɛmfætɪk]
27. [kɛrɪktə˞]
28. [haʊndəd]
29. [vəlgɛrətɪ]
30. [dɪtɜ˞mənd]
31. [ɛmplɔɪmənt]
32. [fæsənet]
33. [prɛʃə˞aɪz]
34. [sætəlaɪt]
35. [sɛnseʃənəl]
36. [sætɪsfæktərɪ]
37. [produsə˞]
38. [inæml̩d]
39. [rɛslə˞]
40. [wɪŋsprɛd]
41. [slipwɔkə˞]
42. [mənɪpjulet]
43. [fɪroʃəs]

4. enamoured
5. pacificism
6. sixteen
7. thermometer
8. representational
9. alliteration
10. encyclopedic
11. hallucinate
12. questionable
13. maharajah
14. mutuality
15. perturbed
16. repartee
17. sweetbrier
18. hypotonicity
19. communique
20. paraphrase
21. scholastic
22. charioteer
23. resurgence
24. rarified
25. shadowy
26. psychodynamic
27. erroneous
28. fluorescent
29. sheathing
30. simulation
31. cavernous
32. celestial
33. multiplicand
34. peculiarity
35. refrigerant
36. employable
37. undoubtedly
38. quiescent
39. anticlimax
40. distillation
41. sacrificial
42. indecisiveness
43. judiciary

M. Polysyllable Words for Phonetic Transcription Practice: (*Cont.*)

44. [mænɪdʒmənt]	44. upholsterer
45. [ʌnkwɛntʃt]	45. enterprising
46. [rinjuəbl̩]	46. coagulation
47. [ɪnstrəmɛntl̩]	47. photogenic
48. [fəsɪlətet]	48. quadruple
49. [tʃɛrətəbl̩]	49. tenaciousness
50. [obidɪənt]	50. vulcanization

N. Put each sentence into phonetics. Transcribe your rapid speech production of each.

1. Harry, when are you coming back?

2. He's going to get a coke and a sandwich.

3. I want to ask him some questions about the examination.

4. Can you help me with some of these problems?

5. I must learn to do them without the book.

6. My notebook is so full I'll have to get a new one soon.

7. Where did I put the newest list of assignments?

8. Is this your outline or is it mine?

9. This formula seems right, but the answer is ridiculous.

10. Will you check it for errors for me?

O. Transcribe each sentence.

1. [ðə rum ɪzn̩t braɪt ənʌf fɚ stʌdɪ]

2. [maɪ læmps tu fɑr əwe frəm maɪ dɛsk]

3. [aɪl bɔro wʌn əkrɔs ðə hɔl]

4. [nau aɪ kən si hwɑt aɪm duɪŋ]

5. [ðɛrz ə nju lɪst əv əsaɪnmənts ðɪs wik]

6. [hɛrɪz gʊd ət ðiz θɪŋz bət wont hɛlp mɪ]

7. [lɛts si aɪ nid ə rulɚ nd ə pɛn]

8. [ɑr jʊr ænsɚ ʃitz əz mɛsɪ əz ðɪs]

9. [aɪ θɪŋk ðɪs ɪz ðə hɑrdəst kors aɪv hæd]

10. [he hɛrɪ aɪ wɑnt tə tɔk tʊ ju ə mɪnət]

P. The following words seem to be difficult for some people to learn to pronounce according to current best use. Look them up if you are in doubt. Transcribe them into phonetics.

guarantee	accident
athlete	pretty
arctic	interesting
larynx	family
often	garage
toward	gradually

P. The following words seem to be difficult for some people to learn to pronounce according to current best use. Look them up if you are in doubt. Transcribe them into phonetics.   (*Cont.*)

chimney	umbrella
library	similar
coordination	familiar
push	piano
Illinios	poor
Chicago	February
double	diapers
across	government
hundred	congress
perspire	abdomen
always	vague
cliff	pleasure
children	egg
United States	prescribe
pronunciation	valuable
casual	wouldn't
president	future

Q. Further transcription practice with word lists containing some of the consonant sounds; [s], [z], [r], [l], [θ], and [ð], are to be found in Chapter 6. The paragraph, "The Old Grad," at the end of that chapter would make an excellent final examination of your ability to use phonetics; it is constructed to contain all the sounds of American English. Practice transcribing it into phonetics. Compare two transcriptions done two weeks apart; have you improved in accuracy?

RECOMMENDED READINGS

Bender, J. *N.B.C. handbook of pronunciation.* (2d ed.) New York: Crowell, 1955.

Chomsky, N., and Halle, M. *The sound pattern of English.* New York: Harper & Row, 1968.

Cooper, F. S., Delattre, P. C., Liberman, A. M., Borse, J. M., and Gerstman, L. J. Some experiments on the perception of synthetic speech sounds. *J. Acoustical Soc. of America,* **24,** 1952, 597–606.

Curtis, J. F., and Hardy, J. C. A phonetic study of misarticulation of [r]. *J. Speech and Hearing Research,* **2,** 1959, 244–257.

Delattre, P. C. The physiological interpretation of sound spectrograms. *Publications of the Modern Language Ass.,* **66,** 1951, 864–875.

Heffner, R-M. S. *General phonetics.* Madison: University of Wisconsin Press, 1949.

Jakobson, R., Fant, C. G. M., and Halle, M. Preliminaries to speech analysis, the distinctive features and their correlates. *Technical Report No. 13.* Cambridge: Massachusetts Institute of Technology, Acoustics Laboratory, 1952.

———— and Halle, M. *Fundamentals of language.* The Hague: Mouton, 1956.

———— and Halle, M. Supplement, Tenseness and Laxness, in Jakobson, R., Fant, C., and Halle, M. *Preliminaries to Speech Analysis, the Distinctive Features and Their Correlates,* sixth printing, Cambridge, Mass.: M.I.T. Press, 1965.

Jones, D. *An English pronouncing dictionary.* (5th ed.) New York: Dutton, 1943.

Kenyon, J. S., and Knott, T. A. *A pronouncing dictionary of American English.* Springfield, Mass.: Merriam, 1944.

Liberman, A. M., Delattre, P. C., and Cooper, F. S. The role of selected stimulus-variables in the perception of the unvoiced stop consonants. *Amer. J. Psychol.* **65,** 1952, 497–516.

Moses, E. Palatography and speech improvement. *J. Speech Disorders,* **4,** 1939, 103–114.

New standard dictionary of the English language. New York: Funk and Wagnalls, 1960.

Peterson, G. E., and Coxe, M. S. The vowels [e] and [o] in American speech. *Quart. J. Speech,* **39,** 1953, 33–41.

———— and Shoup, J. A physiological theory of phonetics. *J. Speech and Hearing Research,* **9,** 1966, 5–67.

————. Elements of an acoustic phonetic theory. *J. Speech and Hearing Research,* **9,** 1966, 68–99.

Potter, R. K., Kopp, G., and Green, H. *Visible speech.* Princeton, N.J.: Van Nostrand, 1947.

Travis, L. E. (ed.) *Handbook of speech pathology.* New York: Appleton-Century-Crofts, 1957, Chaps. 4 and 5.

Wise, C. M. *Applied phonetics.* Englewood Cliffs, N.J.: Prentice-Hall, 1957.

CHAPTER
6

SKILL
IN
ARTICULATION

Important little movements. Crucial. But so habit-
ual—we don't think. Not all habits are good. Let's think. Crucial little
movements—articulation. Details, sequences, coordination. The process of
forming speech sounds by altering the free flow of the exhaled breath
stream. Blockages, constrictions, diversions of the air stream. Part of the
process of speech production: innervation, respiration, phonation, resonance, articulation, and monitoring. A set of anatomical instruments is
involved, the articulators: vocal folds, soft palate, hard palate, tongue,
lower jaw, teeth, and lips. The consonants, you recall, are articulated by
contacts or approximations of articulators. Vowels are formed by resonance conditions set up by positions of the lower jaw, tongue, and lips so,
in a sense, the vowels are articulated too.

The initial learning of articulation, its development and adult control
are, for most people, completely automatic; it is given little conscious

attention. As a child learns he imitates adults around him quite uncon-sciously. He goes through a period of errors and approximations in sound production, but typically by about six or seven years of age, he has mas-tered the speech sounds and produces them as adults do. Through all the years of trial-and-error learning he probably thought little about exact methods of producing speech sounds. Most speech learning is spontaneous and requires little real concern for the exact nature of articulation. That lack of conscious concern about speech persists, in most people, through-out their lives.

A misarticulation occurs when an error in articulator positioning is so extreme that the sound produced belongs, for the listener, to another phoneme; or when the articulator positioning is so faulty that the sound is noticed as strange or unusual; or, of course, when the communication becomes unintelligible to the listener. When one has misarticulations, it is usually necessary for him to *become* aware of speech sounds and move-ments in order to correct his errors. He will probably need assistance from parents and teachers—perhaps even speech-correction personnel—in the process.

Review the information on feedback and the role it plays in speech in Chapter 1. There is no doubt that awareness of positions and move-ments of articulators is very much involved in our producing correct speech sounds. Ringel and Steer found that under conditions of local anesthetiza-tion of the oral region their subjects produced speech that was significantly inaccurate as judged by a panel of experienced speech pathologists. The same research confirmed previous findings of deleterious effects on articu-lation of binaural masking. In other words, if you do not hear and feel what you are doing with your articulators, the results will be inaccurate. You need to be aware of how you are using your articulators to develop habits which will yield the best results.

PRECISION IN ARTICULATION

When a speaker becomes aware of the processes of articulation either to correct misarticulations or simply to study the processes, as you are doing, he may have a tendency to become overly careful and exact in his speech sound production. If he goes too far in that direction, he may shift the attention of the listener from the content of his communication to the manner in which he is producing the sounds involved, thus failing to communicate, or failing to communicate effectively. By being too correct he commits a speech fault as fatal to good communication as that attributable to a new set of dentures or an anesthetized tongue. Speech that is too precise, or affected, can be quite annoying to the listener.

How far should you lean away from precise speech to avoid such affectation? As in most things, it is probably best for you to seek a middle course between the extreme exactness of articulation that becomes pedantic or affected and the extreme laxness that becomes uncommunicative "sloppiness," laden with minor distortions of phonemes.

In natural, conversational speech the small words—connectives, articles, and auxiliary verbs—are often "thrown away," unstressed, because of their comparative unimportance to the meaning. That is a perfectly acceptable procedure so long as speech does not approach "telegraphese," language that completely omits connectives as one might in a telegraph message. "I am arriving at the west station at nine o'clock tonight. I have a guest, so please bring the sedan," might become in telegraph language, "Arriving west station nine tonight. Have guest. Bring sedan." Though the "telegraphese" is intelligible, it is not acceptable language for most speech situations. Normal unstressing occurs in a sentence such as "Give the dog a bone to gnaw." The words "the," "a," and "to" are barely present in the typical production of that sentence. Other connectives frequently unstressed are "an," "for," "and," "but," and "from." The vowels in such words are sometimes moved toward mid-vowel quality when unstressed; they may not be given their usual vowel value.

Then, of course, there *are* times when a small, normally unimportant word demands stress to make the meaning clear. For example, the stress on "their" will vary in the sentence "This is their house," depending on whether the speaker is simply pointing out the house or whether he is making clear the ownership of this particular house. Or, the small word "the" might be emphasized in "That is *the* Smith family," when the speaker must indicate the importance of the family in question. You can probably think of dozens of similar examples. In normal, good speech it is acceptable to unstress most unimportant small words, though there are times when stressing such words is necessary.

It is probably best in conversational situations for you to compromise between the overly precise and the carelessly inexact, using speech that is clear and accurate without calling attention to its precision.

There are times, however, when a situation demands very careful speech. Such a situation might occur when a specific meaning depends on accurate understanding of a word or phrase, when new or unusual words are used, when there is noise or other distraction present, or when the matter under discussion is so crucial that any error in communication would be extremely severe or far-reaching in consequences. Consider the varying need for precise articulation in these situations: a college student reads the minutes of a meeting to a social club; a woman telephones the measurements of a chair for which a slip cover is being made; a new employee introduces himself to his boss; a mechanic explains a malfunctioning transmission to another mechanic; a purchasing agent telephones an urgent order for replacement parts in a broken refrigeration system; a businessman gives a buy or a sell order for current stocks to his broker; the quarterback calls numbers designating the next ball receiver; in a noisy, crowded room a young man makes small talk with a charming girl he has just met; the President of the United States addresses Congress; a pilot gives instructions in flight to the crew of his nuclear-armed bomber. Can there be any doubt that the situation and the conditions of the moment put varying demands on precise articulation for good communication?

Let us recognize, also, that because of his profession or position the speaker sometimes has demands made on him for very careful speech. Consider the varying needs for speech exactness by the speakers in these situations: a professor argues a point before a faculty meeting; a student defends his point of view in a campus club dispute; a college graduate applies for a job in industrial management; a salesman describes to a possible buyer the new developments in this year's automobile; an engineer describes and defends a new or unusual idea before the production board of a large corporation; a scientist reads a highly technical paper before a large group; a medical doctor discusses a severely ill patient's condition in consultation with several colleagues; in court, a lawyer stresses a precedent in law crucial to his client's life. When the situation places emphasis on the special knowledge or skill possessed by the speaker, he should communicate with the accuracy and clarity of articulation that will reflect the accuracy and clarity of his knowledge of the matter at hand.

Summary

Recognizing that most of the time a happy middle course with respect to precision of articulation is best, we must recognize also that sometimes the situation or the demands on the special knowledge of the speaker will call for careful, precise speech. After you have studied the articulation processes and have practiced their use and control, you should be able to use very precise speech *when you need it;* and you should also be able to use the normal, educated but casual speech of everyday experiences. That is the reason we want you to take a critical look at your articulation and to work for increased control.

IMPROVING ARTICULATION IN THE SPEECH LABORATORY

Before you begin work with the following drills, it would be helpful for you to replay the recording you made of your reading early in the course. Listen for any articulation difficulties listed at that time by your instructor and classmates. Play and replay your recording until you are sure you hear the differences that were perceived by your listeners. Listen as well for any other errors that they may not have discovered. Listen especially for any of the following, not infrequently heard, errors and distortions: (1) Final sounds that should be voiced, may be unvoiced, especially the "es" and "ed" endings. For example, the final "s" in "homes" should be voiced but may be articulated incorrectly as a voiceless sound, and final "ed" in "played" should be voiced but may be unvoiced in careless delivery. The opposite error, voicing of unvoiced phonemes, is a less common mistake. (2) Inaccurate placement of the articulators for [l] may give it [w] coloring; "little" may be almost [wɪtə] or "hello," almost [hɛwo]. (3) The [s] is subject to numerous distortions, toward the [θ], toward "slushiness," toward a whistle; or it may be slighted, giving it inadequate strength. (4) The [r] may have [w] coloring or may be slighted almost to omission. (5) The "th's," voiced and unvoiced, may approach the [d] and the [t]. There are numerous other possible errors, of course. If you hear something on your recording that bothers you, but you can't identify it, ask your instructor for help. List and describe the articulation errors or need for general articulation improvement you hear in your recording.

If the articulation errors or distortions are severe enough, your instructor may suggest that you go to your speech clinic for help in your corrective work; or, if he is trained in speech therapy techniques, he may be able to give you special help himself. The work in this book, however, is designed to help students improve basically normal articulation not in need of speech correction procedures. If there is any doubt, perhaps your instructor will ask you to check with your speech clinic and get an opinion on your possible need for therapy.

As you work to improve your own articulation, whether you have special needs for improvement or are merely improving conscious control over your articulators, keep in mind that the monitoring by ear, by touch, and through kinesthetic means matches the result against the mental image of what is desired. In some cases it will be necessary for you to strengthen and sharpen your ideas of what is desired. Ask your instructor or a classmate to help you check your undesirable production of any given sound against a better—best—production. Learn to hear and feel the best production of the sound and to integrate it into words.

Usually, precision of articulation and accuracy of identification by the listener are improved by slowing the articulation process. Schwartz reported that for five vowels slowing rate and prolonging the vowels made them identifiable at consistently lower loudness levels. Apparently listeners receive with more accuracy at lower loudness levels when vowels are prolonged somewhat. The principle probably will assist you in generally improving articulation. Keep it in mind as you work with these exercises.

1. We have selected [s], [z], [r], [ɜ], [ɚ], [l], [θ], and [ð] for specific drill purposes because they seem to be more often misarticulated or distorted than other sounds by otherwise normal speakers. Following are word lists for use in practice on these sounds. When you are doing well with the words, work them into short, simple sentences; then make longer sentences; and finally, for practice read materials from a magazine.

Clinical experience indicates most students can achieve greater awareness of articulatory movements and greater accuracy by over-emphasis or exaggeration of those movements. Admittedly, one would never use such extreme articulation in usual speech. Many "lip lazy" speakers can improve through use of this technique. Exaggerations in practice can lead to moderate, but more active than usual, movements in their habitual speech. As you read the following word lists aloud, watch yourself in a mirror; use large jaw, lip, and tongue movements. Overdo it; don't mind if you feel a bit foolish and awkward at first. Remember your first try at riding a bicycle? You stayed with it till it became natural and easy. The same principle will make articulation movements seem natural, too, if you practice. Read aloud the [s] world lists, concentrating on precise formation of this phoneme in the various phonetic contexts in which it is found. Then follow with the other word lists, exaggerating your articulation on each.

[s]

INITIAL POSITION	FINAL POSITION	MEDIAL POSITION
sock	mass	possible
solemn	grass	roster
sad	pass	passing
satisfy	glass	glasses
said	press	lesser
settled	address	addressing
same	place	pacing
sable	trace	place
sit	bliss	misses

[s]

INITIAL POSITION	FINAL POSITION	MEDIAL POSITION (*Cont.*)
situation	miss	mister
seed	geese	peaceful
seeking	grease	leasing
sought	floss	awesome
salt	moss	bossy
soak	dose	dosage
soldier	gross	roasting
soon	goose	rooster
soupy	loose	boosting
certain	purse	merciful
certify	nurse	person
such	us	fluster
suddenly	fuss	rustle
sigh	nice	pricing
sighted	rice	icy
soil	choice	choicest
soy bean	invoice	invoices
soap	house	household
soundly	blouse	roustabout

[z]

INITIAL POSITION	FINAL POSITION		MEDIAL POSITION
zebra	laws	hands	positive
zenith	as	hubs	razzing
zoo	says	rugs	blazer
zed	plays	hums	pheasant
zipper	fizz	rains	blizzard
zircon	sees	brings	feasible
zoom	gauze	breathes	pauses
zeal	pose	mouths	nosy
zest	news	paths	confusing
zigzag	furs	fills	pleasant
zinc	does	cars	doesn't
zero	prize	rooms	rises
xylophone	toys	pals	loser
zone	plows	blurs	rousing

[r]—[ɜˑ]—[ɚ]

INITIAL POSITION	FINAL POSITION	MEDIAL POSITION
rock	car	parting
rat	pear	parrot
red	tear	character
rate	care	area
rich	dear	fearful
read	hear	parent
wrong	oar	orange
rope	pour	doorway
roof	tour	tourist
room	poor	purpose
rough	cur	hiring
right	fir	fireworks
royal	fire	hourly
round	hour	ourselves

[l]

INITIAL POSITION	FINAL POSITION	MEDIAL POSITION
lock	doll	collar
laugh	pal	Sally
let	tell	yellow
late	pail	failure
lift	till	filler
leap	steal	peeling
loss	crawl	taller
lone	poll	folder
look	full	fullest
loop	school	ruler
love	dull	lulling
loyal	trial	filing
light	spoil	boiler
loud	trowel	growling

[θ]

INITIAL POSITION	FINAL POSITION	MEDIAL POSITION
thank	path	pathway
think	death	mathematics

[θ]

INITIAL POSITION	FINAL POSITION	MEDIAL POSITION (*Cont.*)
thief	with	bathtub
thought	teeth	toothbrush
thigh	cloth	wealthy
thousand	oath	mythical
thin	booth	lethal
thumb	mouth	filthy
thimble	south	fifths

[ð]

INITIAL POSITION	FINAL POSITION	MEDIAL POSITION
than	wreathe	bother
then	breathe	wither
thus	scathe	brother
that	bathe	father
these	loathe	mother
those	clothe	southern
this	seethe	leather

If you have experienced difficulties with other sounds, make word lists for practice similar to those above

2. Now read the lists again with as little lip movement as possible. Watch yourself in the mirror; notice how lifeless you look. Record some of the words; notice how blurred and monotonous they sound. Could you understand the words if you did not have the lists before you? Could you understand similar speech in a room full of talking people?

3. Return to exaggerated articulator movement for a few words. Notice the sharpness of sound. Gradually make your articulation movements smaller until you are speaking with an optimum of movement. Remember that you are likely to judge your usual articulation to be the optimum; have a classmate watch and listen as you increase your articulatory emphasis just a bit above what feels right. It probably does not appear to be too much movement.

4. The "negative practice" technique may help you sharpen your monitoring powers as well as your articulation. Read your practice words, purposely misarticulating the sound you are working on, then correcting it to emphasize the difference in feeling and sound between the "old or "error" sound and the correct sound. You can work with a classmate

this way, testing both your control of sound *production* and his ability to *hear* the difference. If you use negative practice, be certain to finish your drill with emphasis on correct production of the sound; it isn't your object to strengthen the error.

5. Each student might read six words before the entire class, purposely distorting a sound in each of three or four words to check his sound production control and the ears of his class members. The listening students might jot down the words, drawing a line under those sounds they hear as distorted. By informally comparing your notes with those of the other members of the class, after each student reads his list, you will soon discover whether your ears are in need of training to hear speech sounds more accurately.

6. Put three words from each of the practice lists into short, simple sentences. Write them down and practice those sentences with very exaggerated articulation, with almost no articulator movement, and with an optimum of movement. Remember to add just a bit more oral activity than feels natural. Watch yourself in a mirror as you record ten of your sentences. Are you becoming accustomed to the change? Listen for any unclear portions on the recording and again record the sentences involved, being careful with those words that were unclear.

7. If equipment for producing binaural masking noise is available to you, read aloud the summary on page 142 for a tape recording with a high level of masking. Following it by a recording of the paragraph with no masking. Note the inaccuracies in the first reading. This should emphasize for you the importance of auditory monitoring as part of your articulation process.

8. If delayed auditory feedback equipment is available, read the first two sentences under conditions of ¼ second delay with a moderate feedback level. If you have little speech disturbance, increase the feedback level and alter the delay time until interference occurs. Read the first two sentences of the chapter summary. Now, concentrate on tactile and kinesthetic feedback and reread the first two sentences. It is quite possible that you will perform better. This is the effect on articulation of awareness and use of available feedback channels.

9. For practice in recognizing all the sounds that should be present as you talk, and for practice in articulator control, read through "The Old Grad," phoneme by phoneme. You may wish to write it in phonetic symbols at first, but try to break it down into phonemes strictly by ear. Then go through the paragraph, reading it word for word. Remember to articulate carefully. Next, read it phrase by phrase; don't lose phonemes simply because you are reading in larger units. Now read it sentence by

sentence; record it and listen to the playback. Were you able to hear all the sounds? Finally, read the paragraph with the best articulation you can. Have a classmate listen and encircle the sounds that you slight or omit. If there are more than ten such slighted sounds, you probably need to redo this entire exercise.

THE OLD GRAD

No sentimental old grad ever forgets his years on the campus. When he attends a class reunion, he mingles with one group after another, sharing with old cronies his most cherished recollections. "Where's Bob Bogue?" he asks. "You remember Big Bob and the Bogue-to-Church passing combination. What a team that season— speedy Dave Hathaway, tricky Victor Thorpe, and the five-yard powerhouse, Long John Mitchell!" Thus our graying ex-collegian takes pleasure in recounting the exciting athletic events of those early days, and conveniently forgets all the pathetic struggles he had with the books.

10. Read the following pairs of sentences to a listener, holding a sheet of paper eight to ten inches before your face to hide articulator movements. See if your listener correctly discriminates the key words under these conditions.

Will you seal the envelope?
Will you feel the envelope?

Please take a cake.
Please bake a cake.

Do you like to ski?
Do you like the sea?

I said "pad it" not "pat it."
I said "pat it" not "pad it."

Were you walking in the garden?
Were you talking in the garden?

It is beautiful glass.
It is beautiful grass

I want you to meet Philip.
I want you to beat Philip.

Bring me my robe.
Bring me my rope.

I am depending on you to simulate conversation.
I am depending on you to stimulate conversation.

As a quarterback he is certainly game.
As a quarterback he is certainly tame.

He's the best of the fraternity.
He's the pest of the fraternity.

11. Record your reading of some unfamiliar material taken from a magazine. As you play the recording, you and a classmate write down or circle each word on which there was poor articulation. Rerecord the material, taking care with those words. You will discover, especially if you have a tendency toward inaccurate articulation, that this reading-and-playback technique will be of great value to you. Perhaps your instructor can make the recorders available at several times each day so that you can practice as much as you wish.

Student Projects at the end of this chapter will include a performance assignment that challenges your use of good articulation. It provides an opportunity for you to hear and judge the performances of your classmates and to profit from their comments about your own performance. The project involves careful description of an unfamiliar object. As you undertake the project, remember to prepare carefully and to monitor yourself well.

Summary

Perhaps by the time you finish the practice activities and the project assignment, you will have improved your articulation of certain sounds that have given you some difficulty. Or perhaps you will merely have practiced control of the precision and coordination of the movements of the articulators. In either case, you should have become conscious of your *ability* to control articulation, and you should have become aware of the frequent need for people to articulate carefully and accurately in almost every kind of employment. Consider your future work and how your articulation will be important. As a teacher, lawyer, physician, engineer, businessman, salesman, or secretary, for example, you will talk. Any occupation in which one communicates orally with other people calls for good articulation most of the time and excellent articulation some of the time. If you are not concerned about good articulation for occupational reasons, consider that all children learn their speech, whether it be excellent, good, bad, or atrocious, primarily through imitation of their parents. You will want your example to be a good one.

You have learned how to hear and control your articulation; now continue to keep it sharp and accurate and continue to improve through critical self-listening.

STUDENT PROJECTS

CONTENT ASSIGNMENT

A. Briefly describe five situations in your everyday life or your anticipated professional life that demand especially careful articulation.
B. What part does normal unstressing play in determining articulation in connected speech? How does unstressing differ from "telegraphese"?
C. When is a sound different enough to be considered misarticulated?
D. List several examples of unusual stressing of connective words.
E. List typical distortions of the "r," "s," "l," and voiced and voiceless "th," as you have heard them.

LISTENING ASSIGNMENT

Replay the recording you made early in the course (Chapter 2). Review the analyses you did at that time and those done on your speech by your fellow students. List those sounds you can hear that need sharpening, those your fellow students think need improvement, and those your instructor may add to the list.

PERFORMANCE ASSIGNMENT

Select an object with which you are familiar but which most of the class is unlikely to know. Outline a one- to two-minute description of the appearance and use of the object. You may not use the object or drawings or charts to illlustrate your talk. Practice your speech carefully, making each part of the description clear. You might describe a part for, an engine, a laboratory measuring instrument, a specially designed kitchen utensil, a flower of strange shape or appearance, an unusually designed piece of furniture, or something similar. You should be able to think of something both interesting to the class and challenging to your most careful speech.

You may evaluate the performance of each of our classmates and they may judge your work.

RECOMMENDED READINGS

Gray, G. W., and Wise, C. M. *The bases of speech.* (rev. ed.) New York: Harper, 1959, Chap. 4.

Nemoy, E. M., and Davis, S. F. *The correction of defective consonant sounds.*

Ringel, R., and Steer, M. Some effects of tactile and auditory alterations on speech output. *J. Speech and Hearing Research,* **6,** 1968, 369–78.

Schwartz, M. A study of thresholds of identification for vowels as a function of their duration, *J. Auditory Research,* **3,** 1963, 47–52.

Van Riper, C., and Irwin, J. V. *Voice and articulation.* Englewood Cliffs, N.J.: Prentice-Hall, 1958.

CHAPTER
7

SKILL
IN THE
USE OF
TIME

Sixty seconds in a minute, sixty minutes in an hour. Time, the heartbeat of the universe. So much to do, so much to say. So many restrictions on our use of time. "Your three minutes are up, now." "Each student will prepare a one-minute speech of introduction." "For the next quarter-hour you will hear an address by the eminent classical scholar, John William Arbuthnot."

Several chapters ago we mentioned that time as an acoustical variable could be manipulated in human vocal communications. This came as no surprise to you, for you had many times observed the drawling vocal patterns you associated with the speech of certain persons or sections of the country and the clipped, staccato utterances typical of other persons or other regions. Our chapter title, "Skill in the Use of Time," is intended to encompass the drawl, the machine-gun delivery, and various stages between these extremes.

We selected time as an early attribute to be worked on because it is an often-neglected factor, a Cinderella among vocal variables. Moreover, improved control over the time factor can be achieved somewhat more easily than improvement in other characteristics. Finally, despite its simple, somewhat prosaic character, the time factor turns out to be of prime significance as a determinant of intelligibility and judged effectiveness of vocal communication.

Time factors in speech have been respectably, even brilliantly, researched for a quarter century or more. A representative sample of the excellent studies in the time attribute is listed at the end of the chapter. Conclusions reached in them make it possible for us to recommend with some authority, for example, that the reader of factual prose to a small audience should employ a rate somewhere between 140 and 185 words per minute. In the same situation the same communicator is likely to speak extemporaneously at a somewhat slower rate, which probably is just as well. But before further reference is made to the research findings in the area, let us examine what appear to be critical factors influencing rate of verbal output and duration of sounds and syllables.

It must be recognized, first of all, that the ear and the auditory system constitute a physiologically limiting factor in the capacity of the listener to deal with information presented aurally. If the ear is overloaded with competing messages, confused with a message-plus-noise situation, or presented with a succession of stimuli at minimum perceptible values in the intensity attribute, there must be compensation in other attributes (for example, time) if successful transmission of information is to be accomplished.

Sidetone feedback, referred to in Chapters 1 and 2, is conceived to be another important physioneurological limiting factor on the time variable, more so on the speaker than on the listener, but affecting both. That is, if we could get auditory stimuli to the decoding stage faster and more precisely with respect to the form in which the sounds reached us, we could control our own vocal signals better and we could understand the other fellow more easily. Each of us learned to talk in a unique vocal environment. This statement is true even of identical twins, since the interaction of the organism with the things and the people, the objects and the events of his experience, is something which cannot be duplicated exactly. So, unconsciously influenced by rate and duration in our parents' speech, our first teacher's vocal output, influenced by our emerging control over the speech musculature, by our own sounds reverberated back to us in the places where our vocal patterns were most importantly determined, our speech rhythms grew as we grew and became unique elements in our speech patterns. Thus it is that, although population norms (averages) for time factors in speech have been discovered, each person's norms for his own feedback and for the listening channels devoted to other speakers are important. Fortunately, the range of time values within a given language is fairly narrow, so that the listening-feedback time patterns that are a part of your physiological equipment for hearing and producing speech would do almost as well for one of your classmates as they do for you. It is this near interchangeability of patterns based on unconscious learning that makes possible reeducation—the discarding of one pattern and the substitution of another deemed more suitable.

The ephemeral nature of the auditory stimulus long has been recognized as a critical distinction between spoken and written communication. The reader can interrupt the transmission of information at any point for the recall or searching out of a definition. ("Ephemeral," for example, is not one of the 10,000 most commonly used words and might well require looking up by some students who haven't met it recently.)

The listener, in contrast, rarely is permitted the luxury of halting the verbal output of the speaker while he gropes for meaning. Thus the speaker must select his language with care and then must exercise control over rate and duration to achieve maximum intelligibility. The use of pause, not only to recharge the blood with oxygen but to give the listener time to catch up and think about meanings, is strongly recommended.

To this point time factors have been considered largely within an intelligibility-communicability frame of reference. Such, at least, has been our design, for we have always placed our emphasis on optimum transmission of information. However, we wish not to neglect rhetorical and esthetic values, so long as these do not conflict with primary aims. Usually, of course, they do not conflict but actually enhance communication. When these matters of interest and artistic vocal usage are applied as criteria for optimum control over the time attribute, we recognize the desirability of presenting information almost as rapidly as the listener can assimilate it. Almost as fatal to understandability of message as the too-rapid delivery is the too-slow output, a clinically tested remedy for insomnia. Of equal merit as a sleep producer is metronomic vocal cadence: syllable following syllable with the "hup-two-three-four" regularity of a squad of infantrymen. Good communicators instinctively, or as the result of good training, introduce variety of rate into their controlled verbal output.

Perhaps now, in anticipation of a brief review of research, summary statements are in order.

Vocal messages are received by auditory systems that have limitations based on thresholds, competing stimuli, and so on.

Vocal output and optimum perception, from the standpoint of time, are governed to a large extent by learned feedback patterns. Thus all speakers and listeners are unique in this regard, although they tend to cluster around average values, or norms.

Vocal messages are transitory; they move through the atmosphere as the wave train passes and then they are gone, not to be reexperienced except under unusual circumstances. This condition creates an obligation on the part of the speaker to select his message carefully and deliver it slowly enough to be comprehended.

However, rates that are too slow and too regular in beat make for ineffective delivery.

As we've told you, time factors in speech have been objects of research for at least a quarter century. As early as 1934, for example, Lynch in one study and Murray and Tiffin in another study investigated certain aspects of rate-duration. Lynch found one time measure which consistently could be used to distinguish between trained and untrained readers and others which distinguish the two groups in the reading of specific types of material. Trained readers, she found, use longer pauses between phrases in reading various different types of material. This finding was corroborated by Murray and Tiffin, who also found that trained speakers are different from both good and poor untrained speakers in having greater variability of duration of phonation and greater variability of duration of unvoiced segments in vocal output.

Darley in one study and Franke in another sought normative data on rate of reading aloud and verification that reading rate, measured objectively, bears a reasonably close correspondence to audience judgment of speed of vocal output. Kelly and Steer sought much the same information for extemporaneous speaking performances. Darley found an average reading rate for his university student subjects of 166 words per minute, whereas Kelly and Steer reported a slower speaking rate for the same type of experimental subject—159 words per minute. The range of rates for the middle two-thirds of the sample tested was much smaller for the readers—approximately 30 words per minute separating the lowest one-sixth from the highest one-sixth—than for the speakers, where the spread was approximately 47 words per minute.

It was Franke's study that provided the 140–185 words-per-minute range cited earlier as desirable lower and upper limits of output. She also concluded that rate in words per minute calculated from the entire reading passage used in her study provided the index most closely related to listener judgment of rate. Kelly and Steer did not concur in this conclusion. They found best correlation between objective and subjective data when average words-per-minute rates for sentences were arranged against listener judgments. This inconsistency of finding is rather easily explained by the greater proportion of pause time in extemporaneous speech than in reading. Kelly and Steer, incidentally, found a range of more than 200 words per minute from the average slowest sentence to the average fastest sentence in the sample of extemporaneous speech they analyzed.

Research evidence bears out the assertion made several pages ago that time factors influence intelligibility of communication. In separate investigations Harris, Kelly, and Draegert found that increased syllable duration accompanies higher intelligibility, particularly when the communication takes place in high-level noise. Draegert not only found this to be a significant correlation; when he compared the 44 best and the 44 worst communicators in his sample of 555 subjects, he found that the factor of syllable duration was a statistically significant means of distinguishing between the two groups. Pickett and Pollack, however, found that slow and fast short samples of speech, whether spoken in conversation or read aloud, were approximately equal in intelligibility if the duration of the samples was equal. They found "a balanced trade-off between slow, precise articulation of a small amount of text and rapid, slurred articulation of a large amount of text in the same time interval." The explanation for this finding is simply that the larger number of words in the fast sample provides cues for the perception of elements misarticulated and misheard.

There are other ways in which a time variable has shown itself to be significant. Tiffin and Steer, examining the acoustical determinants of emphasis, or sense-stress in vocal communication, discovered that increased duration contributes to stress at least as significantly as increased vocal power, and perhaps even more so. Finally, Fairbanks and Hoaglin showed that certain aspects of time are closely linked with listener identifications of emotions being portrayed.

Summary time again. Based on experimental evidence, you have now good reason to believe the following:

College students reading aloud vary considerably in rate, with the middle two-thirds of this population ranging between about 155 and 185 words per minute. These limits come close to limits judged most effective, though a rate as low as 140 is acceptable for some persons.

Speaking rate is slower than reading rate and has a wider range for the middle two-thirds of the college population. You'll find yourself in this group if you speak extemporaneously at some rate between 135 and 183 words per minute.

Longer and more variable pauses and phonations of greater variability in duration distinguish trained from untrained readers.

Syllable duration is significantly correlated with intelligibility when communication takes place in noise. Moreover, longer syllable duration distinguishes good from poor communication. However, if rapid speech becomes necessary in some circumstances, contextual clues may compensate for misarticulated and misheard message elements.

Increased duration is one of the most frequently used techniques to achieve vocal emphasis. Time factors also help to distinguish portrayals of different emotions.

These generalizations, however, must be qualified in this way: they hold for the speakers, the spoken or read material, and the environmental conditions in the experiments cited. We believe that the conclusions drawn from these studies are valid and generally applicable, but we also believe that the intelligent speaker or reader changes his rate and duration in response to changing conditions. The size of the room and the size of the audience, the amounts of noise present, the level of difficulty of the material, and the emotional content of the material all can and should influence the speaker's rate and duration.

In the pages immediately following we shall suggest some things you might do to develop greater control over this vocal variable. First, however, a few words about control symbols and artificial versus "natural" delivery. To help remind you about slowing down or speeding up, prolonging or curtailing the duration of vocal units, we will use and suggest that you use these two symbols: ⊢———⊣ for something relatively slow or relatively prolonged, and ⊢—⊣ for something relatively fast or relatively staccato. Some students object to the use of these, or any other, symbols in this way. "Anything so artificial detracts from the spontaneity of my speech, makes me stilted and mechanical." (Probably true.) Note that for the large majority of speakers we do not recommend the use of these or other symbols as devices to govern a finished performance. We suggest them to you as a part of the learning process, a part of preparation for public utterance. We hope you will make use of devices such as these while they can be helpful, then discard them before they become crutches or worse.

DEVELOPING TIME SKILLS IN THE SPEECH LABORATORY

Rate

1. What is your normal reading rate? Turn back to page 141 and read "The Old Grad" passage silently, two or three times. Now read

it aloud once or twice. Now time yourself through at least two, preferably four, readings. On a scrap of paper record your total time per reading in seconds. If all the readings are within a ten-second range, sum them and divide by the number of readings to establish average time for the passage. If one time is much longer or shorter than the others, ignore it in calculating your average. If there is no apparent tendency to cluster around one time value, keep timing several more readings until you begin to discern a central tendency in the time values. Once you have calculated an average that seems representative, use this value as the divisor and 5760 (60 seconds times the number of words in the passage, 96) as the dividend in calculating your rate for this passage.

Here is the rate calculation illustrated in a hypothetical example:

Reading 1:   42.0 seconds
        2:     36.8 seconds
        3:     40.2 seconds
        4:     34.6 seconds
  Total $\overline{153.6}$ seconds

Arithmetic mean = 153.6/4 = 38.4

Rate = 5760/38.4 = 150 w.p.m.

Does your calculated rate lie within the recommended 140–185 words per minute range? If not, it may be too fast or too slow. Ask your instructor to evaluate your rate.

2. As a preliminary step in establishing rate control, read the passage aloud several more times, recording reading time in seconds and attempting to cluster the time entries around 40 seconds, which would yield an average words per minute rate of 144, near the slow end of the acceptable range. How did you accomplish this slower rate—by lengthening pauses between phrases? by prolonging syllables? Probably a fairly even balance of these two is the best way to reduce rate, though your instructor may wish to counsel you to concentrate on one aspect more than the other. How do you react to the slower rate? Did the passage seem to drag interminably? You should practice at this end of the rate continuum until you feel comfortable in it; many future speaking situations, for example, in noisy surroundings, will require a slow rate of you. Ask a classmate or your instructor to listen to you. Verify that the slower rate makes for acceptable listening. If it sounds too plodding to your instructor, see what you can do to add interest, but maintain the reduced rate.

3. Repeat, attempting to cluster the time entries around 33 seconds,

yielding almost 175 words per minute, near the top of the acceptable range. Compare this experience with that in the preceding exercise. Was it easier or harder to accomplish? In later months or years you will find this skill is important, too. Could you maintain acceptable articulation at the increased rate? Get a listener's judgment of your vocal effectiveness with this faster delivery. Work to achieve good listener reaction to your rapid reading.

4. Assuming you now have established firm control over your reading rate, at least with "The Old Grad" passage, select a piece of fresh material and read it aloud at preselected slow, medium, and rapid rates. The material may be taken from a newspaper, a newsmagazine, or other popular, general-interest periodical. Do not, at this time, select dramatic, poetic, or special-interest material to work with. In calculating your rate over this fresh material, multiply the number of words by 60 and divide by the number of seconds' reading time.

5. Are you beginning to feel you have rate fairly well under control? Perhaps you have, and that's good. But remember it's *reading* rate you've been working on. There's been no need for you to compose the message before you delivered it. Now see how much control you have over rate when you haven't the help of the printed page. Select some easy topic like "The Street I Live On" or "What I'm Going to Do in the Next Six Hours (Days, Months, Years)." Think about the topic for three to five minutes, then talk about it for 30–60 seconds. It will be most helpful if you can tape-record this exercise. How did you sound? Slow? Fast? Just right for the material?

Now speak on the same topic again, but this time imagine you're on a long-distance telephone line. This is costing you money, so get the message through in the shortest possible time, but get it through! How did you sound this time? Better? Worse?

Finally, deliver the same information as you would to an elderly friend of the family. Don't shout, but speak slowly enough for the old gentleman to keep up with you.

If you have been able to record these three short impromptu speeches, play them back at half-speed, counting words. Then calculate your rate in words per minute as in exercise 4. By this objective measure, did you achieve your goal of control over rate in the impromptu speaking situation? Has this been accomplished without sacrificing clarity or interest? Then no doubt you're ready to go on to other challenges in the control of speech time. In sections to follow, syllable duration, rate of phrases, and duration of pauses, all of which contribute to vocal flexibility, will be brought to your attention.

Duration

As you know, over-all rate in words per minute is a function of the duration of communicated sounds plus the time when no sound is being communicated. This next set of vocal experiences is designed to awaken in you a consciousness of the duration of sounds and control over this factor. If need be, the exercises can be put to work to build new feedback patterns of duration.

1. Read aloud the following list of monosyllabic words:

a) act	f) book	k) head	p) cook
b) add	g) but	l) put	q) debt
c) pad	h) could	m) took	r) egg
d) as	i) get	n) up	s) pick
e) big	j) had	o) bad	t) yet

2. Now read these aloud:

a) age	f) down	k) law	p) real
b) all	g) eel	l) mean	q) school
c) boy	h) far	m) more	r) these
d) call	i) here	n) now	s) use
e) cry	j) knew	o) old	t) wall

What was the difference between the two lists? Which did you read faster? Why? These words, carefully selected for the two lists, represent essentially the same level of difficulty, in terms of the frequency of their use, but they belong to different classes phonetically. List 1 is loaded with short vowels and plosives, whereas list 2 has a loading of long vowels and various types of continuant consonants. It would take a considerable effort to read list 2 faster than list 1. But such control is important, so try it now; read list 1 with a deliberate prolongation of the vowels and list 2 with a deliberate staccato effect.

3. Now return to your natural way of reading and time the two lists, then calculate average duration of the words in each list (total time per list, divided by 20).

4. Now repeat exercise 2, prolonging list 1 and clipping short list 2; calculate average time as in number 3. Were you successful in reversing the natural durations of the two lists?

5. Set yourself a variety of tasks in control of duration. For example, in list 1 prolong word *a*, read word *b* naturally and then word *c* even more crisply than is normal for you, and so on through word *t*. Then

do the same for list 2. Invite comment from a fellow student or your instructor. When your classmate asks *you* to listen and criticize similar efforts, do so conscientiously and honestly. This not only will be beneficial to the other student, but it will also provide you with increased skill in listening, a necessary first step in side-tone control of vocal output.

6. If you have access to a tape recorder, put these exercises on tape and listen attentively to them. Be critical of your recording. Have you achieved real control over duration?

7. Prepare your own lists of words for duration control. Don't limit yourself to monosyllabic words, but increase the syllable count and difficulty level. A good source of words for your lists is *The Teacher's Word Book of 30,000 Words,* for which the complete citation is given in the list of recommended readings at the end of the chapter. With your own lists repeat any of exercises 1 through 6 on which you (or your instructor) feel you need more practice.

Phrase rate

Some of the things we say have considerable internal consistency with respect to the rate at which successive phrases are delivered. It is normal and natural that this should be so for some materials and certain special communication situations. Two of these will be suggested below, with the recommendation that you deal with them appropriately. However, we recognize that this consistency of rate is (and should be) the unusual rather than the typical. In almost any situation you can name, with almost all types of speech materials, there will be phrase-to-phrase variation in rate. Such flexibility is an aid to intelligibility, to the maintenance of listener interest, and to emphasis. Normally we reduce rate on key phrases, those which are most difficult to understand or those we wish to emphasize. In contrast, we find many phrases we can afford to "throw away," to toss off lightly, because they are not essential either to meaning or to the argument we are advancing. Introductory phrases and interpolated phrases often, though not always, are of this nonessential variety. In the exercises below we shall use and recommend to your use the two symbols mentioned earlier in this chapter: ⊢————⊣ for slow or prolonged, ⊢⊣ for fast or staccato. The *degree* of rate retardation or acceleration must depend on your feel for the material and increasing skill in delivery. Remember that we use these symbols in support of the learning process; we do not recommend them for use forever after.

1. The passage below is a paraphrased stenographic transcription of an on-the-spot broadcast of a championship football game. Only the

names have been changed, for obvious reasons. The circumstances and the language join forces in dictating that the selection be read at breakneck speed, without letup. Try it that way and evaluate your success both by subjective judgment and objective measurement as in exercise 3, page 151. For the whole passage, then, ⊢⊣.

We're just under way here in the first quarter, Tulsa getting a big break, recovering a fumble on the opening kickoff. This 1968 CFL championship game being brought to you live and in color from Mobile, Alabama. Ryan to the left, Curtis to the right. Tom Bennett is covering Curtis. Pete Snow will be on Ryan. There's a fake draw play, Onesti firing to Richter . . . wide-open . . . *touchdown,* going against a slight wind. Tulsa leads 6 to nothing, and Bangs has come in for the extra point. The ball is down, it's up, it splits the uprights, and the Cyclones lead 7 to nothing with thirteen and a half minutes left to play in this the first quarter. And now, this message . . . Now the teams have lined up for the Tulsa kickoff, into a slight wind. Here's Bangs' kickoff; it's not too deep, bouncing on the 15. Sorensen has it there, Sorensen's dropped it on the 17. Now he has it again, but he's snowed under on the 21, Horvath the first man to make contact. Now Gerber brings the Cavaliers out to the line of scrimmage. Gerber had a sore arm last year; he took isometrics and weight-lifting all summer and strengthened that arm and had his best health of his ten-year football career this fall. They're in a slot left. Four receivers are out. Gerber is hit by 72, Mel Faulk from the University of Akron, perhaps the most underrated defensive player in the Continental Football League. This is a second down and 17 situation. Morelli nearly went into motion. There's a screen to Morelli at the 45 and Morelli was dropped to the 49 by Steve Sturgis. First and ten, Cavaliers. Morelli's wide to the right, Hart to the left. Gerber fakes to O'Keefe, Gerber throwing deep, deep to his flanker, Nims, and Nims nearly has his head torn off, but the big, strong flanker's in for the touchdown, and the Mobile Cavaliers have stormed right back to come within one point of the Tulsa Cyclones.

2. It would not have been difficult to select, for contrast in rate, a piece of lyric poetry, a chapter from the Bible, or a eulogy delivered to the memory of some great man or woman. Yet we believe there is greater merit, usually, in providing you with speaking materials from everyday life situations or in urging you to provide yourself with these materials. Hence we suggest for you a speaking topic like "The Most Beautiful Scene I Ever Saw," or "The Emotional Impact of the Grand Canyon (a Historic Shrine, or a Place of Worship)." Think, then speak on the subject—slowly. Incidentally, don't be ashamed or afraid of revealing a

little honest emotion, provided you exercise good vocal control. So, 30–60 seconds on the topic, delivery: ⊢————⊣.

3. Another opportunity to use a somewhat slower than average rate is provided by the short passage below, taken from the women's pages of a daily newspaper.[1]

Arnold House, always a warm and hospitable place to visit, was never lovelier than it was Thursday, when the Women's Project Board of the Santa Barbara Historical Society entertained there with a tea for their associates.

A giant Christmas tree, decorated with the old time swags and baubles that were a part of the time when Senator Everett Arnold and his family lived there, was settled by the staircase. Reminiscing beside it was Mrs. Eldon Moore, granddaughter of Sarah Arnold Dempster. She remembered childhood days when she went to grandmother's house and stayed to learn very ladylike things like greeting guests and walking softly, and holding a delicate teacup with great care.

4. Classroom teachers, speech pathologists, psychologists, and doubtless people in other professional categories speak of the benefits to be derived from *negative practice:* deliberately going back to bad habits or performing acts one wishes not to perform. Let's try some negative practice with these materials, convincing ourselves that inappropriate styles of delivery can create almost ludicrous effects. Read the passage in exercise 1 consistently ⊢————⊣. Now speak on the topic in exercise 2 consistently ⊢⊣. Hard to do, wasn't it? Also, not likely to win you public speaking or oral interpretation awards. Nonetheless it was good negative practice, helping you to develop vocal control.

5. Read the following sentences as directed by the symbol that precedes each:

⊢⊣ a) Lay that pistol down!

⊢————⊣ b) Call me later, freshman; they'll have to start school without me.

⊢————⊣ c) I'm dreaming of steak, french fries, a parfait, and coffee with cream.

⊢⊣ d) All those in favor, signify by the usual sign.

⊢————⊣ e) Let's take a summer cruise to Hawaii, Fiji, or Samoa.

⊢⊣ f) Step back from the edge or you'll break your neck!

⊢⊣ g) I want to report a fire at 2922 West Second Street!

⊢————⊣ h) Down through the years, our goals have always been truth and honor.

[1] Permission to use this excerpt was graciously extended by Mrs. Pat Dayton of the staff of the *Santa Barbara News-Press.*

⊢⊣ i) Exercise by the numbers: Arms up, arms down, one-two, one-two.

⊢———⊣ j) Towering redwood trees line the highway down which the motorcade will slowly drive.

6. Now read the following paragraph as directed by the symbols, each of which should serve as a control over the phrase which follows it. You may find two ⊢⊣s in succession or two or more ⊢———⊣s. This does not necessarily mean that successive phrases get more of the treatment (fast or slow) than preceding phrases. Each symbol applies to one phrase without regard to surrounding phrases.

⊢———⊣ "It seems to me," / ⊢⊣ mused the old professor, / ⊢⊣ "that students get brighter every year. / ⊢⊣ Yes, and better looking, too! / ⊢⊣ There's more drive today, / ⊢———⊣ more will to get ahead, / ⊢———⊣ than there was forty years ago, / ⊢———⊣ when I met my first class. / ⊢⊣ This eagerness to succeed, of course, / ⊢———⊣ is admirable. / ⊢⊣ Yet surely there is something to be said / ⊢———⊣ for the contemplative mood, / ⊢———⊣ for learning through reason, / ⊢⊣ not simply the hasty grasp of facts. / ⊢⊣ I guess it all adds up to this: / ⊢⊣ the present generation challenges me and makes me proud, / ⊢⊣ but I'm a little lonely / ⊢———⊣ for the young ladies and gentlemen of yesterday."

Doubtless that paragraph was awkward to read the first time through. Try it again, two or three times, till you can read it smoothly, obedient to the symbols.

Having done this, do you find yourself disagreeing with any of the markings? It is natural that you should, for few people today would argue that there is only one correct or one good way to communicate a given piece of material. Suppose you go over the paragraph and revise the symbolic treatment in accordance with your notions. Now read it aloud again. Better? Good. See if a classmate or your instructor agrees that the revision is an improvement (for you) over the original.

7. Now start with a fresh piece of material. In the paragraph below insert slant lines for the phrases and slow and fast symbols as seems most appropriate to you. Then read the material aloud as in exercise 5, following your own directions.

Think for a moment about fishing. Now, if you will, think about several other leisure time activities. Did you think of any that offers the variety characteristic of fishing? Take degree of participation, for example. The fisherman can be active, or passive. He may drowse in the sun, long cool drink in one hand and pole in the other, motionless and still. Or he may stand hip-deep in a swiftly moving stream, lashing the water with passionate casts. For a change, he may troll in a lake or the ocean, or drop a line from a pier. Consider the range of temptations he may offer his quarry: night crawlers or minnows, a dry fly, bone jig, or flatfish, to name just a few. The fisherman's life is all thrills and excitement ⊢⊣ if that is the way he wants it to be. Or the fisherman's life is the next thing to sleeping, and that life, my friend, is the best life for me.

How much opportunity for rate of phrase flexibility did that paragraph offer you? How many ⊢————⊣s did you use? How many ⊢⊣s? How does this compare with your classmates? How many times did you shift from ⊢————⊣ to ⊢⊣ or ⊢⊣ to ⊢————⊣ on successive phrases? How does this compare with the other students? After you had marked the paragraph did you find it easy to respond vocally to your symbols? Did some of them require change? Do you think you could read the paragraph with more extreme variation in the rate of phrase and keep it sounding natural? Try it with a listener and invite criticism.

    8. As suggested in *Student Projects,* below, your instructor may assign a task similar to that in exercise 6 for you to do out of class. This will involve your selection of a paragraph from another source, marking it with the symbols, and practicing for control of rate of phrase.

Duration of pause

One of the most difficult tasks for the inexperienced speaker is, paradoxically, the one communicative act requiring the least effort⊢⊣to introduce controlled pauses into his vocal output. It is as though the speaker feared his listeners would begin to hiss him, or would walk out on him in the moment or two of silence indicative of a shift of ideas, an approaching climactic phrase, or simply the need, at an acceptable place, to pause to breathe. In Chapter 4 we had a few words to say about the pause. Now it's time for a few more and some practice in the use of this device.

    To begin with, the pause is one of your most effective techniques for achieving and holding attention. Properly placed, the pause tells the listener, "Brace yourself; something important is about to be said." The pause also gives the listener that occasionally much-needed moment to catch up, to recognize and understand a somewhat unfamiliar word or difficult phrase, and prepare himself for what is to come next.

The neophyte's greatest fault is his fear of pauses. He bridges the span between shifting ideas with "Uh," "and," or an obviously artificial cough. Even practiced speakers mistreat the pause, so to speak. Experimental evidence is lacking on this point, but our observation is that the experienced speaker who does mistreat pauses, tends to make them too long and too uniform in duration. You will recall the studies mentioned earlier in the chapter which showed that variation in the duration of pause tended to separate better from less effective speakers and readers. In the exercises below we will use a slightly different pair of symbols: ☐ for a long pause and ☐ for a short pause. You must decide for yourself, with help from your instructor, just *how* short and *how* long the pauses are to be.

1. Insert pauses in the following as directed:

    a) Though given every chance /☐/ he failed to make up the work.
    b) That's all I have to say /☐/; the subject is closed.
    c) The flowers have gone to seed /☐/. Even the house looks shabby.
    d) Man the lifeboats /☐/. The ship is going down!
    e) This is no time for comedy /☐/. The need is urgent.
    f) Turn to your left /☐/; Mark lives on this street.
    g) Since they can be used again /☐/ please save the plastic utensils.
    h) Participation in student government is good /☐/. It prepares one for future citizenship.
    i) When your name is called /☐/ take one step forward.
    j) You students have worked hard /☐/. You are to be congratulated.

Do you think you succeeded in introducing pauses of contrasting length? If you're not sure, run through the sentences two or three times more, counting silently for the symbols. Use a one-count for ☐ and a two- or three-count for ☐. This will have a tendency, at first, to increase the artificial sound of your reading. However, it is good discipline, forcing you to vary the length of your pauses. Again you should request some critical listening from another student. Can he detect your flexibility in this aspect of time?

2. As in exercise 1, vary the duration of pauses as directed in the following paragraph:

Hello /☐/ Hello /☐/ George? /☐/ Good of you to return my call /☐/. Now I know you're busy /☐/ so I'll try not to take up much of your time / [____] /. I'm calling /☐/ as directed by the Executive Board /☐/ to ask you to serve as Chairman of the Social Committee for the coming year /[____]/. Your silence leads me to believe you're not enthusiastic about this honor /☐/—right? /[____]/ Well /☐/ I expected you to feel that way /[____]/. To be honest /☐/ I'd probably feel the same way /[____]/. But George /☐/ it's a job that must be done /☐/ and the Board will cooperate in every way /[____]/. Finally /☐/ once you've done this job /[____]/ they can hardly ask you again for at least five years.

When you have this exercise thoroughly under control—making use of the silent counting technique at first if it helps you—read it for criticism, or tape-record it, or both. Your pauses should be distinguishably different in length, but the reading as a whole should sound as spontaneous as someone else's words can ever sound, coming from you.

3. As a graduation exercise in control and variation of pause length, select a topic, compose a 30–60 second impromptu talk on your subject, and deliver it, preferably to a listener, or to a tape recorder. A description like "The View from My Window" might be a good topic for this exercise. As you deliver this talk, remember that flexibility in your use of pauses is your aim.

Having performed these exercises, you should realize that your work in the time attribute really has just begun if you hope to achieve excellence, vocal skill. You will be moving on, concentrating on other speech attributes now. But hold, not too far toward the back of your mind, the idea that you can and should achieve greater control over the time attribute. It is, after all, the easiest one to work with and it certainly is a rewarding one, in terms of gains in over-all speech excellence.

STUDENT PROJECTS

CONTENT ASSIGNMENTS

A. Review the chapter and bring in for class discussion a list of ten situations in which some aspect of vocal time control would be important. Tell why it would be important and *how* the control would be exerted.

B. Check your library for other books written on speech improvement and compare the treatment on time factors with this chapter. Do you find general agreement? On what points is there disagreement?

LISTENING ASSIGNMENTS

Listen to time factors in the speech of others as directed below and report what you heard. If perfunctorily done this assignment will contribute little to your vocal development.

A. Listen to 5 students reciting in other classes; evaluate for *slow, normal,* or *fast* rate.
B. Listen to 5 students talking conversationally, evaluate and report.
C. Your instructor will suggest a radio or TV newscaster whose rate is noteworthy; describe his delivery in considerable detail.

PERFORMANCE ASSIGNMENT

Your instructor may assign a two- or three-minute extemporaneous speech to be prepared with special attention to time factors. "How to ———" is a possible topic. Alternatively, you may discuss a concept or operationally define a word from your major field of interest. You will present this speech for evaluation by your classmates.

RECOMMENDED READINGS

Draegert, G. L. Relationships between voice variables and speech intelligibility in high level noise. *Speech Monogr.,* **18,** 1951, 272–278.

Fairbanks, G., and Hoaglin, L. An experimental study of the durational characteristics of the voice during the expression of emotion. *Speech Monogr.,* **8,** 1941, 85–90.

Hanley, T. D. An analysis of vocal frequency and duration characteristics of selected samples of speech from three American dialect regions. *Speech Monogr.,* **18,** 1951, 78–93.

Kelly, J. C., and Steer, M. D. Revised concept of rate. *J. Speech and Hearing Disorders,* **14,** 1949, 222–226.

Pickett, J. M., and Pollack, I. Intelligibility of excerpts from fluent speech: effects of rate of utterance and duration of excerpt. *Lang. and Speech,* **6,** 1963, 151–164.

Pollack, I., and Pickett, J. M. The intelligibility of excerpts from conversation. *Lang. and Speech,* **6,** 1963, 165–171.

Snidecor, J. C. A comparative study of the pitch and duration characteristics of impromptu speaking and oral reading. *Speech Monogr.,* **10,** 1943, 50–56.

Thorndike, E. L., and Lorge, I. *The teacher's word book of 30,000 words.* New York: Teachers College, Columbia University, 1952.

Tiffin, J., and Steer, M. D. An experimental analysis of emphasis. *Speech Monogr.,* **4,** 1937, 69–74.

CHAPTER
8

SKILL
IN THE
USE OF
LOUDNESS

The disturbance we create with our vocal cords, quite apart from any communicative impact it may have, is physically measurable. This "more-or-lessness" of sound was touched on under the headings of intensity and loudness in Chapter 2. There you learned that sound strength or power usually is reported in decibels (dB), a system based on calculation of sound power or pressure ratios; hence it is a relative rather than an absolute system.

Not only are these units relative rather than absolute; they are very difficult to interpret in terms of human perception. The assertion that decibels represent minimum perceptible differences among auditory stimuli is without substance or merit. Actually, there are some pairs of sounds that can be discriminated though only one-fourth decibel separates them, and there are other pairs that require as much as 10 dB difference in level before the observer can say with confidence, "These are different."

This inconsistency notwithstanding, the dB is the best unit we have for expressing quantitative information in this acoustical region and the term will recur often in discussion of the intensity-loudness attribute. Keep in mind that it was never intended to express the reactions of people to sound levels; with this reservation you are not likely to misinterpret data presented in decibels.

Levels at which sound becomes perceptible and painful are known to the audiologist and other professional people interested in hearing. Certain normative data about sound levels of human voices are known, too. A great deal of this basic information was collected in the Bell Telephone Laboratories in the nineteen twenties and thirties, and later research has produced only minor changes in key values. For the most part this excellent early work is substantiated. We can say with considerable confidence, for example, that the average level of human vocal sounds is 65 dB above an arbitrarily chosen zero reference level of 0.0002 microbar when the sound measuring instrument is held three feet from the speaker's lips. We can also state with some assurance that there is a range of approximately 140 dB from the threshold of sound detectability to the threshold of pain in the frequency region where hearing is most acute. Stated another way: if zero decibels (0 dB) is the sound level where you just hear a pin drop, then approximately 140 dB higher is the point at which the power of the sound becomes almost more than you can tolerate.

Now these statistics perhaps are fascinating to the scientist, but what is their relevance to vocal skills? What is the basic importance of sound power—loudness to the speaker? How can and should information of this nature be used? First of all, it is desirable to establish a range of values within which we should be working. As we shall point out shortly, this will not be easy to do. Next, it is well to consider the possibilities with respect to vocal flexibility. Perhaps most significantly we need to evaluate this sound attribute in the light of what we believe and what we know about vocal feedback.

Our assumption, you remember, is that what we say passes in review before an internal evaluative mechanism. This mechanism approves or modifies the vocal output in terms of learned patterns of what is "good" or "normal" and what is "bad" or "abnormal." Now for this mechanism to function, the output must be above the threshold of the receiver. That is, the signal must be strong enough to be matched against the pattern. Failure of the signal to achieve this minimum level is itself enough to trigger the error signal in the mechanism and bring about automatic adjustment. Interestingly enough, this triggering is accomplished, not on any absolute basis, but on a relative basis that we term "signal-to-noise ratio."

A comparison of the power present in the meaningful stimulus with the power in the meaningless audible hash through which the message must fight its way is implied in the signal-to-noise ratio.

The concept of strength of signal being related to noise level returns us to the first mentioned of the reasons for studying and working with loudness intensity: the desirability of establishing the limiting values within which vocal signals should be spoken. At what point does your voice fade into imperceptibility or burst into intolerability? When we search the literature for these critical points, we encounter mild frustration; norms are hard to find, and for a very good reason. As mentioned earlier, there is research to tell us that the average level of a person's voice *in the protected environment of a speech laboratory* is 65 dB, measured three feet from his lips. There is also research which indicates, while not demonstrating conclusively, that 65 dB is a preferential level for listening to speech. So far, so good. But there is an intervening variable between the talker and the listener that sharply limits the applicability of these 65 dB levels as guideposts to the strength of vocal signals. This intervening, supervening variable is environmental noise.

How much of your 65 dB message will get through in competition with 80–90 dB of knife, fork, plate, and voice clatter in your campus cafeteria? Are you ever aware of a feeling of fatigue upon finishing a meal there? Doubtless the struggle to communicate is responsible.

Environmental noise, then, is a deterrent to the establishment of voice level norms. Distance is the other major deterrent. That 65 dB level of voice is just fine if your listener is at the three-foot distance where the normative measurement is made. But what if he is thirty feet away? The inverse square law in acoustics states that intensity is inversely proportional to the square of the distance from the source. The acceptable level at three feet becomes a weak signal at thirty.

With this acoustical information as background, let us examine a few of the research studies in this area, drawing from them whatever conclusions seem warranted regarding the development of loudness skills.

As you would expect, there is complete unanimity of research evidence bearing on the relation of strength of signal to intelligibility (or what some researchers, unfortunately we feel, term "articulation"). This strong correlation has been reported for phonemes by Fletcher, monosyllables by Kryter, dissyllables by Stevens and his associates. Draegert, in the study referred to in Chapter 7, showed how important signal strength in the presence of noise is for the military communicator. His good and poor communicators were as distinguishable on the speech signal level criterion as they were on syllable duration, and the correlation between level and intelligibility was even higher than that between duration and intelligibility. Black and his associates also concluded that vocal intensity is a significant contributor to the intelligibility of military voice communications.[1]

One qualification should be inserted here. Whereas a strong relation between signal strength and intelligibility has been demonstrated over and over again, the relation holds only within a limited section of the total range of audition. Perception of speech begins about 15–18 dB (at the listener's ear) above zero reference level. Almost total intelligibility is reached in the neighborhood of 78 dB above the zero level. Hence the rise in intelligibility associated with a rise in power takes place over about a 60 dB range. Below and above the critical levels there is what amounts to zero and perfect intelligibility, although there is some evidence to show that as signals approach the threshold of pain there may actually be a decrement in intelligibility. Of course the lower and upper limits here cited would necessarily be shifted upward when noise is introduced into the listening environment.

So signal strength is important; you must be loud enough to be heard. And signal-to-noise ratio is important, too. It is not enough just to be loud; you must be loud enough to contend on fairly equal terms with the noise in your environment. Interestingly and fortunately, your vocal servosystem is quite helpful in this regard. Hanley and Steer, in a study of 48 young adult males, discovered a very consistent tendency among them to elevate vocal intensity when distracting noise level was increased. This effect appeared to be somewhat automatic, taking place below conscious levels.

The need for adequate loudness level of voice is obvious. What more control of this attribute need the person skilled in speaking be able to exert? He must be able to use more or less as the situation and the nature of his material require. Lewis and Tiffin, analyzing six voices selected to cover a rather wide range of speaking ability, found that the subjects made little differential use of average vocal level, but that the better speakers tended to make use of a larger number of shifts of intensity. There was also a fairly clear-cut distinction in the relative prominence given the various grammatical elements. The better speakers used less vocal power on articles, conjunctions, and prepositions than the poorer

---

[1] As in many other places in this book, the authors have selected a few scientists to support a specific position with research evidence. Many other scientists, whose work is equal in merit, might have been selected. Their names would have been mentioned if the primary aim of this text were scientific exposition rather than the functional objective described in Chapter 1.

speakers. In this sense the better speakers were more flexibile. Murray and Tiffin, whose research has been mentioned in an earlier chapter, reached much the same conclusion, trained voices were different from judged good untrained voices, which in turn were different from judged poor voices, in having slower and wider intensity pulsations.

The effect of this variation in sound pressure level in speech almost goes without saying; certain grammatical elements, words, phrases, and the like, are given more or less prominence, depending on their significance in the total communication. These elements are stressed or emphasized, and relative loudness plays a large role in the process. In fact, at least nine out of ten of your friends would equate stress with loudness, would insist that the terms are virtually synonymous. Qualified support for their position would be provided by the research of Tiffin and Steer, mentioned in the preceding chapter, who ranked vocal intensity very high as a determinant of stress.

Now for a series of summary statements, indicative of your goals with respect to loudness:

Your over-all level must be loud enough for ready comprehension, equivalent to approximately 65 dB at the ear of the listener in an ideal acoustical environment.

Under conditions that are less than ideal, your level should be loud enough to compete successfully with environmental noise. There is experimental evidence to show that connected speech 10 dB above noise level results in intelligibility scores above 90 percent.

You should make use of loudness to achieve syllable, word, phrase, and even paragraph stress.

Your selection of words, phrases, and so on, upon which to exert loudness stress should be well planned and executed so that key words rather than connectives stand out in your speech.

The practice materials in the pages following are designed to help you accomplish vocal control in the loudness attribute. Equally, of course, the materials are designed to help the student overcome faults of loudness, if he has any. The weak voice, the overloud voice, the inflexible voice, the too-flexible voice, and the inappropriately flexible voice all will be targets for these exercises.

We have said very little about vocal stereotypes up to this time. There's been little or no mention of the character analysis people are purported to do, based on vocal characteristics of the subject. The reason we have avoided such voice-personality tie-ups is that we are not convinced that there is much validity in it, *for the normal speaker.* It seems to be true, however, that extremes of deviation from the norm in any vocal attribute do take on personality stereotypes. The far too weak voice is A. Paul O'Jettique or Rita Goosebump; the bellowing delivery belongs to Horace Blowhard or some other authoritarian individual; the stressless voice to Sadie O'Paque, a colorless girl if there ever was one; and the oddly, wobbly stressed output to Hysteria Trayfort, the superficially enthusiastic soul we try so hard to avoid.

You are none of these characters, understand. But to the extent that you achieve intelligent control of loudness, you remove yourself farther from the remote possibility that someone might tag you with one of the labels.

DEVELOPING LOUDNESS SKILLS IN THE SPEECH LABORATORY

We'll make use of certain symbolic and typographical conventions in this section, just as we did in the laboratory section of Chapter 7. Our reasons for the use of symbols are the same. First, we can save time and space by conveying suggestions through this shorthand of a sort. Second, and of far greater importance, we can help you break down established vocal habits by this technique. You can then re-establish the old habits or adopt some new ones, depending on the critical evaluation given them by you and your instructor.

Two different symbolic approaches will be used. Our suggestions for the increase of syllable or word power, contrasted with adjacent syllables or words, will be conveyed through capitalization of the SYLlables or WORDS we think you should add the power to. When it comes to phrases, and paragraphs, however, we'll return to a symbolic usage first brought to your attention in Chapter 2. At the beginning of any grammatical unit on which added power is urged, we'll insert a large-amplitude circle: ○. Where conversational speech power, without particular stress or emphasis, is your objective, we shall so indicate with a moderate-amplitude circle, with a slash: ∅. Finally, we shall recommend for occasional, sparing use a technique known as unstressing-for-stress, and suggest its use with a small-amplitude circle: ○.

The possibility that you are at work on the loudness attribute without first having read Chapter 7 and worked with the time attribute has not escaped us. If this is the case, we urge you to lose no time in turning back to page 150, there to read our arguments for the use of symbol cues in developing vocal skills. If you have read the chapter, let us remind you that the use of these conventional signs is recommended to all students for a short time, but to almost no one for very long. Their potential contribution to stilted, artificial delivery is freely acknowledged, with their present use being justified as a kind of shock treatment for more or less acceptable vocal habits. Now to work.

Loudness level

1. The first exercise isn't a very forceful or dynamic task. We suggest only that you engage in a few moments of introspection about your vocal loudness. Do you describe yourself in any of the stereotype terms mentioned on page 168? Are you O'Jettique or Goosebump, Blowhard, O'Paque, or Hysteria Trayfort? Do people frequently ask you to speak up, or do they remind you that you're communicating over a distance of six feet, not six counties? It's our experience that young women are a little more likely to be judged wanting in over-all loudness than young men. This is neither a physiological nor an acoustical sex-linked phenomenon, we think, but rather a cultural one. In our society little girls learn to be little ladies ("Irma, little ladies don't shout!") at about the time little boys learn to speak up or the extra piece of cake goes to Rollo, who did speak up. Well, think it over. Get expert opinion (roommate?) if need be. See if you can decide in advance what your loudness skills and deficits are.

2. If you regularly get a turn on a tape recorder, put the opening paragraph of this chapter on tape for later critical evaluation and comparison. A 30-second impromptu speaking sample—"My Route to the Campus," or the like—could well be recorded at the same time. As we have told you, we believe firmly that your vocal patterns *as revealed in words of your choosing* are of prime significance as bases upon which to build vocal skills.

3. This exercise requires the participation of a speech lab partner. Go, if possible, to an empty classroom. Station yourself at the front of the room and your partner (a) in the first row, (b) in the middle row, (c) back in a corner (not necessarily in this order). With your eyes closed, keep up a running flow of words on some familiar topic, *speaking throughout as though to a friend not more than three or four feet away.* Ask your partner to evaluate your over-all loudness, the carrying power of your voice, over these relatively short distances. You should do the same for him. If a sound-level meter or a sound-survey meter is available to be used with these exercises, so much the better. You and your partner will have objective data to record.

4. Redo exercise 3 with your eyes open. As you see your target, the listener, do you succeed better in maintaining optimum over-all loudness?

5. This exercise requires not only your lab partner, but class participation as well. We hope that conditions at your school are such that this participation can be worked out, because the exercise has worked very well for us. We shall describe the exercise as though you were the only subject, but obviously each class member takes his turn being "it."

You are stationed at the front of the class, back to it. Your instructor, or someone appointed by him, stands between you and the class, facing the class; we'll call him the Director.

> a) Director instructs you to begin reciting nursery rhymes or something equally familiar (this you will continue to do throughout the exercise).
> b) Director points to student No. 1, who begins to count to 100 in a conversational voice.
> c) Director points to student No. 2, who counts *down* from 100 in a conversational voice.
> d) Director points to student No. 3, who begins to speak the letters of the alphabet in a conversational voice.
> e) Director points to student No. 4, who speaks the alphabet backward, starting with "z."
> f, g . . .) Director points successively to students 5, 6, 7, 8, . . . , who join students 1–4 in creating a noise barrier to communication.

Your lab partner, in the back row if possible, checks on a listener sheet:

(A) Whether you make automatic responses to increased noise; (B) whether your responses are adequate; and (C) how many conflicting voices it takes to render you less than 50 percent intelligible. (One researcher asserts that four voices will quite effectively mask out a single voice, but the conditions in the experiment he describes are somewhat different from those in this exercise.)

By the time the masking exercise is finished and you have reviewed your lab partner's judgments, you should have the bases for a good diagnosis of your average vocal power. Being the kind of person you are in the kind of class this is, it is unlikely that you depart seriously from an optimum level, either on the more or less side. However, if you do have a problem of some severity, you and your instructor should discuss the desirability of a work-up for you (including thorough audiometric check) in a speech and hearing clinic.

If you have a borderline average loudness problem, your voice occasionally falling below a level adequate for good communication, you should first of all return to Chapter 4 and review breathing and phrasing exercises. Next you might undertake the three exercises described below.

1. Often the voice that is inadequately loud is so because vocal sound gets trapped in the speaker's mouth and fails to find its way to the listener. This condition, sometimes described as the "San Quentin Syndrome," is the result simply of failure to open the mouth wide enough. "Oral inactivity" is the technical name for it. Try reciting the names of the days of the week and the months of the year with the smallest amount of oral activity you can manage. Now, making no other change in your delivery, do the same thing with your normal amount of movement. Finally, exaggerate the movement a little—not enough to make your facial appearance grotesque, but noticeably more than average. A mirror will help. Contrast these three degrees of oral activity, using the criterion of vocal loudness. If you find differences favoring increased oral activity, you should pursue exercises of this type further. Read aloud from newspapers and popular magazines, exaggerating oral activity. Establish kinesthetic feedback recognition of inadequate movement. (You recognize the word "kinesthesia," don't you? It is the sensation of movement in muscles, tendons, and joints.) Establish kinesthetic feedback patterns of what is optimum movement for optimum clarity and loudness.

2. Next, an exercise for reinforcement of good breathing habits. You will recognize this as a minor variation on some of the work described in Chapter 4. This exercise works best with a lab partner, a stop watch, and a sound-level meter or the VU (volume unit) meter, or a sound-level glow lamp on your tape recorder. Your objective is to take a normal breath, start to phonate on the peak of the inhalation, and, maintaining a constant predetermined level, continue to phonate as long as you are producing "good" sound. Start with the vowel [ɑ] and set yourself a fairly low sound level to sustain. For how many seconds can you hold the tone? Now make the problem more difficult; demand 5 dB more power of yourself if you are working with a sound-level meter, or lower the level of amplification in your tape recorder (thus requiring more sound if the VU meter needle is to hover around the zero mark or the glow lamp is to maintain a constant glow). Ask your partner to time "good" sound. Now make the task 5 dB more difficult. What is the time on this phonation? Now shift to the vowel [i] and run through the series again. Then the vowel [u]. How do the vowels compare? You might make up a table which reveals the results for three vowels and three degrees of vocal power. Then repeat the exercise regularly in your

room and in the speech lab. Try to extend your time. You will be building good feedback patterns of muscle action and the sound of sustained tone.

3. Finally, another exercise that works best if you have some electronic help. If you have a tape recording of the masking noise situation described on page 170, play the tape again and again and speak extemporaneously or read aloud over the noise. (If you can listen to the tape through earphones you'll create less general room noise to disturb your fellow students.) Play back the tape at a fairly low level, at first. Gradually increase the strength of the masking noise and test your capacity to react appropriately.

If your minor loudness problem was the result simply of habit, a feedback receptor system that typically accepted as normal vocal loudness levels insufficient for others to hear and understand, the three exercises just described should be effective in breaking the habits and helping you institute new ones.

Accent

Now it is high time we turned our attention to flexibility of loudness, variations which contribute to more intelligible and more effective speaking performances. You remember that variations in vocal power may be applied to syllables, words, and longer grammatical units. Interestingly, the descriptive term for what is done tends to vary with the size of the unit affected, though this is not always the case. More vocal power applied to syllables is termed *accent;* to words it is *stress;* and to longer units it is *emphasis.* Many people use the terms, particularly *stress* and *emphasis,* interchangeably. For convenience more than because of semantic conviction we'll make the distinction indicated above as we describe some exercises to you. First, accent. Here more vocal power is applied to a syllable within a word, often to distinguish that word from another spelled the same but somewhat or greatly different in meaning. More often than not nouns and adjectives receive primary accent on the first syllable, whereas the verbs with which they might be confused receive their primary accent on a later syllable. There are many finer points of historical and practical interest that linguists find to say about accent. We are tempted to pursue the subject further, but recognizing that certain boundary lines must be respected we content ourselves with recommending the chapter-end readings to the interested student.

1. Read the following pairs of words, responding appropriately to the indications for syllable stress or accent.

a) CONtent   — conTENT
b) PROduce   — proDUCE
c) SUBject   — subJECT
d) COMbine   — comBINE
e) PROceed   — proCEED
f) RECord   — reCORD
g) SURvey   — surVEY
h) PROGress   — proGRESS
i) CONtract   — conTRACT
j) PERfect   — perFECT
k) PROject   — proJECT

Notice how vowel quality changes with the shift in accent?

2. Now take the same list and build sentences around the contrasting words. Make sure you can effect the desired shift of meanings as you shift the accent. If in doubt of your success, ask a classmate to listen to you. We will provide you with sample sentences for the first three word-pairs, then urge you to carry on.

a) Are you conTENT with the CONtent of this chapter?
b) The PROduce store depends for its goods on what the farmer can proDUCE.
c) Please change the SUBject and don't subJECT me to any more complaints.
d) You're on your own for this and the other pairs of words in exercise 1, above.

Stress

Now to stress, word stress in particular. In this frame of reference more of vocal energy is applied to one word than to the others in a phrase or sentence, making it stand out from its fellows. Most of the time, stress is applied simply as a means of enhancing intelligibility, of making meaning clear. In furtherance of this aim, stress usually is applied to action words, idea words, picture words, rarely to connective words, structure words. (Lincoln's *of, by* and *for* the people, as interpreted by some readers, is a notable exception to this generalization.)

Word stress sometimes is applied more to reveal state of mind or attitude than to prevent misunderstanding of meaning. However, the difference usually is a matter of degree of stress rather than the selection of a different word to stress. For example, "I *favor* the idea" puts stress on the verb to prevent misunderstanding, but "I FAVOR the idea" (stronger) indicates that real feeling is involved. Both uses of word stress will occur in the exercises below.

1. Examine the possibilities for word stress in this sentence: You can lead a horse to water.

> a) YOU can lead a horse to water (but you'll never catch *me* doing it).
> b) You CAN lead a horse to water (in spite of your opinions to to the contrary).
> c) You can LEAD a horse to water (but you can't push him in that direction).
> d) You can lead A horse to water (but just try leading six or eight of them).
> e) You can lead a HORSE to water (but did you ever try to lead a goat?).
> f) You can lead a horse TO water (leading him away from it is another matter).
> g) You can lead a horse to WATER (whereas leading him to coffee is a waste of time).

Seven-word sentence, seven shades of meaning. Read the sentences aloud, first with the inclusion of the material in parentheses, then without. Are you conveying these fine shades of meaning? Does anyone else think so?

2. With the following sentences repeat exercise 1, shifting the word stress for shades of meaning. You supply the parenthetical material, of course. If you can get this exercise on tape its value to you will be increased.

> a) June is the month for brides.
> b) Our football team shows great promise.
> c) Employers in industry are interested in the well-rounded college graduate.
> d) When do you plan to turn in your term paper?
> e) I started learning Spanish in grade school.
> f) Centreville is only fifty miles away.
> g) Walk to the nearest exit, then turn left.
> h) Have you forgotten the peanut butter sandwiches?
> i) Ken and Esther are going steady now.
> j) The biology lecture today was grim.

Doubtless you learned in this exercise that sometimes word stress, misapplied, can do more to conceal than to enhance meaning. That is, stress applied to certain words in certain contexts leads only to listener confusion. This is a lesson that was never learned by Hysteria Trayfort, mentioned earlier. She chatters on at great rate, with boundless enthusiasm, applying stress at random or according to some statistical design unrelated to syntax. The results, like the results of some of the word stresses in the exercise above, are unfortunate.

3. Here is a not-very-important word-stress exercise: count aloud, one-two-three- . . . , stressing each digit a little more than the previous one. The number of digits you can manipulate in this way tells you two things: the range of speech power at your command, and the delicacy of your control over this attribute. If you are forced to stop at the count of three or four, then apparently you need to practice this exercise a good deal to gain more vocal control. On the other hand, if your count goes up in the teens, there is some reason to suspect that you are hearing imaginary differences in loudness between digits. Tape record the exercise and ask someone to verify your score.

Emphasis

Next, emphasis. Now comparative vocal power is used to facilitate comprehension, reveal conviction, show comparison and contrast of objects, events, or ideas, and generally add interest to vocal delivery. In this section we will use the comparative symbols ◯ and ⊘ for greater and lesser degrees of vocal power, respectively.

1. Read the following short selections aloud, responding appropriately to the symbols as they occur.

   a) ⊘ To err is human ◯ to forgive divine.
   b) ⊘ Although she is tiny ◯ she's full of spirit.
   c) ⊘ You go your way ◯ I'll go mine.
   d) ◯ Don't cross that line ⊘ it's against the law.
   e) ◯ You seem so sure of it ⊘ perhaps you're right.
   f) ⊘ Mark is conservative ◯ but Irene is liberal.
   g) ◯ The final exam ⊘ from what I hear ◯ is easy.
   h) ⊘ When the dam breaks ◯ head for the hills.
   i) ⊘ Hope likes to paint ◯ but she loathes cleaning brushes.
   j) ⊘ I can't sketch with this pencil ◯ it's much too hard.

2. Now reread the sentences, reversing the stress symbols. Note that some of them still read well, though there is a shift in meaning. Others

sound very strange with the reversed stress. Can you derive a rule for phrase stress from this exercise?

Do you think you performed numbers 1 and 2 well, responding as you should to the symbols? If you believe that you need more practice, repeat 1 and 2, then turn back to exercise 1 on page 159 in the preceding chapter. Pencil in the loudness symbols as you think appropriate and run through these several times. When you decide that you have reasonably good control, ask your lab partner to listen to one of these exercises. Then go on to the exercise below.

In the next two exercises we serve up larger chunks of material for you to cope with. Your aim, though, is the same: to achieve flexibility of loudness. above an optimum level by emphasizing certain phrases in contrast to certain others. In exercise 1 be obedient to our directive symbols, and in exercise 2 write in your own symbols and respond appropriately. Sometimes there will be two or even more "less loudness" symbols in succession, sometimes two or more "more loudness" symbols in succession. You must decide whether to give equal loudness under these conditions or to weight one more than the others.

1. (The following news items, with names changed, are taken from NBC News broadcasts through the courtesy of the National Broadcasting Company.)

$\emptyset$ METROPOLIS. / $\bigcirc$ Governor Martin R. Martin / $\emptyset$ told a new board of state college trustees today / $\bigcirc$ that education and economy should not be enemies / $\emptyset$ in the state. / $\emptyset$ In a half-hour session with the trustees / $\emptyset$ the governor declared / $\bigcirc$ he is not for short-changing education / $\bigcirc$ but he is for economy. / $\emptyset$ He warned that the time is coming /$\bigcirc$ when capital expenses will be as constant / $\bigcirc$ as the salaries we have to pay. / $\emptyset$ Martin told a news conference later / $\bigcirc$ he is greatly concerned with overorders of textbooks. / $\emptyset$ He also said / $\emptyset$ he is at a loss to understand / $\bigcirc$ how music books get out of date. / $\emptyset$ In response to questioning / $\emptyset$ he said that he can foresee / $\bigcirc$ no wage increases for college professors now / $\emptyset$ but added / $\bigcirc$ the situation may change / $\emptyset$ in two months or so.

2. (In this selection, also an edited news broadcast, insert your own phrase markers and loudness symbols. If you can tape record this exercise and receive listener criticism, the work will be more valuable to you. It will help you, too, to play back the selection and compare your intentions—the marked passage—with the outcome, the recording.)

METROPOLIS.   The hunt is on   in the governor's mansion . . .
for two pet hamsters . . . Mary and Harry.   The hamsters—
furry rodent-type animals—   arrived at the mansion a week ago
as a gift for four-year-old Ruthie Martin   from a little boy in West
Migrate.   Mary and Harry lost no time   in breaking out of their
cage.   The first time they got loose,   Mary was found   in
the governor's study,   Harry in his bedroom.   But last night
       the hamsters made a clean get-away.   And the mansion staff
is combing the halls   for the two pets.   Hamsters—   like
rabbits—   multiply rapidly.

3. Was exercise 2 a successful vocal experience for you? If not, if
you feel you need more practice in effecting loudness contrasts, turn
back to the paragraph on page 157 in Chapter 7. Insert your loudness
symbols in that one, practice reading it aloud, then read it for criticism,
if possible tape-recording your delivery.

4. As your last exercise in emphasis, work up a short impromptu
speech on some topic of personal interest to you. As you speak, to listener,
to tape recorder, or just to yourself, be alert for opportunities for loudness
flexibility. Be critical of your delivery. Repeat this exercise until you derive
some satisfaction, a sense of accomplishment, from it.

Unstressing

Now, *unstressing* as a stress technique. This is an interesting vocal
maneuver, one that can be quite effective if used in moderation. A certain
silver-tongued politician we've observed uses the device so often that it
stands out for the trick he obviously makes of it. As implied by the
name we've given to this practice, it simply involves applying *less* than
normal loudness to a key word or phrase, near or at one of the subclimaxes
in a speaking performance. Almost any departure from the expected, and
this certainly is that, can have the effect of jolting a drowsing audience
into wakefulness, or sharpening the attention of an already attentive group
of listeners. Its best use, we feel, comes after a momentary pause in
delivery. Try the technique in the short sentences below, pausing at the
slant lines and then delivering the climax-word at a level barely above
your listeners' threshold. The small symbol reminds you to unstress.

a) The ballots have been counted and the motion is / ○ lost.

b) They're untangling players and the ball's recovered by / ○
Southwestern.

c) What do you think was the cost of the new gymnasium? / ○ one million dollars.

d) Gentlemen, there is just one word which describes this action / ○ stupidity.

e) The greatest artist of our time / ○ Carl di Carlo / ∅ could do no better.

f) Time for the mile run was / ○ four minutes, flat.

g) On that date, it is believed, occurred the first successful / ○ lunar landing.

h) And now, the event you've all been waiting for / ○ the three-legged race.

i) Fellow students, the queen of the Golddiggers Ball will be / ○ Vivian Smith.

How did those sentences sound? Some of them had a hollow ring, didn't they? That's because this vocal device often is, we feel, truly artificial. Once again we caution you against overapplication of unstressing. Learn to do it well, gain the necessary shock tactic, but apply conservatively.

Well, you've been exposed to a good many vocal experiences in the loudness area, we trust to good effect. Our emphasis throughout has been on vocal variety in loudness, rather than increased loudness as an end in itself. However, even in this era of the microphone and amplifier, a word might be said in favor of practice for sheer vocal power. Microphone cables do get broken; amplifiers sometimes short out. You might even, some day, find yourself speaking in public without any electronic help. This can be a debilitating and unnerving experience. To prepare for it we recommend the Demosthenes approach—declaiming to the waves, if available, to the wide open spaces if not. Work with a substantially larger than normal air charge and use greater than average oval activity. (The pebble-in-the-mouth refinement used by the old Greek orator, we believe, is contraindicated.)

If you undertake this project seriously, you will learn something of your vocal strength and limitations. Don't give up after 30 seconds; stay with it for two, five minutes at a time. Extend your time to 15 minutes. If you can still dominate your natural environment at the end of that period, you have good prospects of communicating to a human audience, unaided, for a similar period or longer. But, caution—undertake the project conservatively. When you feel vocal strain, slack off. Review your breathing habits. Locate, if you can, local sources of muscle tension and seek, through relaxation techniques, to eliminate them. Your entire vocal mechanism must be well tuned if this exercise is to be successful.

STUDENT PROJECTS

CONTENT ASSIGNMENT

A. After reviewing Chapters 2 and 8 in the text, write down ten facts about intensity of loudness.

B. Describe, in writing, three different speaking situations calling for differences in control of the loudness attribute.

C. Compare and contrast vocal control in the loudness and time domains as reflections of the strength of the speaker's convictions about his topic.

LISTENING ASSIGNMENTS

A. Listen to 4 radio, TV, or movie actors for loudness flexibility. Evaluate them on -3 to $+3$ scale. Add any pertinent comment.

B. Observe your own over-all loudness level under various conditions of noise: a restaurant or dining hall, the library, walking between classes, and so on. Report your findings.

C. Write a critical evaluation of your loudness usage in the tape-recorded exercise 2, page 169 of the text.

D. Evaluate your lab partner's loudness in exercises 3, 4, and 5, page 169 of the text.
   1. Does he (she) respond automatically to increased masking?
   2. Is the response adequate?
   3. Did masking noise render him (her) less than 50 percent intelligible? If so, how many voices were required to reduce him to that level?

PERFORMANCE ASSIGNMENT

Only one more experience now remains and the decision as to whether it should be applied must be your instructor's. The culminating assignment in control of loudness is an extemporaneous speech for class evaluation and instructor's grade. Topic: "I'm Dissatisfied with _____!" (Sometimes inelegantly referred to as a gripe speech.) Work hard on the preparation. Maintain an optimum level. Introduce variation in accents, stress, and emphasis.

RECOMMENDED READINGS

Draegert, G. L. Relationships between voice variables and speech intelligibility in high level noise. *Speech Monogr.,* **18,** 1951, 272–278.

Fletcher, H. *Speech and hearing in communication.* Princeton, N.J.: Van Nostrand, 1953. Chap. 4.

Hanley, T. D., and Steer, M. D. Effect of level of distracting noise upon speaking rate, duration, and intensity. *J. Speech and Hearing Disorders,* **14,** 1949, 363–368.

Hudgins, C. J., Hawkins, J. E., Karlin, J. E., and Stevens, S. S. The development of recorded auditory tests for measuring hearing loss for speech. *Laryngoscope,* **57,** 1947, 57–89.

Kenyon, J. S. *American pronunciation.* (10th ed.) Ann Arbor, Mich.: Wahr, 1958.

Kryter, K. D. Effects of ear protective devices on the intelligibility of speech in noise. *J. Acoust. Soc. Amer.,* **18,** 1946, 413–417.

Miller, G. A. *Language and communication.* New York: McGraw-Hill, 1951. Pp. 52–63.

Tiffin, J., and Steer, M. D. An experimental analysis of emphasis. *Speech Monogr.,* **4,** 1937, 69–74.

CHAPTER
9

SKILL
IN THE
USE OF
PITCH

"There is in oratorical discourse, a kind of tune, differing from that of Song and [from the melody] of Music, only in degree, but not in kind or quality." So wrote Dionysius of Halicarnassus, a Greek historian and teacher of rhetoric who flourished around 20 B.C. James Rush, a Philadelphia physician who wrote a ponderous treatise on the voice in the early nineteenth century, quotes Dionysius and then proceeds to expand on the functions of pitch in vocal communication:

> If we listen to his [man's] ignorance, his fears, superstition, selfishness, arrogance, and injustice, we hear them under the forms of vivid vocal expression. We have the rising intervals of the third, fifth, and octave, for interrogatives, not of kindness, but of the fierce and persecuting. Catechists of our life and faith; the downward third, fifth and octave for dogmatic, or tyrannical command; waves for the wonder of ignorance, the snarling of ill-humor and the curling voice of

contempt; the piercing height of the falsetto for the scream of terror, the brawls of intemperance, and the shouts of the fanatic around the stake of the martyr; the semitone for the peevish whine of discontent, and for the puling cant of the hypocrite and knave, who thus strive in vain to conceal their crafty designs. Then listen to him on those rare occasions when he forgets himself and his passions, and has to utter a useful thought or plainly to narrate, and you will hear the second, the unobtrusive interval of the scale, in the admirable adaptation of Nature, made the simple sign of the dispassionate perception of her wisdom and truth.[1]

The departure from our general pattern of emphasis on the functional rather than the scholarly, represented by the quotations above, was deliberate. We wished to show, first, that for two thousand years or more there has been recognition of the rise and fall characteristics of the communicating human voice. Second, we believe there is significance in Rush's vigor-

(Somebody's) Mother   (Anybody's) Horse

Figure 9.1.

ous description of the use of intonation in what he describes in another place as "the just use of its intervals, for denoting the states of mind in thought and passion."

The rise and fall refers to pitch, to level and intonation, which is pitch movement over such speech units as the phrase. We believe, with Rush, that this vocal attribute can be most effective in revealing "the states of mind in thought and passion." Reference now to Figure 9.1 will indicate to you what intonation (or more properly in this example, inflection) will do for some languages, but not for ours. The objects depicted in Figure 9.1 are a mother and a horse. Phonemically the Chinese words for these objects are identical: [ma]; they differ only in *tone*. In this context "tone" means level or inflection. As a matter of fact, there are several other words that are also pronounced "ma" in Mandarin

[1] The spelling in this passage has been modernized.

Chinese. One could compose a sentence made all of "ma's": "mā mà mǎ ma." Translation: "Does mother scold the horse?" "Mā" is spoken on a fairly high level pitch, "ma" from fairly high falling to medium-low, "mǎ" is fairly low, rising at the end, and "ma" is neutral but, when spoken at a higher level than what precedes, indicates a question. If the ear of the listener is keen and is attuned to the dialect of the speaker, he will distinguish one of these meanings from the other possibilities by detecting the subtle difference in inflection that makes each word unique.

Dew and Hollien even demonstrate that pitch movement, in contrast to level inflection, is of negligible value in listener identification of vowels; Diehl, White, and Satz present experimental evidence to show that pitch movement contributes almost nothing to audience comprehension of spoken material, though audience preference, as you would suppose, is greatly on the side of the inflected as opposed to the monotonic delivery.

Pitch movement in Chinese, you see, conveys meaning. Pitch level, inflection, and intonation in English (and other Indo-European languages) convey information about the speaker and his attitudes. But pitch does not convey meaning in English, at least in the sense of differentiating between homonyms.

Let us, then, reflect on what we can learn from hearing pitch level and pitch movement in a person's voice. In the absence of visual and other contextual cues we can identify the speaker by sex (Pronovost; Snidecor) and age (Fairbanks and others; Curry; Mysak). There is, moreover, nearly universal agreement among authorities (for example, Heffner; Herman and Herman; Hockett; and Jones) and a small body of experimental evidence (for example, Hanley) to the effect that a speaker's native language and even his dialect within the language may be revealed to the trained ear by pitch levels and intonational features of his utterance.

What more? Personality characteristics? As we mentioned with respect to loudness factors, we are inclined to discount much that has been written relating vocal behavior to personality, but we are bound to admit that pitch stereotypes do exist in the public mind. The high-pitched male voice is associated with effeminacy and low-pitched female tones with what we may conservatively term hyperfeminity. Terango reported recently a study of 40 college males, half of whom had been stigmatized by their instructors as having effeminate voices. Surprisingly, the median pitch level for these young men was *below* the median level found to be average or normal by earlier investigators, though considerably higher than the level for the other half the experimental sample, judged to have masculine voices. The less masculine voices were also found to use a much faster rate of pitch change during inflection than the more "manly" subject.

An overabundance of falling-rising inflections at phrase ends, which we'll discuss in some detail later, are thought to characterize the indecisive person, whereas a repetitious pattern of abrupt falling inflections, unrelieved by level or rising ones, is a vocal stereotype of our friend Horace Blowhard from Chapter 8. Remember, we don't take much stock in this type of analysis, though we cannot deny that extreme forms of pitch usage may stigmatize a person.

A review of the literature by Kramer, a psychologist, leads him to the conclusion that "the presence of so-called vocal stereotypes is not really so empty a finding after all."

What of the relation of pitch usages to attitudes? Here it is, we believe, that pitch skill may be of greatest benefit to the speaker. As you will demonstrate to yourself in the laboratory section of this chapter, a well-placed, skillfully executed circumflex inflection can be as convincing and effective in denying an otherwise affirmative statement or confirming a negative one as an elevated eyebrow or a sardonically curled lip in a wide-screen close-up. One of the major virtues of pitch control, then, is subtlety of communication, extending beyond the informational values inherent in the language we use.

It seems to us that pitch, without very much in the way of a specific role to play in communication, contributes as much to vocal excellence as any other attribute. Perhaps more. There is some inconclusive but persuasive research evidence to support our position, which we'll write about in a moment. Additionally, there is a great deal of concurring authoritative opinion to be found in other books. Thus we find ourselves writing about an attribute for which we have considerable enthusiasm, and in succeeding paragraphs we shall try to summarize in such a way as to be of practical value what is presently known or generally believed about pitch.

Pitch level is the first topic to engage our attention and the most important thing we have to tell you about your own pitch level is, *let it alone.* Research findings for superior young adult male and female speakers are that their average ("habitual") pitch levels are approximately C_3 and $G\#_3$ respectively (Pronovost; Snidecor), or one octave and two musical tones, respectively, below middle C. Despite these findings and in flat disagreement with many textbooks in this field, we urge you to make no attempt to relocate your average pitch level, whatever you know or believe it to be. If, in your instructor's opinion, your habitual and optimum pitch levels are too far apart, he will work with you individually or will make an appropriate referral to a physician or a speech clinic. But far too many persons, in our experience, self-diagnose "too high" (rarely "too low" for either sex) pitch levels, set about lowering pitch, and by so doing perhaps lay the groundwork for future serious vocal disturbances.

Why should it be that altered pitch level is blamed for laryngeal pathology? Pitch (frequency) is a function of balances among length, tension, and mass in the vibration of a taut string, which your vocal cords resemble to a considerable degree. In your vocal mechanism these balances or adjustments have been arrived at over a span of many years. Your average level changed from infancy to childhood to young adulthood, where you now stand. In the absence of better information, we believe, it should be assumed that your physiological maturation has been as normal in the larynx as it has in your upper arm, or ankle, or any other anatomical locus. If this is true, if you have normal cords that vibrate under normal tension, then the frequency at which they vibrate most often is the best, most effective, most efficient frequency, the optimum pitch level, the one at which you can produce sounds longest, with least effort. Temporary movements away from that frequency are good, for obvious reasons. But an ill-considered shift of any magnitude away from that habitual level can result in vocal strain and other more serious effects that are not within our province to discuss here.

Now our positive statements about pitch level are as follows. Be aware of the average pitch of your voice. Listen for it and to it, both live and in recordings. It changes, doesn't it? Note that the level changes throughout the day with changes in your freshness or fatigue, generalized tension or relaxation, ease or difficulty of communication, loudness or softness of voice. Adapt your pitch level to the material being communicated, shifting up or down a little if it seems appropriate to do so. Gain control over level, so that you may accomplish temporary relocations. If anything, you might even be a little pleased should you somehow discover that your average level is higher than the hypothetical population average for your sex. Lewis and Tiffin, in a study previously mentioned, found that the subject judged to be their most effective speaker had an average pitch level almost two musical tones above the average for their sample of male voices. This finding may be explained by McIntosh's later discovery of a positive relation between pitch level and vocal flexibility; when subjects are instructed to increase or decrease one, the other rises or falls too.

To summarize our advice about pitch level: learn to know and control it, as you do your other vocal attributes, but institute no program of relocation without consulting authority. Assume, until proved wrong, that your average or habitual pitch level is exactly equivalent to your hypothetical natural or optimum pitch level, that frequency of vocal cord vibration best suited to the physiology and mechanics of your vocal structures.

The speaker can no more find his "lost chord" and phonate forever on that optimum pitch than he can produce sounds at an unvarying optimum rate or optimum loudness. There must be flexibility of pitch. In fact, as we've suggested earlier, pitch flexibility may be the most significant of the bioacoustical contributors to judged excellence of vocal delivery. What are the components, the determinants of pitch flexibility? Authorities in the past, both teachers and researchers, have listed these: (Note that different authorities attach different labels to the same phenomena. Often there is little save unreasoned personal preference to choose between alternate terms, which we list parenthetically.)

A. Total Pitch Range—that difference, in musical units or cycles per second, between the lowest and highest tones produced over a stated span of time or unit of phonated material.

B. Functional Range—again a difference in musical units or cycles per second between high and low tones, but a statistical limitation that excludes a stated percentage (usually 5 percent) of upper and lower vocal frequencies is applied. The frequencies excluded are considered to be somewhat accidental or uncontrolled tones, often terminal phonations at ends of phrases.

C. Inflections (slides)— changes in pitch level, up or down, up-down, down-up, down-up-down, and so on, taking place without cessation of phonation. Inflections which involve one or more changes of direction within a phonation are called *circumflex*. A special case and seeming contradiction in terms is the *level inflection,* which signifies a phonation with insignificant change of pitch level.

D. Skips (steps, shifts)—changes in pitch level, up or down, between phonations.

E. Other—these are highly specialized observations made by voice scientists and often related by them to perceived or judged aspects of vocal performance:

1. Mean rate of pitch change: average extent of inflection divided by the average period of time required to complete the pitch movement.
2. Pitch sigma (standard deviation of the distribution of vocal frequencies): a purely statistical description of a vocal performance, reflecting the variability of the performance around the mean or median. Philhour's research showed this measure to be more closely related than any of the others to judged flexibility of pitch usage.

Comes now brief mention of a few research findings, pointing up the virtues discovered in some of these aspects of pitch flexibility. Armed with such evidence, we can confidently engage in some voice laboratory exercises tailor-made, we hope, to the vocal demands placed upon educated persons today.

Both width of range and magnitude of pitch sigma were considerably wider for the trained subjects in Lynch's study than for the untrained readers. Extent of inflection also distinguished the two groups, with the wider glides characterizing the delivery of the trained readers.

Lewis and Tiffin confirmed the Lynch results only to a limited extent. Their findings supported the hypothesis that an extremely narrow range is a limiting factor on a speaker's effectiveness. However, in the interpretation of their results they stressed the desirability of adequate spread of pitches around the median, rather than breadth of pitch range as such. This spread doubtless corresponds to what we have identified earlier as pitch sigma.

Pitch range in the study reported by Murray and Tiffin again was a measure which distinguished trained and untrained groups of speakers and judged good and poor speakers within the untrained group. The investigators, however, noted many instances of individual displacements or reversals within the latter two groups. When extent of inflection was examined, even more instances of individual reversals were found, this time being concentrated more in good and trained groups. Interestingly, wider inflections on stressed words than on the same words unstressed were reported by Tiffin and Steer to occur in 84 percent of the observations they made. This is a larger incidence than was found in their analysis of intensity of stressed and unstressed words.

Failure to confirm either range or extent of inflection (or any other physical measure of variability, for that matter) as highly related to general excellence or pitch excellence was reported by Philhour.

We fall back on our own classroom observation and critical attention paid to artistic performance, buttressed by limited support from the studies cited, in arriving at the following position with respect to pitch flexibility. As controlled by intelligent and disciplined speakers and readers, pitch range, extent of inflection, and pitch sigma all contribute importantly to the general effectiveness of delivery.

Further support for the significance of pitch factors in artistic performance is to be found in a study reported by Fairbanks and Pronovost. These investigators found that a semantically ambiguous reading passage could be delivered in such a way that any one of six emotional states could reliably be identified by listeners. The six different patterns of delivery were identifiably different with respect to pitch characteristics.

It is imperative that stress be placed on the notion of intelligent, disciplined delivery. Mere wide range, or sweeping inflections, or accumulations of vocal frequencies spreading out from the average pitch level are not enough. These pitch movements must be applied where and when they will do the most good.

It is a curious thing that many texts we examined recommend development of a range of an octave or more. Curious, because in published research one rarely finds a report of a subject with a range smaller than an octave. When such a report is found, as in the Murray and Tiffin study, the character of the speech sample may help to explain the limited range. We stress this point because we feel that extending the pitch range is, in itself, a probable waste of time for the normal person. What is wanted, in our view, is intelligent, extended utilization of the range one already has. To this end we shall set you to exploring your range and building confidence in your ability to move about meaningfully within it.

In anticipation of your laboratory work, let us acquaint you with some new symbols, for inflections and skips. It is unnecessary to symbolize pitch levels, since these can easily be specified verbally at the beginning of an exercise. For rising and falling inflections, respectively, we shall make use of $\nearrow$ and $\searrow$. When the line connecting the notes is broken, $\nearrow$ and $\searrow$, the same *directions* of pitch change are symbolized as with the solid lines, but the movement is by pitch *skip* rather than inflection. Finally, the subtle circumflex may be indicated as follows: $\wedge$, standing for a rising-falling inflection. Other progressions, of course, are possible.

These pitch symbols, like those for time and loudness, are intended to help guide you through early stages of acquisition of pitch control. They will not compensate for a tin ear or unintelligent delivery. Used slavishly, they could contribute to patterned, lifeless communication. Used thoughtfully, they can have the effect of replacing the commonplace with the interesting, the bland with the arresting in your conversation and more formal speaking efforts.

DEVELOPING PITCH SKILLS IN THE SPEECH LABORATORY

Average level

We don't know what your pitch level should be, and we're not convinced that anyone else does, either. Pronovost in one study and Thurman in another demonstrated the unreliability of several rule-of-thumb methods for locating optimum and habitual pitch levels. The former demonstrated reliability for one interesting technique applied to a small group of superior speakers, but we are not aware of experimental validation of any method applied to normal speakers. So, as we've advised more than once before, don't try to pin down in absolute values either your habitual or that hypothetical optimum pitch level. But don't ignore level altogether. Become aware of the average pitch of your voice, alert to changes in it. Learn to listen to this attribute in yourself and others.

1. Establish yourself comfortably in a chair. Sit erect, but not stiffly so. Try consciously to reduce tension in your chest, shoulders, throat. Breathe naturally for a half-minute or so, then take two or three slightly deeper-than-average inhalations. Release the last of these in a sigh, gradually adding voice to the outflowing column of air. Listen to this sound. Repeat the whole process. Listen to the vocalized sigh. Did it come out on just about the same pitch as the first one? Now do the whole business again. Listen to that vocalized sigh. Same pitch? So far as we're concerned that sound you've produced is neither your habitual pitch nor your natural pitch, but it's probably not far from either. Almost surely it's in the lower half of your range, but somewhere above the lowest tone you can sustain. There, according to the best research evidence and the most respected authorities on voice, is the general region where both these levels are to be found. Now you have a tone, a pitch level to listen for. Can you repeat this whole exercise with a tape recorder? Now listen to the electronic reproduction of your vocalized sighs. Compare these with live voice. Which is lower? Which sounds better to you? Your recorder's reproduction of your voice is much more like what your listener hears than the synchronous feedback you enjoy as you produce sound. Try to decide whether your recorded sounds are "normal" in pitch level. Invite other opinion. Confer with your instructor if you have any doubts or feelings of insecurity about your pitch.

2. We are fairly sure this next approach will take you quite close to your average pitch level, a tone to which, by definition, you return more often than any other. Resume the comfortable position described in exercise 1 and, starting at the beginning of this chapter, read aloud for a minute or two. Read normally, with no particular attempt to introduce vocal flexibility. Listen for some central pitch tendency in your voice. Gradually confine your vocal sound to this central tendency, working toward a true monotone, or monopitch. When you think you've achieved it, stop on some easily prolonged vowel sound and hold the tone. Listen carefully to it. Compare it in your auditory memory with the vocalized sigh of exercise 1. Do a vocalized sigh. Compare it with the tone you've just prolonged. Lower? Higher? Now read on. Listen to your pitch level.

Work to monopitch and prolong a vowel. Listen to that sound. Put this exercise on tape, if you can. Listen carefully when you play back what you have recorded. Make the judgment you made in exercise 1. Is your pitch level pleasing to you? It is "normal"? Resolve any doubts, if you have them, by inviting comment from your instructor. An interesting variation on this procedure is suggested by Franks and asserted by him to be accomplished more easily than conscious narrowing of the range. He suggests, as we and others have done, that you start reading normally, but he recommends a departure from normal reading in *rate*. Read normally, then at ever-increasing speed. His subjects became monotonic, and you may too. Try this approach and compare it with the others. Remember that in this section we are trying only to create awareness of something which comes close to being habitual pitch level. We are *not* laying the groundwork for a change in level. When you feel your ear has developed some sensitivity, some pitch level sophistication, you will be ready to undertake work on range. It goes without saying, we trust, that listening to classmates perform this same exercise will contribute to your aural sophistication.

Pitch range

The objective here, as we conceive it, is to achieve optimum utilization of range, rather than to extend it. Certainly there are persons whose range is so limited that extension would be prescribed, but if you are one of those persons we are greatly surprised.

1. Explore your range. Really explore your range. Unless you are trained in vocal music, this may be one of the most difficult tasks we will set for you. Few of us relish displaying our operatic limitations. But cast aside your inhibitions. Here is how you set about exploring your range: Take the position described in 1, page 189, and vocalize a sigh. Take that as a point of departure and produce, at random, a tone of different pitch. Now another, and another. Move up, move down. Use [ɑ], [i], and [u] as tones to produce. Now hum these random-pitched tones. Sometimes it helps to close your eyes during this exercise. If you find yourself humming a tune, make a deliberate effort to break it. Don't abandon this exercise until you have achieved some degree of mastery over it, until you can skip about within your range rather effortlessly, until you are producing random sounds two to three musical tones below your habitual pitch level, four to six musical tones above it. Surely someone in your lab class will be able to check you out on the extent of your

variation around your average pitch level. Listen to others perform the exercise. Return to this exercise from time to time as you work on pitch flexibility. We think it can do a good deal to release you from self-imposed limitations on the use of range.

2. Now explore your range a little more formally. Hum or sing a scale. Can you achieve a span from "do" to "do"? Try starting with a comfortable note in mid-range, hum to your lowest sustainable tone, then start up the scale. Don't stop if you hit a sour note. Carry on. Then make the return trip down the scale. How wide is your singing range? Wider than an octave, we're quite sure. And if you can sing those tones, you can speak them.

3. Now explore your range monotonally with verbal material. That is, select a page or more from a popular magazine, a column from a newspaper, a column from this book and read it aloud on a preselected monopitch (a) Start with a pitch close to your habitual level. (b) Repeat, at a perceptibly higher level. (c) Repeat, at a perceptibly lower level. (d) Repeat, extending your range outward from the level originally selected. Do not pursue this exercise to the point where you are croaking at the low end and squeaking at the high end. If either of those extremes is reached, stop the exercise. Engage in some ear training by listening to other students, or return to some of the earlier exercises. But come back to this one. Build self-confidence in your ability to communicate on pitch levels other than the one you habitually use. This exercise, like the first one in this section is worthy of many repetitions.

4. Demonstrate to yourself the value of this ability to assume and sustain a pitch level different from your own. The short selections (a) through (c) below, reflect different emotional states and different degrees of emotional loading. Read each one three times, once at your normal pitch level, once generally above it, and once generally below it.

a) Dear Folks:

Here it is the first of the month again and I find I haven't written since the last time I flipped a page on the calendar. That's the way it is in your senior year—time races by so fast you can hardly believe it.

Well, here is a rundown on what has happened since my latest letter. I've had hourly exams in all my courses and did quite well in four of them. The fifth almost tripped me because I misinterpreted one of the questions, but I did well enough on the others to salvage a "B—."

I've taken time off from the books to go to all the basketball games and to see a road company performance of "The Blue Jay." This I thought was so funny it was out of sight.

You will be surprised to learn that there is almost $22 in my checking account. Looking forward to being on my own next year, I'm practicing economy.

Back now to the studies. Please give my best to Bud and Helen.

Love,

J.

b) "Sir, I've just come from the registrar's office, where I got my grades. I believe there's a mistake in the one for your course. A 'C,' Mr. Sheehan. You didn't give me a 'C,' did you? I'm afraid I don't understand that grade, sir. I worked hard in this course and I deserve better than that—a lot better. Maybe I didn't get top grades on the tests, and I guess I missed a couple of the quizzes. But how about my class participation? And what about my term paper? I got a 'B—' on that and you said if it had been a little longer it might have been a 'B.' I'd like to know what you have to do in that class to get a 'B.' I'd also like to know who decided it should be a required course for graduation. It was the dullest, most confusing course I ever sat through and I guess I'm just real happy my grade is high enough that I don't have to repeat it!"

c) "Students, you'll notice one of your classmates is absent today. I don't normally make a point of class absences, but this is one you should know about. Bob Turner isn't here because Bob's friend couldn't bring him. King, who has been Bob's eyes ever since the boy lost his sight in high school, was run down by an irresponsible driver last evening. That Bob, too, was not run down was a miracle. So we'll miss one of our class members for a meeting or two and then he'll start showing up again. Maybe one of you will walk with him from the dorm. And then one day there will be another King, and he'll be a skillful guide and devoted friend, too. But the first King is gone, not to return. I, for one, will miss him. So will most of you. But none of us will miss him like Bob Turner. How does a man feel who's lost his eyes twice?"

Now, having read those selections each at three pitch levels, what judgments have you to offer? Were different levels appropriate to different passages? If you couldn't make that judgment on your own reading, could you do it for one of your classmates? Do you have the material on tape? Play it back, listening carefully. Make sure, first of all, that you were successful in sustaining three different levels for each passage. Then decide whether this control stood you in good stead in presenting this material. As we have suggested so many times before, solicit some unbiased opinion from your instructor or another student. A favorable report? Good. Now on to work in inflections.

Inflections

Rereading our earlier working definition of inflections, you will discover no limitation as to the *place* where an inflection can occur. Correct; there is no such limitation. An inflection can occur within the phrase as well as on onset and terminal phonations. However, observers in the past typically have reported on these onset and terminal phonations, particularly as they relate to dialectal variations. In General American speech, for example, the normal intonation for a declarative sentence involves an initiating upward inflection and a strong downward terminating inflection. (Intonation, you remember, is pitch movement over a phrase or larger grammatical unit; it is a term that represents the melody of speech.)

Inflections and intonation serve the important function of conveying a speaker's attitude to his listener, the "tone of voice" going beyond the strict verbal denotation of his utterance. Irony and sarcasm depend on skillful pitch control if their full effect is to be appreciated. So, for that matter, does the asking of questions—of all the pitch functions one of the most important. Now, going from easy to hard, simple to complex, we suggest you set about gaining greater mastery over the inflection.

1. First, the level inflection, ⌒—o , on single phonemes only. Phonate the following with no pitch change: [m], [ɑ], [o], [u]. All these phonemes can be used, alone, as meaningful utterances. Did they sound meaningful to you?

2. Now try them on rising inflections, ᴼᴼ : [m], [ɑ], [o], [u]. Did you succeed in giving them rising inflections? Will someone testify to that effect for you? Enlist a listener, and volunteer your services for the same function. Now, assuming success, did you give meaning to each phoneme by your inflection? What meaning? Explain to your listener.

3. Reverse the inflection on the same phonemes; direct them downward, ᴼᴼ : [m], [ɑ], [o], [u]. Successful? Meaningful? How different from number 2, above?

4. Finally, in this series, the subtle circumflex inflection, ᴼᴼ on the

same sounds: [m], [ɑ], [o], [u]. That was harder to do, wasn't it? But you did it. And now what meanings could you attach to the sounds you made?

5. No book of this nature is complete without this exercise: do the following words on (a) level, (b) rising, (c) falling, (d) rising-falling, and (e) falling-rising inflections:

> Yes
> No
> Maybe
> Who
> What
> When
> Where
> Why
> How

Do you hear the meaning shifting as you change inflections? This seems to be a good place to comment on questions, because the punctuation mark, ?, can only be revealed vocally by the pitch attribute. How? Rising inflection? Not always. In fact, more often than not the question takes the same intonation, ends on the same downward inflection, as the declaration. Questions containing interrogative words—the who, what, and so on of this exercise—do *not* terminate with a rising inflection except in the special case where the speaker is saying: "Did you ask . . . ?"

6. In the following questions use both rising and falling inflections as directed by the symbols placed before the terminal words. Note that assigning pitch symbolization to the terminal word only is a gross over-simplification. From Rush to the present day, voice scientists and linguists have concerned themselves with intonation pattern rather than with simple inflections. Elaborate systems of notation have been employed. However, it is our belief that much benefit is to be derived and rather small chance for error will be introduced if the exercises are carried out as recommended here and in the pages following. Listen for shifts of meaning in the paired sentences on the next page.

a) Where is ⤵ Lois?
b) Where is ⤴ Lois?
c) Who's ⤴ there?
d) Who's ⤵ there?
e) How did the experiment ⤴ go?

    f) How did the experiment ↘ go?
    g) When does that class ↘ meet?
    h) When does that class ↗ meet?
    i) What did he say before ↗ that?
    j) What did he say before ↘ that?
    k) Why are you shaking your ↘ head?
    l) Why are you shaking your ↗ head?
    m) Is it OK to ↘ leave?
    n) Is it OK to ↗ leave?
    o) Did he get there on ↗ time?
    p) Did he get there on ↘ time?

What did you notice about the last two pairs of questions, (m) through (p), above? They contained no specific interrogative words, they could be answered "Yes" or "No," and the terminal inflection that made them ask the question as intended was a rising one. When the question was delivered with a falling terminal inflection the effect was essentially the same as a rising terminal inflection in a question of the other type—that is, to inquire, "Did you ask . . . ?" Did you get the intended meanings out of your questions in this exercise? We refer you again to your helpful listener and again we recommend your participation in the listener role. You will find your control becoming surer, more precise, as your ear gets keener in detecting these fine pitch movements in your voice and the voices of others.

    You've shown yourself one important use of the rising inflection: to ask certain kinds of questions. Another function of the same inflection is to inform the listener that there is more to come before the sentence or idea-group of words is finished. This may be an end-phrase inflection, terminating an introductory phrase, or it may be a within-phrase inflection associated with two or more words in series. Of course it may be used to terminate phrases in series also. All three of these applications are made available for your practice in the next exercise.

    7. Read the following, in each case letting the symbol guide you through the inflection to be applied to the word that follows it:

    a) If we win this ↗ one, we're in the playoffs.
    b) Where Edith ↗ is, there you'll find George also.
    c) Before you ↗ go, check your name off the list.
    d) The campus chest drive should have the support of ↗ fraternities, ↗ sororities, and ↘ non-orgs.
    e) All my classes meet on ↗ Monday, ↗ Wednesday, and ↘ Friday.

f) The three busiest streets are ↗ Main, ↗ Columbia, and ↘ Ferry.

g) My advice is borrow no ↗ money, lend no ↗ money, and spend as little as ↘ possible.

h) Charles can write like a ↗ poet, paint like an ↗ artist, and sing like a ↘ crow.

i) Between Master's and Doctor's degrees one must demonstrate reading knowledge of a ↗ language, pass qualifying or preliminary ↗ examinations, and submit an acceptable report of independent ↘ research.

If you have done that exercise two or three times and listened to someone else perform it, doubtless your ear has been sharpened to the preception of inflections which imply continuation, sometimes called the undropped second shoe. Now each of the words and phrases in series, with which you have just dealt, terminated in a downward inflection, indicative of completion of idea expressed. Go through exercise 7a) through i) once more, concentrating this time on the terminal inflections. One of the most consistent faults we detect in normal speakers is a tendency to elevate the pitch very slightly on the end of a downward inflection. This error, which we call "fishhook" inflection, imparts some hesitancy, a tinge of indecisiveness, to the delivery. The listener is made vaguely uncomfortable by this fault when it becomes too noticeable. So, eliminate the fishhooks, if you have any, in exercise 7. Then go on to exercise 8, where again your attention is directed to terminal downward inflections.

8. When an idea is expressed with finality, leaving no doubt that the thought is complete and the speaker unwavering in his attitude about it, the sense-group of words terminates with a downward inflection. This is true also, and even more strongly, of a directive or command. Read the following sentences with the same rigorous control over the terminal inflection that you exerted in exercise 7. The appropriate symbol is inserted as a reminder.

a) Many schools have adopted the sixteen-week ↘ semester.

b) This makes possible a three-semester ↘ year.

c) A student could graduate a year ↘ early.

d) However, this might leave him academically ↘ exhausted.

e) Problems of athletic eligibility could ↘ arise.

f) Pay fees at the next ↘ window.

g) Shut off the ↘ light.

h) Pass on the left ↘ side.

i) Mind your own ⌒o business.

j) Blow ⌒o square!

No fishhooks? Sure? Put the exercise on tape, if you can, and listen closely. We think the final downward inflection is a critical one and we suspect your instructor does, too. Hence you're well advised to do and redo this exercise, then construct a number of declarative and imperative sentences of your own. Practice these until a fishhook inflection is detected automatically and corrective measures are set off in your vocal mechanism.

Finally, an oral examination in inflection. Administer exercise 9, below, to yourself and to a classmate. Do you agree on all your answers?

9. For the shades of meaning assigned to the following words, first write the symbol for the inflection you would use, then speak the word as the symbol specifies.

a) Don   1. Response to "Who's There?"

a) Don   2. "Come here!"

a) Don   3. Response to "He's the guilty party."

a) Don   4. Response to "Guess who got the A."

b) Rain   1. Indian medicine man commands the event to happen.

b) Rain   2. "Did you say rain?"

b) Rain   3. "Surely you can't believe it's going to rain."

b) Rain   4. Response to "What's making that noise on the roof?"

c) Really   1. "I mean it."

c) Really   2. "Are you sure?"

c) Really   3. "What a disgusting thing to say."

c) Really   4. "Yes it's true—I think."

What was your score? How many rising inflections? falling inflections? Did you use any circumflex or level inflections? How much agreement was there between you and your classmate? Try scrambling the alternatives to see whether your partner can detect which you're producing. Now start fresh with a new list of words and ascribe different interpretations to them. Test your interpretations on a listener as you apply different inflections to the following three words.

d) Help

e) More

f) Lying

Did you convey your intended subtleties of meaning? If not, try, try again. If you are able consistently to reveal attitudes in this way, then you can move quickly into and through skips.

Skips

The subtlety of the inflection is lacking in the skip. One phonation terminates on a given pitch level; the next begins on another level. Typically, in General American speech, upward skips outnumber downward ones. This is in contrast to inflections, where the reverse is true. Skips seem to occur naturally and correctly in the speech of normal persons such as you are, being particularly noticeable (if one is skip-hunting) following the very brief pauses between words or phrases in series and following the slightly longer pauses that occur after a complete thought has been expressed in a sense-group of words. In the former case, the direction of the skip typically is down, whereas in the latter typically it is up. As we've said, these two types of skips occur quite naturally. We'll give you a little practice on them, but we doubt that you'll need much. Two other kinds of skips also tend to occur fairly naturally, but they can be encouraged and extended for better effect. These are the skips that set apart parenthetic words and phrases, those which may be used to enhance contrasts in meaning between words and phrases.

1. Read the following aloud, attending to the symbols between words and phrases in series.

  a) Speech feedback involves audition ⌒ vision ⌒ and touch.
  b) Sam's car lacks lights ⌒ horn ⌒ and muffler.
  c) Red ⌒ yellow ⌒ and blue are primary colors.
  d) Walk three steps ⌒ turn right ⌒ and walk three more.
  e) The wind in the trees ⌒ the surf on the shore ⌒ and rain against a window are three of my favorite sounds.
  f) We deplore the everlasting critic who hears no good ⌒ sees no good ⌒ speaks no good.

2. Now speak the following. Note the direction of skip after a complete thought has been expressed.

  a) Carol left her book. ⌒ Call her.
  b) The dance has been re-scheduled. ⌒ Aren't you glad?
  c) I'll be home at Easter. ⌒ So will Brian.
  d) You should come to the picnic. ⌒ Everyone will be there.

e) They're paving the path to the dorm. ⟋⟍ Which way shall we walk?

Exercises 1 and 2 should have been easy for you. Were they? Could you detect the upward and downward pitch movements in your own voice, in the voice of the person next to you? If not, better go through the exercise again. Also repeat exercise 7, in the inflection section, concentrating this time on the skip between words and phrases. When you're satisfied with your control, go on to exercise 3 below.

3. In the following sentences use skips of pitch leading into and away from parenthetic elements. Respond to the symbols. Perhaps you should go through this exercise twice, working to extend the skips.

a) I believe ⟋⟍ however ⟋⟍ that we should keep trying.
b) The last to arrive ⟋⟍ it seems ⟋⟍ is always the first to go.
c) The Adam's apple ⟋⟍ or thyroid cartilage ⟋⟍ belongs to Eve also.
d) Tom is counting on you ⟋⟍ by the way ⟋⟍ to bring your car.
e) Control of the pitch skip ⟋⟍ sometimes called "shift" ⟋⟍ is rather easily acquired.

We ended this exercise with sentence e), because we believe this is so. If your ear is keen enough to detect and monitor the subtle pitch changes suggested in the preceding section, it can surely be relied on in connection with shifts. Hence the preceding short exercises and the final short exercise to come.

4. In this one the skip of pitch is used to point up contrasts present in the language used, but benefiting from vocal emphasis in the form of pitch manipulation. As always, read the sentences aloud and let the symbols direct the rise and fall of your voice between the indicated phonations. Read the sentences twice, extending the skips the second time.

a) I said ⟋⟍ "pitch" ⟋⟍ not "fish."
b) You may think that's funny ⟋⟍ but I surely don't.
c) While Beth was studying ⟋⟍ Karen was out having fun.
d) Martin would rather be ⟋⟍ right ⟋⟍ than ⟋⟍ popular.
e) Judy doesn't know ⟋⟍ left ⟋⟍ from ⟋⟍ right but ⟋⟍ she always gets there.

Now read exercise 3 and this one again, reversing the direction of shift in every case. Still make sense? If you read with care it will. This is, after all, a technique for making words and phrases stand out by setting them apart in pitch from the context in which they are embedded. This skipping about within the range can be done in either direction, though sometimes it seems more natural to skip upward; at other times the effect is enhanced when the skip is downward.

Integration

As a final exercise before demonstrating your pitch control for a grade, as suggested in *Student Projects,* here is an opportunity for you to integrate into one reading selection all the pitch techniques you have been working on. Actually, two selections are offered, the first more appropriate for a male student and the second for a girl. Read the selection carefully to yourself, copy, and pencil in appropriate symbols for important inflections and skips. When the selection has been orchestrated to your satisfaction read it over several times to gain mastery. Then if possible tape-record it and listen critically to the playback. If you can't record the selection, at least read it for a critical listener.

1. For the men. Here is a continuation of that football game you were describing in Chapter 7. Use pitch control now to convey the excitement of the contest.

First down and 10 to go at the 13 yard line.

Johnny O'Keefe is only 193 pounds, would seem small for a big fullback which he is. He runs like a 220 pounder, and he looks even bigger. We watched him on the practice field a couple of times, and he's a big, strong boy, belying his size, and he just carries men with him as he did on the last play. Now, Flood has come out of the ball game and Arnie Nichols is in there offensively. Nichols, No. 23, is in and Flood is out. First and 10, 13 yard line. In close to O'Keefe. He keeps going but is thrown back before he gets to the 10 yard line. Buddy Clyde at the bottom of the pile. And we pause briefly for station identification. This is the UBC Television Network. KUBC, Mobile. This is Roger Nash with John Pullman in Mobile, bringing you this 1968 Championship game. Tulsa playing for the first time in any bowl game. Second and eight at the Cyclones' 11 yard line. Now a quick switch. It's Arnie Nichols and he is hit down at the line of scrimmage by Terry Oates, a first-year defensive right end. No gain. At the moment, Sam Gerber has completed three passes out of four attempts for 34 yards. We mention that because it's third down and big yardage about the ten. There may be a little less than that so he might have to go the air to keep the drive alive. Rick Flower comes into the ball game. Arnie Nichols comes off the field now for Mobile. Flower, a fine blocker, coming in there now as the Monitors try to move the ball on third down. It's third and seven. Curly Dye is slipped to the right side. That's Sam Gerber, goes to Dye and he's down at the five-yard line and makes the catch. It is not a first down. It's short of first down it'll be fourth. Mal Faulk just made the tackle. It'll be fourth down and about two yards to go. Bert Whitmore is the holder for Mobile and Gerber will attempt a field goal. At the moment, he's at the side line right next to Coach John Snider. Mobile is taking a time out. Action will continue here at Mobile, the score is Tulsa 7 and Mobile 7. Now they're back in action and Gerber's throwing and it is complete, the ball settling right in the arms of split end Dan Hart. Touchdown, Mobile!

2. Now for the girls. Can you work some feeling, suitably projected by variations in pitch, into these accounts of social events? Think it through, copy, put in some symbol-cues, practice them, then record or read for a critical listener.[2]

A. It was a cold winter night in Santa Barbara but the reception for Mr. and Mrs. R. Theodore Shelton at the home of the Vernon Buchanans couldn't have been more warming.

Guests were greeted by twinkling lights strewn along the front hedge, a large, merry Santa waving from the balcony, a sparkling dove signifying peace on the front door, and prancing reindeer. The porch was bathed in spotlight.

The holiday theme flowed from the porch into the reception hall. In the center a fluffy pink Christmas tree towered over the festive party scene, and colored lights of another tree cast their reflections into the pool. The guest house also was aglow with multicolored lights.

B. Fiesta had another grand opening last night. Ask anyone who was at Noche de Gala. The guests who wined, dined, and danced their way through the boom-cha of the dance band, the brassy sound of the mariachis, and the clickety-click of tiny feet were a colorful, almost motley sight to behold.

All the guests in their brilliant array of costumes mingled during the cocktail hour while Spanish music softly serenaded. At intermission the guests were entertained by the authenic mariachis, circling the bandstand, while tiny tots in buckskin jackets won hearty applause for their rendition of Mexican dances.

---

[2] For permission to use these two items from the women's pages of the *Santa Barbara News-Press*—names changed, of course, the authors are grateful to Miss Mary Every of the *New-Press* staff.

Linda Seymour, who was chairman of Noche de Gala, was a lovely hostess with her blonde hair done up in soft swirls befitting her full-length gown, featuring a velvet pink bodice and a lime green multi-tiered taffeta skirt.

When exercise 1 or 2 has been completed to the satisfaction of all concerned, you will be ready, we think, for the project-for-grade. Actually, we are recommending *two* projects-for-grades in this vocal attribute, as you will see below. Since we believe so thoroughly that pitch control is the key to real speech excellence, we have expanded the laboratory section of this chapter. As in our own teaching, we use two finishing-off projects. One is a reading of lyric or narrative poetry, the other a reading selected from the climactic moments of some noteworthy public address of the past. Both assignments are discussed in greater detail in *Student Projects*.

STUDENT PROJECTS

CONTENT ASSIGNMENTS

1. Write a short paragraph describing the pitch characteristics of the superior speaker, as revealed in research.
2. Describe three speaking situations in which inappropriate pitch usage would be disastrous.
3. Sometimes people who undergo laryngectomy—surgical removal of the voice box—replace vocal force with an artificial larynx, often one with a buzzer-like tone on a monopitch. Describe, with illustrative sentences, the limitations imposed on such a speaker.

LISTENING ASSIGNMENTS

A. Evaluate on criteria of pitch level and flexibility one performance by a representative of each of the professions listed below. Remember, you're cheating your favorite person (you) if you do this assignment without actually *listening* to performances such as these.

   1. Teacher   3. Minister
   2. Actor   4. Politician

B. Check your own average pitch level at five intervals through a typical day. Write a report of what you heard.

PERFORMANCE ASSIGNMENTS

A. Select from your library's collection of famous speeches one that is distinguished by depth of feeling. Prepare to read the climactic two or three minutes of this speech for class and instructor evaluation of your pitch level and flexibility.

(NOTE: Unless you have great confidence in your vocal prowess, avoid speeches like the Gettysburg Address and Patrick Henry's "Give me Liberty," about which your listeners probably have strong preconceived notions.)

B. Similarly prepare and read a two-minute excerpt from an epic or a narrative poem (for example, "The Highwayman" or "Young Lochinvar") and a two-minute excerpt from a lyric poem (for example, "To a Skylark"). As in (A) above, avoid the too-familiar. Approach this assignment with confidence. Poetry is *not* hard to read. On the contrary, the poet has made his material easy to read by selecting words with good sounds, putting them together so that there is a built-in flow or fluency.

RECOMMENDED READINGS

Curry, E. T. The pitch characteristics of the adolescent male voice. *Speech Monogr.,* **7,** 1941, 48–62.

Dew, D., and Hollien, H. The effect of inflection on vowel intelligibility. *Speech Monogr.,* **35,** 1968, 175–180.

Diehl, C. F., White, R. C., and Satz, P. H. Pitch change and comprehension. *Speech Monogr.,* **28,** 1961, 65 68.

Fairbanks, G. An acoustical study of the pitch of infant hunger wails. *Child Develpm.,* **13,** 1942, 227–232.

———, Herbert, E. L., and Hammond, J. M. An acoustical study of vocal pitch in seven- and eight-year-old girls. *Child Develpm.,* **20,** 1949, 71–78.

———, and Pronovost, W. An experimental study of the pitch characteristics of the voice during the expression of emotion. *Speech Monogr.,* **6,** 1939, 87–104.

————, Wiley, J. H., and Lassman, F. M. An acoustical study of vocal pitch in seven- and eight-year-old boys. *Child Developm.,* **29,** 1949, 63–69.

Franks, J. R. Determining habitual pitch by means of increased reading rate. *Western Speech,* **31,** 1967, 281–287.

Hanley, T. D. An analysis of vocal frequency and duration characteristics of selected samples of speech from three American dialect regions. *Speech Monogr.,* **17,** 1951, 78–93.

Heffner, R.-M. S. *General phonetics.* Madison: Univer. Wisconsin Press, 1949. Chap. 8, Sec. 9.

Herman, L., and Herman, M. S. *Foreign dialects.* New York: Theatre Arts Books, 1958.

Hockett, C. F. *A course in modern linguistics.* New York: Macmillan, 1958.

Jones, Daniel. *The pronunciation of English.* (4th ed.) Cambridge, England: University Press, 1956. Chap. 14.

Kramer, E. Personality stereotypes in voice: a reconsideration of the data. *J. Soc. Psychol.,* **62,** 1964, 247–251.

Mysak, E. D. Pitch and duration characteristics of older males. *J. Speech and Hearing Research,* **2,** 1959, 46–54.

Pronovost, W. An experimental study of methods for determining natural and habitual pitch. *Speech Monogr.,* **9,** 1942, 111–123.

Rush, J. *The human voice.* (7th ed.) Philadelphia: The Library Co., 1893. Sec. 7.

Snidecor, J. C. The pitch and duration characteristics of superior female speakers during oral reading. *J. Speech and Hearing Disorders,* **16,** 1951, 44–52.

Terango, L. Pitch and duration characteristics of an oral reading of males on a masculinity-femininity dimension. *J. Speech and Hearing Research,* **9,** 1966, 590–595.

Thurman, W. L. Frequency-intensity relationships and optimum pitch level. *J. Speech and Hearing Research,* **1,** 1958, 117–123.

Tiffany, W. R. Vowel recognition as a function of duration, frequency modulation, and phonetic context. *J. Speech and Hearing Disorders,* **18,** 1953, 289–301.

Tiffin, J., and Steer, M. D. An experimental analysis of emphasis. *Speech Monogr.,* **4,** 1937, 69–74.

CHAPTER
10

VOICE QUALITY AS A SKILL

Richness, pleasantness, charm, vibrance, color. Human gifts to sounds. Actors use them, announcers develop them, speakers often hurt for lack of them. Quality. "Timbre," sometimes. Beauty, depth, character, personality, certainly difference.

If you heard tones in succession from a violin, a saxophone, and a clarinet, in the next room, you could identify each, couldn't you? Make it more difficult. Same note for each, same loudness, same length of time; you could still identify them. Make it singers; say all sopranos—same note, loudness, time. You could recognize the voice of the opera star among the voices of her less talented sisters. In fact, you could identify the voices of your friends and many of your acquaintances with no dependence on pitch or loudness or duration. It is a useful and delightful aspect of sound that makes such judgments possible; we call it "quality," although sometimes "timbre" is used to mean the same thing. Musical instruments depend, partly at least, on their qualities for their characteristic sounds; and quality differences give individuality to human voices for both singing and speech. Richness, pleasantness, charm, vibrance, gruffness, tenseness, unpleasantness, and many other "colors" are imparted to human utterances by qualities.

The value and importance of tone quality in vocal effectiveness has long been recognized. Rush, in his 1833 writing on human voice, discussed "the qualities of voice employed as means of expression." During the middle and late nineteenth century, many other writers were concerned about vocal quality, along with other aspects of voice. Almost every text on voice, public speaking, interpretation, and stage speech during the first sixty years of *this* century has discussed voice quality.

As is frequently pointed out in such writings, every person who communicates orally has quality characteristics and variations different from those of every other person. Most people have little or no conscious control of voice quality characteristics and variations—they just happen. Yet in daily professional and casual communication, not just in speech from the stage or the speaker's platform, quality is a major factor in vocal effectiveness. Anyone with an interest in developing his own best communicative or creative speech must become alert to this aspect of voice.

PRODUCTION OF VOICE QUALITY

How do we produce this voice quality? Where in the vocal mechanism is it determined? Recall the discussion in Chapter 2 of wave-form complexity? It was stated there that the quality of a tone is determined by the number of harmonics or overtones present, as well as their frequencies and strengths. For any fundamental tone, instrumental or vocal, there are many possible combinations of overtone patterns, many quality possibilities. For most musical instruments and for the voice, in addition to the nature of the original sound-producing vibration, the sizes, shapes, and numbers of resonance cavities, and the manner of their couplings are critical factors in determining overtone patterns. The French horn, the trumpet, and the trombone, for example, get their initial sounds from the vibrations of the players' lips, much the same vibration in each case; but, because the resonance chambers of those horns are different in size and shape, their tone qualities are distinctive. Different parts of the original tone are resonated or built up and different parts damped or reduced. The complex vocal resonance system of the human being, made up of the pharynx, oral cavity, and nasal cavities, is also capable of producing many overtone combinations.

The discussion in the preceding paragraph is based on the "harmonic theory" of resonance which is generally recognized as an important concept of sound behavior. It is worth noting that Helmholtz experimented with resonance chambers before the turn of the century, contributing considerable evidence in support of this resonance concept.

So the human resonance chambers do contribute to the final voice tone; and because vocal resonance structures vary greatly in relative size, shape, and coupling, natural differences in resonance occur, producing distinctive individual qualities. A speaker may voluntarily change the size, shape, and, to a certain extent, the surface tensions of two of the resonators, the pharynx and oral cavity; and he may use, partly use, or entirely shut off the nasal cavities. Such adjustments change the amplification and damping of parts of the vocal cord tone and so change the quality of the voice.

For the most part, adjustments in the resonance system, especially the oral cavity, are used *phonemically,* to effect changes in vowel and semivowel quality as the speaker moves from one phoneme to the next in rapid, connected speech. However, resonator adjustments also contribute importantly to voice quality and vocal distinctiveness. In summary, there are individual voices because of the nature of the structures; and a degree of control over vocal quality is possible because adjustments in the resonance system are possible.

We make impressions on our listeners with our voices. Listeners make judgments about us and our messages on the basis of what they hear. The judgments are not all spurious. Markel and others found, for example, that judges listening to recordings of schizophrenics and nonschizophrenics could differentiate between them on several semantic rating scales. They concluded that their results "indicated the validity of the hypothesis that specific impressions of a speaker's physical characteristics and demeanor are determined by that speaker's voice qualities." We believe the same concept applies to judgments made by most listeners.

Your desire for general effectiveness in creative speech should be reason enough for you to want to develop voice quality control; but there is another very good reason. Some qualities, almost always unconsciously used, can be extremely detrimental to the effectiveness of simple, everyday speech as well as to creative speech efforts. However, when properly used and controlled, voice quality can be a strong positive factor.

You probably are not aware of the qualities you produce and the effects they have on your listeners; most people are not. But if you are to achieve real vocal skill, it is quite important that you should learn to *hear* and *evaluate* your own voice quality, realizing that it is only partly determined by structural limitations of your individual resonance system. You should also learn to *control* quality for improvement of your habitual speech, if necessary, and for effective variety in public speaking, acting, and reading aloud. The practice activities presented later in this chapter are designed to help you to accomplish those aims—hearing, evaluating, and controlling quality.

We are not going to be concerned with correcting the extremely undesirable deviations of a clinical nature, but with helping you to develop awareness of quality and control of its production in your voice. However, since "good" quality is generally defined as an absence of certain negative tonal characteristics, our approach will be to describe the various deviant qualities and guide you through exercises designed to develop control over the objectionable features. This should help you to improve your habitual voice and to develop versatility of voice quality for creative uses to which you will wish to put this powerful aspect of delivery.

TERMINOLOGY

It is difficult to discuss voice qualities with exactness because there is no universally accepted set of names or terms for them. One finds contradictions and disagreements in this respect among writers of textbooks on speech pathology, general voice usage, interpretative reading, public speaking, and acting. Nonetheless, most such writers do recognize the importance of quality differences and advocate control of quality for the most effective use of the voice.

We shall attempt partly to solve this problem of terms by using the six listed below. Thurman found experimentally that a large group of judges, chiefly speech clinic staffs and graduate students at a number of midwestern universities and colleges, could use these terms adequately in an experimental situation. The terms were taken from among the dozens used by various authors, and the descriptions were originated by the experimenter. Although they were first applied only to clinically significant quality deviations, we believe the quality types exist in lesser degrees in voices within the range of acceptable, though imperfect, habitual quality and that they provide useful labels for quality variations which may be purposely assumed for acting, public speaking, or reading aloud.

Nasal quality is characterized by strong modification of the vocal cord tone by resonance from the nasal cavities during the production of sounds normally essentially nonnasal.

Breathy quality results when the vocal cords are not brought closely enough together during the production of tone, and air rushing through the glottis produces friction heard as a whisperlike noise in addition to the vocal cord tone.

Thin quality is essentially lacking in resonance. It is flat and colorless, and it gives the impression of "smallness."

Strident quality sounds hard and piercing; it apparently is caused by strain and tenseness in the resonators during voice production.

Harsh quality is unpleasant and rough; it is caused, apparently, by strain and great effort in the larynx.

Hoarse quality is characterized by a rasping, grating, sometimes husky sound such as is often heard in persons with laryngitis. It may also be a result of misuse, such as too much shouting at a sports event.

This is not to say these are the only quality types that exist, nor that these are the only terms that can be applied to them. However, we believe that these terms, as described, represent types or categories useful for our purposes.

One hears examples of these voice qualities almost daily on the radio, on television, and in the movies, to say nothing of in the drugstore, on the bus, in the bookshop, in the barbershop. Before you can change television channels or radio stations you may find yourself listening to a soap opera; perhaps the slow-talking dispenser of homespun philosophy speaks with a nasal voice. Or a threatening bully, the "bad guy," may use a harsh quality. You surely have heard a sultry blonde who uses a half-whispered breathiness to achieve her vocal effect. The stereotyped "henpecked" husband often has a tiny, thin voice; and piercing stridency may be the weapon of his forceful, domineering wife. Hoarseness is not as common as the other quality types, but that too may be heard, for example, in the voice of the actor playing an overworked army sergeant. These are only a few examples; you can probably think of many others.

Put your listening skill to work. Two Listening Assignments in this chapter's *Student Projects* suggest that you locate and report examples of voice quality types to sharpen your ear and to develop your awareness of this vocal factor.

The range of acceptable qualities is very wide; not all occurrences of the six types described above are undesirable. The skilled speaker, in fact, uses his voice quality to help achieve a desired effect just as he uses pitch, loudness, and duration. Such skill is quite apparent in the actor who assumes a voice to fit the character he portrays, but it is also important to the platform speaker who seeks an effect, "Crying out against injustice," for example.

You probably will find mixtures of qualities and varying degrees of quality differences in the actors and speakers you observe for the Listening Assignments, as well as in the people around you. Possibly you will hear wider variations among the actors' voices than among voices in your surroundings. However, keep in mind that actors reproduce or imitate typical voices; they do not invent them entirely.

One frequently hears a voice in his surroundings strikingly unfitted to the possessor's age, sex, personality, occupation, or position in life. The breathy voice, for example, may be excellent for the blonde bombshell actress but not so fitting for a young teacher of social studies in high school. The harsh voice, quite appropriate for the villain of a dramatic piece, is probably a detriment to an aspiring young lawyer. The little, thin voice may be useful for a television role but a serious handicap to the quarterback of the football team and a real professional liability to an otherwise competent engineer. In such cases, modification and control of voice quality are not only desirable but urgent.

Any of the qualities described earlier, *in the extreme,* may be severely handicapping for the speaker. Medical advice and the services of a speech correctionist should be sought for such extreme problems.

QUALITY RELATED TO OTHER FACTORS

Let us bear in mind that it is not possible completely to separate quality from pitch, loudness, and duration; they influence one another. Laase found, for example, that when his subjects changed pitch or intensity levels the overtone structure of the vowels used, [ɑ], [i], and [u], changed measurably. Tiffin, Saetveit, and Snidecor concluded that the manner of vibration of the vocal cords probably caused changes in the acoustical make-up of [æ] and [ɑ] as intensity increased. Williamson concluded that a voice that is pitched too low sometimes will take on a harsh or hoarse quality. Several observers have commented that strident tone resulting from resonator tensions may or may not be heard, depending on pitch and loudness factors in a voice. A loud breathy voice is not commonly heard because the loudness will usually eliminate the breathiness. You may discover other useful relations among these factors in your own tone control efforts.

As we have already noted, natural differences in individual phonatory and resonance structures make for individual voices. We could never all sound alike even if it were desirable; the awkwardly made, inexpensive fiddle can never have the quality of a Stradivarius. But the poorest instrument, when carefully played, sounds better than when it is used without skill. *Even those of us who do not have, by inheritance, what might be called "good voices" can develop and learn to control the best qualities of which our vocal instruments are capable.*

DEVELOPING VOICE QUALITY SKILLS IN THE SPEECH LABORATORY

Now it is time for you to evaluate your vocal feedback with respect to quality. Record "The Old Grad" paragraph (page 141) in your usual voice. When you have finished reading the passage, sustain the vowels [i], [æ], [ɑ], and [u] for three seconds each at a natural, easy pitch level. Play the recording through several times, listening carefully for your voice quality characteristics. Write a brief analysis of what you hear.

Increase your quality consciousness and versatility by practicing at least some of the materials given for each quality type on the following pages. These suggestions will also be helpful to students who discover on the playback of "The Old Grad" that they need to improve certain undesirable quality tendencies in habitual speech. Perhaps your instructor will help you decide whether or not you need to concentrate especially on certain of the quality drills. Work very carefully and do not strain your voice at any time, especially if you attempt to produce harsh and hoarse qualities.

Remember you are working toward conscious control of your tone production. As you work with recorders, mirrors, and other external monitors, bear in mind that they are props which you must discard as soon as possible. You must learn to evaluate your output by strengthening old or even by establishing new auditory and kinesthetic monitoring patterns. You must hear the sounds and feel the muscle movements that give the desired results. The eventual success of your work here depends on your sharpening your self-monitoring ability.

WARNING NOTE: *These are voice awareness and improvement exercises. If, after you try the drills for improvement of any of the quality types, you and your instructor still find an important, undesirable quality difference in your voice, you should seek professional help. Your instructor can advise you in this matter. Do not persist in drills and exercises when you are not achieving the desired result. A physician or speech pathologist should be consulted.*

Relaxation

Before you undertake a program of voice quality control or improvement you must learn to relax. Tension and vocal strain are recognized by speech pathologists as causes of numerous vocal difficulties, among them quality distortion. It is easier to achieve efficient, effective voice production if you can relax your entire body to a level of tension just adequate to the job at hand. Outstanding among the writings designed to make us relaxation conscious are those of Edmund Jacobson. Especially useful is his *You Must Relax,* a book describing specific techniques for relaxation. A very tense person, who has difficulty relaxing, may find the Jacobson techniques very useful. Perhaps your instructor will explain and demonstrate.

The following procedures, patterned somewhat after Jacobson, will assist you in relaxing the muscles of the neck, pharynx, larynx, face, and mouth. Jacobson emphasizes that relaxation is "simply a negative"; one must learn to recognize tension to know what not to do. Holding the shoulders down, tighten the muscles of the neck, concentrating on the feeling of tension; then relax them, concentrating on the feeling of nontension. In the same way tighten the muscles of the throat and inside the mouth, then relax them. Repeat this procedure. Now slowly pull the lower jaw down as far as possible and tense the tongue; feel the tension. Letting the jaw hang slack, holding the tongue relaxed, feel the nontension. Drop the head back as far as possible. Rock the head forward, then back, several times. Roll the head around several times in one direction, then several times in the other direction. The procedure should be accompanied by deep breaths and concentration on the feeling of lassitude, of "letting-go," that comes to the muscles of the area.

To maintain relaxation, you must approach voice drills easily, without a feeling of urgency. Some students may have difficulty in relaxing the speech mechanism. Repeated use of these procedures both in and out of class will improve your ability to maintain an optimum relaxation-tension balance for speech.

Nasality

Whether you have an occasional bit of unintentional nasality to bring under control or want to learn how to produce the nasal voice purposely, the following materials should be helpful to you. Bear in mind that nasal voice is produced by inadequate closure of the nasal port by the soft palate and associated structures. Hixon found in X-ray studies of nasal and nonnasal vowel production that there may be an incomplete closure of the nasal port for normal vowels. *Adequate* closure, then, need not mean *complete* closure, but it would help for you to develop awareness of the location and movements of the soft palate.

1. Before a mirror produce the sound [ɑ] and watch the movement of the soft palate. Make a nasal, then nonnasal [ɑ]. Note that the palate goes up and back during the nonnasal sound. Strive to keep the tongue down and forward as much as possible. Hixon's nasal subjects showed much high-back tongue humping. Such tongue posture would tend to block sound from the oral cavity and encourage nasal emission. Practice each of the vowels and diphthongs with nasal, then nonnasal sound. (In these exercise instructions we shall speak of vowels with the understanding that the diphthongs are also included.) Train yourself to feel and hear the desired nonnasal production. Be particularly careful with the high vowels. Kelly found in examining amounts of nasal resonance that [i] and [u], the highest vowels, had the most nasality. When the tongue hump is high, apparently oral resonance is diminished and the nasal-oral balance may be difficult to keep on the nonnasal side. Ask classmates to listen and verify your nasality or nonnasality; it will help develop their listening ability as well as your voice control.

Open your mouth as wide as possible for the vowel sounds without introducing distortion. Kelly found experimentally and Williamson confirmed from clinical observations that wider mouth opening and more active articulation help to produce nonnasal voice. Practice before a mirror may be helpful in that respect. If you feel somewhat foolish opening your mouth wider than usual, remember that a change of habit seems strange until you become accustomed to it. Do not let the initial feeling of strangeness discourage you.

Adler suggests that louder voice production helps eliminate nasality, possibly because it is accompanied by wider mouth opening. Good breath support and moderately loud tone is almost always helpful with voice improvement. If you have difficulty on the following drills, remember breath support and loudness may help along with wider mouth opening and more vigorous articulation.

2. If you have difficulty getting voluntary movement of the soft palate, try the nasal snort. Close your mouth and breathe through the nose as usual. On an exhalation make an explosive sound through the nose. Do not make a glottal plosion; that would be something like a cough. Be sure the tongue is lying relaxed in the mouth; make the plosion with the soft palate. Perhaps your instructor will check your production of the nasal snort. Now, if you had difficulty with exercise 1, try it again.

3. When you can produce nasal and nonnasal vowels at will, combine them with nonnasal consonants, *not* [m], [n], or [ŋ]. First, use vowel-consonant combinations such as [ɑt], [ɑp], [ɑf], [ɑʃ], and [ɔd], [ɔk], [ɔb]. You may wish to make your own lists of five vowel-consonant combinations for each vowel. A short pause between the vowel and the consonant may help control nasality at first, but eliminate the pause soon, connecting the vowel and consonant elements.

Try the exercise in the same way with the vowel following the nonnasal consonant, for example [tɑ], [kɑ], [fɑ], and [dɔ], [pɔ], [ʃɔ]. You may wish to make practice lists of five such combinations for each vowel. Practice them as described above for the vowel-consonant combinations.

Now put the vowels between two nonnasal consonants, for example, [tɑk], [bɑs], [lɑd], and [sɔk], [tɔp], [bɔʃ]. Again you may wish to make lists of five such combinations for each vowel. Practice them as described above.

You may use the tape recorder on these exercises to help you learn to hear and recognize your nasality, both purposeful and accidental; but depend on your own ear for monitoring during production just as soon as possible.

4. Now go on to these short words with only nonnasal consonants. Remember to get wide mouth opening and active articulation to help you produce nonnasal vowels. If you are working with a partner or in a group, produce the words in sets of four, making two nasal and two nonnasal vowels. Ask your fellow students to identify the nasal sounds.

ONE-SYLLABLE WORDS WITH NONNASAL CONSONANTS

odd	la	pop
at	baa	cat
etch	bet	red
ache	bay	face
it	tip	bit
eat	see	feet
ought	caw	caught
oak	toe	poke
ooze	too	toot
up	pup	rub
earth	fur	perk
ice	buy	fire
oil	toy	boil
out	cow	bout

TWO-SYLLABLE WORDS WITH NONNASAL CONSONANTS

otter	eager	earthy
actor	auto	ivy
echo	oboe	oily
acre	oozy	outer
itchy	upper	awful

5. If you are trying to eliminate unnecessary nasality in your habitual speech, you may have discovered by now that you have more difficulty producing certain vowels nonnasally than others. If so, go back and practice those difficult vowels in the various consonant-vowel combinations (as in exercise 3), then set up word lists of your own: five with each troublesome vowel before the consonant, five with the vowel following the consonant, and five with the vowel between two consonants. Remember these are to be all nonnasal consonants. Practice your words aloud, record them and listen critically to the playback. If you continue to have difficulty with particular vowels, ask your instructor for assistance.

6. If you have easily controlled nasal quality in all the foregoing exercises, you may wish to skip this exercise. If not, work on the following words with no nasal consonants. Watch your articulation in the mirror, and over-articulate for practice. Record your work if it helps you, but depend on your own immediate monitoring, if you can. Nasalize an occasional word purposely; see if your drill partner can hear the change; then repeat the word nonnasally to emphasize the difference for your ear.

DISSYLLABIC AND POLYSYLLABIC WORDS WITH NONNASAL CONSONANTS

poppy	holiday
sadder	passages
baby	capable
wretched	catalogue
river	situate
teepee	peaceable
sawtooth	talkative
rodeo	motivate
footpad	put away
toothless	studious
rugged	butterfly
server	purposeful

DISSYLLABIC AND POLYSYLLABIC WORDS WITH
NONNASAL CONSONANTS   (*Cont.*)

highway	right-of-way
loiter	loiterer
powwow	roustabout

7. When you have successfully controlled nasality in vowels with non-nasal consonants, you begin a more difficult task. Nasal tone sometimes "spills over" from the nasal consonants to adjacent vowels (assimilation nasality, a common fault). To avoid such excess nasality you must actively use your soft palate to close the nasal port. Combine nonnasal vowels with the nasal consonants [m], [n], [ŋ]: for example, [ɑm], [ɑn], [ɑŋ], and [ɔm], [ɔn], [ɔŋ]. You may wish to make a list of such combinations for each vowel. Practice first with a short pause between units, if it helps you; then eliminate the pause so that you combine the units as one would in continuous speech. Be especially careful when attempting nonnasal resonance on the high vowels.

Proceed to this list of short words. For nonnasal vowels get good mouth opening and emphasize the consonants. Practice the words in sets of four, making one nasal vowel to test your drill partner's ear.

ONE-SYLLABLE WORDS WITH NASAL CONSONANTS

am	I'm	tame	soon
aim	earn	hen	put
in	ant	pin	turn
on	and	team	fine
own	Tom	song	round
an	tan	tone	

8. Now work with nasal consonants followed by vowels in syllable drills as in exercise 7: for example, [mɑ], [nɑ], [mɔ], [nɔ]. Practice all the vowels and again be careful with the high vowels. When you are doing them well, go on to these words.

ONE-SYLLABLE WORDS WITH A NASAL
CONSONANT BEFORE EACH VOWEL

map	neat	mud
nap	naught	nerve
Ned	mope	nice

ONE-SYLLABLE WORDS WITH A NASAL
CONSONANT BEFORE EACH VOWEL   (*Cont.*)

make	nook	noise
mitt	move	now

9. Finally, put a nasal consonant between two vowels or diphthongs: for example, [ɑmɑ], [ɑnɑ], [ɑŋɑ], and [ɔmɔ], [ɔnɔ], [ɔŋɔ]. Be careful that both vowels remain nonnasal; there may be a strong tendency for you to carry over the nasality from the nasal consonant to the second vowel. Practice all the vowels as described in exercise 7. When you have been successful, go on to these words. Practice them with both nasal and nonnasal vowels to train your ability to identify the feel and sound of nasal and nonnasal speech.

TWO-SYLLABLE WORDS WITH A NASAL
CONSONANT BETWEEN TWO VOWELS

honor	omit
Annie	tuna
any	unmasked
Amy	earner
innate	timer
enough	downy
tawny	joiner

10. Again you may find it more difficult to control nasality on some vowels than on others. Make lists of words using those difficult vowels in the three positions with nasal consonants. Following are such practice lists for three vowels and two diphthongs which seem frequently to give students difficulty:

WORDS COMBINING NASAL CONSONANTS WITH VOWELS

[i]	ream	meat	mean
	steam	need	anemic
	clean	meal	Armenian
	seem	mead	Jeanine
	team	kneel	meantime
[æ]	ham	map	man
	fan	gnat	Nan
	rang	mat	remand
	tang	Maggie	command
	sang	nap	finance

WORDS COMBINING NASAL CONSONANTS WITH VOWELS   (*Cont.*)

[u]	soon	move	moon
	room	mood	soon
	spoon	nude	noon
	loon	newel	innumerable
	loom	movie	numerator
[aɪ]	time	might	mine
	climb	night	nine
	fine	my	ninety
	I'm	knife	mining
	chime	snipe	nineteen
[aʊ]	town	now	mound
	brown	mouse	noun
	down	mouth	mountain
	around	haymow	announce
	found	nowadays	amount

11. It will be a good test of your progress in control of the nasal tone for you to record the following paired lists of similar words, being certain that both have clear, nonnasal vowels.

SIMILAR WORDS IN NONNASAL-CONSONANT AND NASAL-CONSONANT PAIRS

pod–pond	tot–not	bob–Mom
pat–pan	pat–gnat	bad–man
red–wren	bed–net	bet–men
rate–rain	bait–mate	babe–maim
pit–pin	bit–mitt	bit–mint
seed–seen	beat–meek	bead–mean
wrought–wrong	taught–naught	bought–morn
toad–tone	dope–mope	boat–moan
suit–soon	rude–mood	boot–moon
rug–rung	bud–mud	dud–none
bird–burn	purge–merge	Bertha–Myrna
fight–fine	bite–might	died–nine
doubt–down	house–mouse	bowed–mound

12. Now you are ready to use your control of nasality on longer words containing both nasal and nonnasal consonants.

POLYSYLLABIC AND DISSYLLABIC WORDS CONTAINING NASAL CONSONANTS

nominate	remodel
management	enamored
menacing	unmentioned
maintain	remaining
mingling	administrate
meantime	anemic
morning	remorse
moaning	unmown
moonbeam	enumerate
money	unnumbered
merging	unmerciful
miner	reminder
noiseless	annoyance
mounting	insurmountable
nimble	annual

Produce these words in groups of three, introducing excess nasality on one. Check the sound on the tape recorder or ask a classmate to test his ability to spot the difference. Also, your instructor may wish you to read part of this list before the class, making three or four words purposely too nasal to give the class practice in spotting the quality difference.

13. Here is a list of sentences such as any student might use any day. You may wish to underline each vowel that is adjacent to a nasal consonant. Read the sentences aloud, articulating carefully, opening your mouth wide. Record them and judge their nasality on playback, then see if you can judge yourself on a second reading without recording them. Produce a very nasal sentence now and then to emphasize the difference between the nasal and the nonnasal sounds.

1. Good morning, how are you feeling today?
2. It is a fine morning.
3. I am going to speech class now. So-long.
4. My watch has stopped. What time is it?
5. Do you have time for a cup of coffee?
6. I think the test is today but maybe not.
7. If it isn't very difficult, I'm ready.
8. When did he say those term papers are due?

  9. We thought the bell would never ring.

  10. I enjoy a class that involves performance.

  14. Reading aloud from a magazine or similar material will give you practice in applying your control of nasal resonance to continuous speech. Read a paragraph; then summarize it in your own words. Recording will help you judge your performance, but depend on your ear as much as you can. Notice that when you introduce nasality, the voice seems to take on "character" aspects; it is somewhat different from a voice with clear, nonnasal quality.

  15. Whether you have used these exercises to learn to produce nasality and use it at will, or to eliminate some undesirable nasality in your voice, go back now and record "The Old Grad" again, first putting in nasality purposely, then in as good, nonnasal voice as you can produce. You should hear a great difference between your two readings. If the second recording has no unpleasant excess of nasal tone, you are ready to work with other quality types. If you are in doubt, consult your instructor. Remember that all this practice is of no value unless you use voice control in your habitual speech and in your creative speech efforts. Incidentally, the repetitious use of "The Old Grad" passage is intentional: it provides you with a well-remembered standard with which to make comparisons.

Breathiness

Bear in mind that excessively breathy voice is produced by inadequate closure of the glottis during phonation. You can develop awareness of glottal closure by making a gentle cough. Recall that in Chapter 5 we said that a glottal plosion is achieved by your holding the vocal cords together while air pressure is built up, then opening them suddenly.

  1. To further your awareness of vocal cord closure, produce a glottal plosion by whispering an [ɑ] sound loudly, stopping the air stream abruptly in the throat, and releasing it suddenly. Remember the primary strength for the air stream comes from the abdomen. Now vocalize the vowel, making a loud [ɑ]. Again stop and start the air stream at the glottis. Concentrate on the muscle sensations in the larynx as the glottal closure is made and released. Breathy quality is produced when that closure is inadequately maintained during vocalization.

  2. Produce a number of vowels, first with breathiness, then with firmness. Listen for and feel the differences between the two qualities. Ask classmates to listen and confirm or correct your judgments of breathiness and firmness.

3. Typically, loud vocalizations are less breathy than quiet tones. Produce an [ɑ] at high, medium, and quiet loudness levels. Can you hear less breathiness? Think of producing a *firm* vowel sound. Practice until you can control levels; listen for the breathiness to creep in. Again produce a loud [ɑ]; gradually produce it more and more quietly until you hear the breathiness begin to occur. Now use a glottal plosion to begin the vowel at this loudness. Think of producing a *firm* vowel sound. Practice until you can control the breathiness. Gradually make the vowel quieter until you can produce it at conversational level without excessive air escape.

You may wish to work with a number of different vowels. If you discover particular difficulty in controlling the quality of certain vowels, leave them till last, until you have mastered the firm tone on the others.

Be careful that you do not become overly tense in muscles not involved in glottal closure. It may be helpful to place your thumb and forefinger of one hand on the sides of the laryngeal bulge in your neck to concentrate your attention on the area in which the "firming up" of the tone must be accomplished. If you find you are becoming tense and tight in the face, neck, and shoulder areas, review the relaxation procedures and then concentrate on containing the "firming up" in the larynx.

4. Murphy says that breath support does more to help eliminate breathiness than tightening the laryngeal area. We believe that in some people the concept of a strongly supported breath stream may be easier to achieve and may be achieved with fewer undesirable accompanying tensions than the concept of a "firmness" in the larynx. If you had indifferent results on the first three exercises, try reviewing the drills in Chapter 4 on breath support. You will find that when you produce more pressure in the abdominal area, your tone will be louder. The accompanying result will probably have a less breathy quality. If this approach is more helpful to you, by all means continue to stress breath support rather than laryngeal "firmness."

5. Try this experiment to convince yourself of the value of louder voice in improving breathiness. If binaural masking by earphones is available to you, record the first paragraph of this chapter with no masking, gradually increasing to 75 to 85 dB of masking. Play the tape and listen for loudness changes; you will find automatically increased loudness as the masking became louder. Play the tape again and listen for the quality changes accompanying the increased loudness. It is very probable that the breathiness decreased significantly, perhaps entirely.

6. Record with the binaural masking again. Set it at a fairly high level, 80 dB. Read aloud, concentrate on the kinesthetic feedback you

receive. You are probably producing a less breathy voice than usual. Concentrate on how it feels. Suddenly turn the masking off entirely; try to maintain the breath support, loudness, and firm quality. Note where in the reading material you turned off the masking. Play the tape and listen to your voice with and without masking. Did you retain an improved quality? Repeat the procedure several times. You will find you will become more conscious of kinesthetic monitoring and will become more accustomed to a different voice quality with practice.

7. If results of drill 6 were promising, repeat the procedure, gradually using less intense masking noise on repeated recordings. The result will be a gradual reduction in loudness. As suggested in drill three, lower the intensity but maintain the "firm" quality. If you find breathiness creeping in again, go to slightly louder masking and work down the masking gradually.

8. When you are ready, practice these vowels and words, eliminating undesirable breathiness. Practice one column at a time; they are progressive in difficulty. Do not leave a column until you have mastered it.

VOWELS AND WORDS FOR CONTROL OF BREATHY TONE

[ɑ]	odd	dot	sod	hod
[æ]	at	bat	pat	hat
[e]	ache	bake	take	hate
[ɛ]	Ed	bed	Ted	head
[ɪ]	it	bit	pit	hit
[i]	eat	beat	seat	heat
[ɔ]	all	ball	shawl	hall
[o]	ode	dope	soap	hope
[ʊ]	rook	nook	took	hook
[u]	ooze	dues	choose	whose
[ʌ]	up	rush	cup	hush
[ɝ]	earth	dearth	surf	hers
[aɪ]	eyed	bide	side	hide
[ɔɪ]	oil	boil	foil	hoist
[aʊ]	out	bout	shout	hound

9. Now, read the vowels and words of exercise 8 in horizontal rows. Be sure the vowel sound retains its firm quality as you read across the page.

10. Following are sentences you might use in everyday conversation. Produce each in a breathy voice, then in a firm voice; finally, produce the entire list in a good, firm voice.

1. Did anyone call while I was out?
2. I hope you got the number so I can call back.
3. Have you a date for the dance on Friday?
4. Everyone will be there before nine o'clock.
5. Why don't you go with my friend from Chicago?
6. No, the dance is not formal.
7. You will enjoy the music of the new orchestra.
8. The tickets are on my desk.
9. What time must we be ready to go?
10. I'm glad you are going; it will be fun.

Your instructor may wish you to read several sentences before the class to test the students' ability to identify a purposely breathy sentence.

11. These sentences are more difficult because they are loaded with the breathy consonant, [h]. In spite of the tendency to let the breathiness spill over from the "h's" to the vowels, keep the vowels firm.

1. Harry walked ahead with the heavy hopper.
2. I hiked to the highest hill with heavy heart.
3. The hoist swung heavenward with its load of hemp.
4. How many hats have you, Helen?
5. The house was hit hard by pounding hail.

12. Strengthen your control of breathy quality by reading aloud from a magazine or similar material. Read a paragraph, then summarize it in your own words. The recorder will help you judge your performance, but depend on your immediate feedback evaluation as soon as you can.

13. When you are satisfied with the results of these drills, return to "The Old Grad" or use a paragraph of similar length in a magazine. Read and record the paragraph in a breathy voice, then in a firm voice. You should hear a great difference on playback; notice the difference in total impression of the speaker you get from two such recordings. Finally, record it in as good, firm voice as you can muster. Your instructor may wish to help you check your performance. If your recording is adequate, you are ready to work with other qualities. Remember the final value of these drills lies in your using what you have learned in everyday and creative speech.

Thinness

Thin voice seems to be produced by pinched, tightly narrowed oral and pharyngeal resonance chambers. The objective in improvement drills for thin voice quality is more resonance, bigness, openness of tone. If you need some practice in that direction, relaxation will probably be helpful to you. Begin your work sessions by relaxing your face and neck muscles as described earlier.

1. Usually, a wider mouth opening will help accomplish better resonance. Practice the [ɑ] sound before a mirror, getting as wide mouth opening as possible. During this drill you should be able to put the first joint of your thumb upright between your upper and lower front teeth. Concentrate on a relaxed, open feeling in all the oral and pharyngeal structures as you do this exercise. Practice each vowel, getting as wide mouth opening as possible without introducing distortion, then produce each vowel in a small, tight, thin voice for contrast.

2. Since thin voice is frequently found in connection with too high pitch level, reevaluate your pitch level as described in Chapter 9. If you are trying to improve your resonance, perhaps you will need to work on pitch level and thinness together. Remember also to get good support behind the air stream. Review the exercises for strong breath support in Chapter 4.

If you are trying to develop ability to produce a thin voice, try raising your pitch level and speaking with less force as you tense and narrow the resonance areas.

3. The following words and sentences are selected to aid in open, resonant production. As you practice them, remember relaxation, mouth opening, and breath support. Occasionally produce a word or sentence in a thin, tight voice, then in an open, relaxed, resonant voice to emphasize the tone difference. See whether your classmates can hear your intentional quality change.

WORDS AND SENTENCES FOR INCREASING RESONANCE

round	prime	lodge	remain	mallet
oval	close	bellow	alive	mellow
value	roll	lily	liable	football
alone	brawl	lemon	telephone	moonglow

1. The ocean rolls and roars its mighty song.
2. The bull bellows across an open meadow.
3. His mind was alive with memories of Gloria.
4. The yellow of a lemon is a vibrant color.
5. I want to be alone.

6. No one man can climb all mountains.
7. *Roaming in the Gloaming* is a famous old song.
8. Morning light comes slowly along the bayou.
9. Rubies and emeralds are valuable stones.
10. I hope my tone is open and resonant.

4. The following sentences are more likely to occur in everyday speaking situations. Give them the same open, resonant sound you used in the last exercise. Notice that each would probably be spoken to a group of ten people or more.

1. Now, children, everyone watch Ronald.
2. The floor is open for nominations.
3. All together, men, pull!
4. I urge you to vote for Holman; he knows the job.
5. Stop; fold your test papers and pass them to your right.
6. In my judgment, this proposal is sound and we should begin production at once.
7. Open the door; this case is heavy.
8. The cause is worthy; make your donation now.

5. The following sentences are not loaded with open, resonant vowels. They are conversational sentences; try to give them full, resonant quality.

1. Let's go home for Easter vacation—shall we?
2. Is the car ready to travel a thousand miles?
3. We can be packed in about an hour.
4. I think we can study during the vacation.
5. Bring your books and notebooks along.
6. Spring has arrived earlier this year.
7. Where did you get that hat?
8. If we leave now, we can be there by midnight.
9. The moon makes the night beautiful.
10. Drive slowly, I want to enjoy the view.

Read them in groups of five, reading two sentences in each group in a thin voice; your drill partner should easily identify the thin quality. Perhaps your instructor will wish you to do this exercise before the class to help develop their ability to hear thin quality.

6. Practice reading aloud from magazine or similar materials. Read a paragraph, then talk about it: summarize it in your words. Remember mouth opening, resonance, fullness of tone, and strong breath support.

Record and play back to help you hear your errors, but depend on self-monitoring as soon as possible.

7. When you are satisfied with your improvement, read and record "The Old Grad," or a similar paragraph from a magazine, first in a small, tight, thin voice, then in a good, fully resonant voice; on playback note the striking difference in sounds. Perhaps your instructor will help you judge your performance. Remember that your work on the these exercises is valuable only if you use your tone control in habitual and creative speech.

Stridency

Since stridency appears to be related to excessive tension in the resonators, the relaxation techniques previously described will be very important to a student learning to produce and control strident quality.

1. Relax as well as you can, then produce the following vowels and diphthongs in as quiet, easy, open tone as possible: [ɑ], [ɔ], [ɛ], [aɪ], [aʊ]. Produce each sound in a tense, strident quality, then in an open, relaxed quality. You may have difficulty at first in shifting from tension to relaxation in the resonators. If so, go back to the relaxation exercises and practice the relaxed sounds alone; then do each vowel openly, easily, following it with a tense, strident production. Concentrate on both the sounds and the feelings of the relaxed and tense vowels.

2. In the same manner, practice the other vowels and diphthongs. Stress open, free, relaxed production, using the stridency only to emphasize the contrast in sound and feeling. Produce a series of vowels for your drill partner, or for the entire class, if your instructor wishes, to judge with respect to presence or absence of stridency. Before leaving this drill, produce all the vowels and diphthongs in a good, nonstrident voice.

3. Since strident voice is usually accompanied by excessive muscle tension in the laryngeal area, pharynx and neck, you may find yourself distorting your head posture, pulling your chin down and inward when you phonate. Elevate your chin until your head is as far back as you can easily move it. Now open your mouth and produce an [ɑ] sound. You will find the tension created in the neck by moving the head back will be relaxed when the mouth is opened. Move your head forward and downward about a half an inch and produce the [ɑ] again. Continue until your chin is about halfway between the extremely elevated position and your usual phonation position. Concentrate on making the [ɑ] easy and open. Practice other vowels and diphthongs in the same manner.

4. Practice the words and sentences given earlier for helping control thin quality. Directions given there will also apply to your efforts to handle stridency. Remember, for nonstrident tone, keep your pharynx open and relaxed. If you find you have difficulty with certain vowels, make practice word lists containing those vowels in the initial, medial, and final positions in words. Ask your instructor to help you learn easy, open production of those difficult sounds.

5. Read and summarize in your own words several paragraphs of magazine or similar materials, maintaining a good, nonstrident voice. Use the recorder to help judge your performance, but work without it as soon as you can successfully monitor yourself.

6. Read and record "The Old Grad," or a similar paragraph from a magazine, first in a strident voice, then in as good, open, relaxed voice as you can produce. You should hear a difference between the performances on playback. Ask your instructor to help you judge the adequacy of your performance. Remember your efforts are best rewarded by your use of what you have learned.

Harshness

Differentiating between harsh and hoarse qualities is somewhat difficult. In fact, there may be an area of overlapping in their characteristic sounds. The definitely hoarse quality and perhaps some qualities labeled harsh can be caused by organic problems in the larynx. Swelling, growths, paralysis, or other organic problems can cause laryngeal malfunctions which are likely to produce hoarseness or harshness. In the doubtful event that the Listening Assignment used at the beginning of this chapter revealed excessive hoarseness or harshness in your voice, and you believe this condition is chronic, consult your instructor about the possible need for a medical referral. A laryngoscopic examination will either make it possible for the physician to clear you to proceed with vocal practice or to indicate need for medical attention. If medical therapy is necessary, there is a likelihood that voice retraining will be needed as well. In such cases it should be carried out with the physician's consent and under the guidance of a speech pathologist. The possible need for medical consultation in cases of hoarse or harsh voice cannot be overemphasized; such quality deviations may be the first signs of serious laryngeal problems.

If it is decided that your harshness is functional and the speech pathologist approves, you may begin working to eliminate harsh quality.

Since harshness or hoarseness or a combination of the two can be involved with physical disorder of the larynx, either as a cause or as a result, it probably is not wise for you to attempt to produce these qualities other than in a very easy, nonstraining fashion. It would be most unfortunate for you to cause a laryngeal injury through trying too diligently to produce harshness or hoarseness. Hence, drills for these two qualities are directed toward elimination or control of an existing tone distortion, rather than toward development of the ability to produce harsh or hoarse voice. If you try to use harshness to achieve a special vocal effect, do so with great care.

A noisy quality often considered similar to harshness is called "glottal fry." Michael and Hollien found judges consistently differentiated between harsh voices and those with intentional glottal fry; harshness and glottal fry are not perceptually identical. We observe, however, that they sometimes occur in the same voice. Their similarity and their occasional occurrence in the same voice prompts us to include both here.

Glottal fry is a popping, crackling, "frying" vocalization. Most of us learned to make this sound when, as children, we used vocal play to annoy our elders. If you will say [ɑ] down your frequency range and let the intensity decrease as you get very low in pitch, you may produce a glottal fry. Hollien, Moore, Wendahl, and Michel described the phenomenon, pointing out that it is probably a normal downward extension of the pitch range of the voice just as falsetto is a normal upward extension. McGlone and Hollien found ten subjects produced fry between 10.9 and 52.1 Hz. This is below the usual pitch level of the human voice.

1. Functional harsh quality is believed to be produced by excessive tension in the larynx. Therefore, the relaxation techniques previously described will be very useful. Learn to produce relaxed, easy, open tone as described under Stridency and Thinness in this chapter. Concentrate on the sound and feeling of smooth, firm tone.

2. Harshness is often heard on the ends of vocalizations where the voice makes a natural downward inflection. The preceding discussion of glottal fry would lead us to expect that. If that is the case in your speech, you may be using a pitch level that is too low. Seek the advice of your instructor if you suspect this is the case. Also, many speakers lower the loudness and breath support of the voice at the ends of downward inflections, causing strain in the larynx, and consequently bringing about improper functioning and harshness. Demonstrate this for yourself by saying a vowel sound with a falling inflection and diminishing strength. This condition can be counteracted by your maintaining adequate breath support and loudness to the ends of phrases and by your avoiding dropping too low in pitch level.

McGlone and Hollien found the air flow rates during production of glottal fry to be less than the literature reports for modal (usual) phonation or falsetto. We might assume, and clinical experience supports the assumption, that stronger breath support and greater air flow rates would tend to eliminate the harsh sounding "fry" quality. In this drill keep good strong breath flowing.

Practice these sentences with typical downward intonation, being very certain to maintain relaxed, fully supported tone to the end of each.

1. I am going to the movies now.
2. I shall stop for John; he's going with me.
3. The picture is a new musical comedy, I think.
4. You would enjoy it; I'm sorry you must study tonight.
5. It will be on through Friday; you can go later this week.
6. My notes are on the desk; use them if they would help you.
7. My diagrams are accurate; I checked them carefully.
8. I forgot; my blazer is at the cleaner's this week.
9. I'll just wear yours, since you won't need it.
10. I'll be home by ten-thirty; see you then if you're up.

Repeat the sentences, letting each become weak and harsh toward the end; then repeat each sentence with good firm quality. Ask a classmate to identify your harsh (or glottal fry) and nonharsh downward inflections as you vary them randomly.

3. In a short magazine paragraph, underline in red the last word of each sentence or phrase which normally would be inflected downward. Read the paragraph aloud, being careful to avoid dropping the pitch too low and being careful to maintain the loudness support for those last words. At the same time, however, avoid the fishhook upward inflection. Now summarize the paragraph in your own words, maintaining the same support and good quality at the end of each downward inflection. Do the same with other paragraphs which you have not marked.

4. If your harshness is not restricted to the ends of sentences and phrases, work with the relaxation procedures and sentence exercises under Thinness in this chapter until you are producing a relaxed, smooth tone. Rees found that isolated vowels are more harsh than vowels preceded by [h] and both are more harsh than consonant-vowel-consonant comparisons. It would be well to begin with single-syllable words rather than with vowels as was recommended in the discussion of thinness. You might proceed from words such as "cat," "pond," "take" to single syllable words beginning with [h]: "had," "hope," "held." Finally, you could practice

the vowels alone. When you can manage to produce such combinations with little or no harshness, practice reading aloud from magazine paragraphs and summarizing in your own words. Sherman and Linke found that harshness was heard more on low than on high vowels and more on tense than on lax vowels. If you discover that particular vowels or diphthongs give you unusual difficulty, you may wish to work from high to low or from tense to lax vowels. At any rate, create a list of practice words with the difficult sounds in initial, medial, and final positions. Rees found consonant environments to be important to amounts of harshness on vowels, with voiceless stop-plosive elements accompanying least vowel harshness, then voiced stop-plosives, voiceless fricatives, and voiced fricatives in increasing severity. It may, therefore, be best to begin with your troublesome vowel(s) next to voiceless plosives in such words as "pot," "caught," "tip," and to work into the more difficult environments. Ask your instructor for help if results are slow.

5. When you have harshness under control, reread "The Old Grad," or a similar paragraph from a magazine, first introducing a small amount of harshness purposely on only a sentence or two; then read the paragraph in the best, relaxed, smooth tone you can use. Listen for the difference on playback. Perhaps your instructor will help you judge your performance. If it is satisfactory, you are ready to work with other qualities. Remember these drills are rewarding only through your use of new voice control ability.

Hoarseness

Read the discussion under Harshness, referring to the importance of possible medical examination for a larynx that produces this quality. A hoarse voice is rarely, if ever, a purely functional problem. Hence no laboratory work is suggested for this quality. If there is some hoarseness in your voice, consult your instructor about referral to medical and speech correction specialists. Because you have come to this point in a voice improvement course, any need for such referral probably has been met earlier.

As was previously stated, attempts to produce hoarseness could result in laryngeal damage. It is probably not wise for you to try to develop ability to produce a hoarse quality. Hence, we give no directions here for producing hoarseness. If, on occasion, you feel a need to use some carefully controlled hoarseness to achieve a special voice effect, undertake such quality production only with the *greatest* care. Do not strain your voice and do not prolong the hoarse quality.

FINAL PERFORMANCE—QUALITY

You are now satisfied by evidence from your practice and your recording of a paragraph of your speech that you have not only learned to produce and control a variety of voice qualities, but also have eliminated all, or most, undesirable qualities from your habitual voice. Demonstrate those achievements for your classmates in a reading performance such as that described in *Student Projects*. Each student may record his judgment of the performances of all the others who have been working for quality improvement. Perhaps your instructor will make available to you the judgments of your performance by the other members of your class.

An alternative assignment is provided in *Student Projects* for the members of the class who have been working primarily for ability to produce and control the various quality types rather than for improvement of habitual quality. Everyone will have an opportunity in this performance to demonstrate his ability to use the qualities effectively. Follow the directions in *Student Projects* for preparing a child's story or a play cutting so that you can use wide quality variations. Each student may rate the performance of the other class members. Your work will be graded, and perhaps your instructor will make the evaluation sheets on your performance available to you.

Improvement of habitual voice quality or of voice quality control is valuable only when put to use. Now that your ear for quality differences has been sharpened, be alert for unpleasant or inappropriate use of this aspect of your voice. You may discover that at certain times, under certain circumstances, or with certain people, you are likely to be at your worst in voice quality control—perhaps all vocal control. That happens to most of us sometimes. Put yourself on the alert; listen for undesirable qualities and eliminate them.

You will have opportunities to use voice quality variation in many of your efforts in speech and drama. Include this facet of voice in your preparations for speeches, new dramatic parts, interpetative readings, and radio performances; you will find it gives you another dimension with which to achieve richness and depth in your speech work.

Remember that everyone who talks has voice quality characteristics, mostly unconsciously controlled. Whenever you talk, act on a stage, lecture before a hundred people, read aloud to a child, beg forgiveness for an unintended slight, insist on committee cooperation, gab about dates or football games, and so on, you *have* voice quality; why not *use* voice quality? This is not a device for improving you as a speech major, as a future teacher, as an actor, or as a college graduate, but as a *talker*. See that these exercises have not been wasted; apply what you have learned about voice quality skills.

STUDENT PROJECTS

CONTENT ASSIGNMENT

A. Review Chapter 3 if necessary, and identify accurately the resonance cavities and speech structures designated by numbers on this drawing:

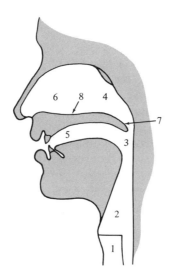

B. Define the quality types discussed in this chapter: nasal, breathy, thin, strident, harsh, and hoarse.
C. Write answers to the following questions about the text:
   1. What are the differences among pitch, loudness and quality?
   2. How is quality related to vowel characteristics?
   3. What other vocal structure, in addition to the resonators, produces quality differences?
   4. How is wave form complexity changed to produce quality differences?

5. When does a quality difference become a problem for a speaker?
6. Is complete closure of the velo-pharyngeal port necessary for good voice? Why?
7. Which of the voice qualities discussed involve excess tension? Where in the voice mechanisms are the tensions located?
8. How are harsh and hoarse qualities different? Why do you not try to produce a hoarse voice?
9. How might articulation practice in Chapter 6 be incorporated in drills for nasality?
10. What is the purpose of creating muscle tension as part of relaxation drills?
11. In improvement of which voice qualities would you expect relaxation to be helpful?
12. How would you expect emotions and tensions in daily life to effect voice quality?
13. Which of the voice quality types, used extensively and repeatedly, could cause damage to the voice mechanism?
14. Identify the following people on the basis of material in this chapter: Hixon, Murphy, McGlone and Hollien, Kelly, Helmholz.

LISTENING ASSIGNMENTS

A. Find two examples in radio, television, or movies of each of the quality types. Give the name of the performer, and if possible, the name of the play or program, and briefly describe the character depicted. You may draw on memory of performances you have seen or heard in the past year, if necessary: nasal, breathy, thin, strident, harsh, hoarse.
B. Listen to your acquaintances and others around you for traces of the six quality types discussed in this chapter. Describe briefly each of four persons in whom you found one of the qualities (do not use names). Describe each voice. How does the quality influence the reactions of his (her) listeners? How did it influence the impression you formed of the speaker?
C. Listen to your recording of "The Old Grad," and the four vowel sounds as described on page 211. Identify your voice quality characteristics. List the classification(s), if any, in which your voice seems to fit, and list the 10 words on which it seems most marked.

Also list the isolated vowel(s) on which you hear the quality. If your voice doesn't fit in a classification, listen for any tones of distinctive quality and list the words or vowels on which you hear them.

D. Is your quality distinction, if any, likely to be helpful or harmful to you in speech activities? In your future professional life? Why?

PERFORMANCE ASSIGNMENTS

A. If you have been working for improvement of an undesirable voice quality, select a one- to two-minute paragraph from a short story or essay, preferably narrative material. Practice it well, and read it aloud in the best voice you can command: that most suited to you, to your position in life, and to your concept of the way you want to sound. Remember that pitch, loudness, breath support, mouth opening, and relaxation may be involved. Strive for a pleasant, effective quality.

B. Select a child's story for reading before the class, or select and cut a portion of a play. Use a story or play cutting that involves conversations among several characters—at least three. *Peter Pan* or a cutting from *Arsenic and Old Lace,* for example, would be very suitable for this kind of project. Assign each character a voice quality appropriate to his role. Summarize the story in a few sentences to the point that you begin to read a one-and-a-half or a two-minute excerpt, demonstrating use of voice quality for character differentiation. Practice the project thoroughly so that you will be in good form.

RECOMMENDED READINGS

Adler, S., Some techniques for treating hypernasal voice. *J. Speech and Hearing Disorders,* **25,** 1960, 300–302.

Bloomer, H. Observations on palatopharyngeal movements in speech and deglutition. *J. Speech and Hearing Disorders,* **18,** 1952, 230–246.

Curtis, J. F. Disorders of voice. In W. Johnson (ed.), *Speech handicapped school children.* (rev. ed.) New York: Harper, 1956.

Fletcher, H. *Speech and hearing in communication.* Princeton, N.J.: Van Nostrand, 1953.

Hixon, E. H. An X-ray study comparing oral and pharyngeal structures of individuals with nasal voices and individuals with superior voices. Master's thesis, State Univer. of Iowa, 1949.

Hollien, H., Moore, P., Wendahl, R., and Michel, J. On the mature of vocal fry. *J. Speech and Hearing Research,* **9,** 1966, 245–247.

Jacobson, E. *You must relax.* (4th ed.) New York: McGraw-Hill, 1957.

Kelly, J. P. Studies in nasality. *Arch. Speech,* **1,** 1934, 26–43.

Laase, L. T. Effect of pitch and intensity on the quality of vowels in speech. *Arch. Speech,* **2,** 1937, 41–60.

McGlone, R., Air flow during vocal fry phonation. *J. Speech and Hearing Research,* **10,** 1967, 299–304.

Markel, N., Meisels, M., and Houck, J. Judging personality from voice quality. *J. Abnormal Soc. Psych.,* **69,** 1964, 458–463.

Michael, J., and Hollien, H. Perceptual differentiation of vocal fry and harshness. *J. Speech and Hearing Research,* **11,** 1968, 439–443.

Moore, G. P. Voice disorders associated with organic abnormalities. In L. E. Travis (ed.), *Handbook of speech pathology.* New York: Appleton-Century-Crofts, 1957.

Murphy, A. *Functional voice disorders.* New York: Prentice-Hall, 1964.

Rees, M. Some variables affecting perceived harshness. *J. Speech and Hearing Research,* **1,** 1958, 155–168.

Rush, J. *Philosophy of the human voice.* Philadelphia: Grigg and Elliot, 1833.

Sherman, D., and Goodwin, F. Pitch level and nasality. *J. Speech and Hearing Disorders,* **19,** 1954, 423–428.

———, and Linke, E. The influence of certain vowel types on degree of harsh voice quality. *J. Speech and Hearing Disorders,* **17,** 1952, 401–408.

Thurman, W. L. The construction and acoustic analyses of recorded scales of severity for six voice quality disorders. Doctoral dissertation, Purdue Univer., 1953.

Tiffin, J., Saetveit, J., and Snidecor, J. C. An approach to the analysis of vibration of the vocal cords *Quart. J. Speech,* **24,** 1938, 1–11.

Van Riper, C. *Speech correction principles and methods.* (3d ed.) Englewood Cliffs, N.J.: Prentice-Hall, 1954. Chap. 8.

———, and Irwin, J. *Voice and articulation.* Englewood Cliffs, N.J.: Prentice-Hall, 1958. Chaps. 7, 8, 9.

Williamson, A. B. Diagnosis and treatment of eighty-four cases of nasality. *Quart. J. Speech,* **30,** 1944, 471–479.

———. Diagnosis and treatment of seventy-two cases of hoarse voice. *Quart. J. Speech,* **31,** 1945, 189–202.

CHAPTER

11

THE
SUM
AND
SUBSTANCE

Final chapter. End of the line. Full exposure to a philosophy and pragmatic approach to the development of vocal skills. You have had very little of the "How now, brown cow" to contend with, almost none of the traditional Byron and Shelley and Keats treatment. We geared our lessons and assignments to the communication needs of normal educated persons in today's world—to the extent that we are able to understand today's world and those communication needs. We hope that we have assessed the situation accurately and that you will be the long-term gainer thereby. So, we provide you with a final summary and concluding assignment in the paragraphs to follow.

Almost all human relations depend strongly for their success on accurate, efficient, and pleasant communication. The speech and hearing processes provide the most frequently used of our communication systems, for both practical and artistic purposes. Yet, in spite of the seemingly obvious importance of speech to human relations, in most people speech "just grows," with only the most rudimentary guidance or training. The average parent gives some attention to the speech development of his child; but unless there is a real communication breakdown or a severe difference in the child's speech, he probably learns little in his early years at home about how he talks and how he can talk more effectively. Then he goes to school. The average grade school teacher is overloaded, teaching a filled-to-capacity class many completely new skills. It is hoped that she will be able to give some attention to oral communication, but she is unlikely to have time or opportunity to emphasize speech improvement in proportion to its importance in human affairs.

Probably a few of you college readers had a speech unit in an English class or a half year's speech course in high school; fewer yet had a year of speech. For most of you this course is the first effort that has been made to help you learn about speech sounds, about your speech mechanism and how it operates, and about ways of making your speech versatile and effective.

However, you now have at least made a beginning. The most efficient, accurate, and pleasant use of the speech process is promoted by an understanding of the instruments of speech and their operation, together with application of techniques for their use. Call to mind now that you have learned in this course about the nature of sound and its dimensions, the nature of your speech and hearing mechanism and its operation, as well as the phonetic representation of the sounds of American English and details of their production. Recall also that you have examined and tried to improve your efficiency and effectiveness in breathing for speech, pitch, loudness, timing, quality, articulation, and, perhaps most important of all, critical self-listening. The information about speech and the details of ways to improve skills were laid out for you.

You are urged to retain and use as much of this information and as many of these skills as you possibly can. If you continue as a major in one of the phases of speech work, you will have more reminders and practice opportunities than most students have; but even if this is your terminal contact with formal course work in speech, you would do well to make habitual the techniques you have learned. Further, you should continue to improve. One never knows all about his own speech habits. Continue to listen to your speech and get to know your own speech better. Without continued self-listening, you are likely to permit your speech habits to deteriorate and to find yourself, one day, unexpectedly, operating far below the peak of your ability. Even the best speakers must remain alert for decay of speech skills and for opportunities to improve speech effectiveness.

You know that an athlete must work out in a conscientious manner at frequent intervals if he is to achieve and retain the peak of perfect form that helps him put the ball in the hoop from midcourt, take the last lap of the pool at full speed, or lift himself that extra half inch over the high jump. The musician trains and works, too, to be accurate in the fast, sensitive runs in a piano concerto. So does the operatic star in order to reach the high notes easily and with full, clear, tone in an aria. The dancer works daily at the *barre* and rehearses almost continuously, whether in performance or not. Explore a skill that is in any way comparable to the use of speech, and you will discover its practitioners accept as necessities the practice, self-criticism, and renewed efforts that we recommend to give if you are to improve and retain your peak in speech skills.

We want you to remember, also, that this is a beginner's course in speech skills. Probably it is an early college course for you. We have only started you on a road which can lead to much broader understanding of oral communication and to surprising, rewarding discoveries of your own capabilities in speech. This is a jumping-off place, a beginning; if you are willing, you can find much of value to learn in the broad academic areas in speech. You may also discover someday that you can add to our knowledge of man's primary communication system.

Let us say a final word before we discuss your last performances. This textbook, projects, and drills have been concerned with the "how" of speech, the mechanics. We intended it to be so; but we wish to point out the overwhelming importance of the "what" in speech. Skilled manipulation of the vocal instruments by a person with nothing to say—or, worse yet, by a person with false, misleading, or slanderous things to say—is at least deplorable, perhaps even criminal. From among the earliest recovered writings of the Egyptians, from the writings of the Greeks, the Romans, through the Renaissance to the present day, we read concern for man's ethical concepts as reflected in his speech. The ability to examine evidence, to think clearly, to reason logically, and to speak with honesty are indispensable to the kind of human beings we hope you strive to be.

Heinberg discovered, experimentally, that delivery is almost three times as important as content in determining the effectiveness of persuasive speaking. Delivery *is* important; we have written and you have read a book based on that premise. But we suggest that the experimenter, by holding content constant in his study, did not explore fully the implications of his subject. "The medium," it is asserted, "is the message." If this dictum is taken to mean, as it rather commonly is, that mere sight and sound are adequate and appropriate substitutes for content and substance, then we must disagree. We continue to believe that delivery is a means to an end, never the end itself. Vocal skills are to be used honestly and reasonably to accomplish the goals of the speaker.

Nor do these reasonable uses of oral communication come as easily as it might seem. Most of us live in some degree of confusion partly because we misunderstand and misuse words. In consequence, we misunderstand the things that words represent. We sometimes warp our own concepts of reality and warp our reasoning about reality through misuse of language. It was neither possible nor desirable to make the study of ethics or general semantics part of this text. Nonetheless, if these paragraphs nurture in you a concern about *what* you say as well as *how* you say it, then attention can once more be turned to the basic objective: development of vocal skills.

Your voice is a wonderful and valuable human instrument. Appreciate it as such; use it accurately, effectively, and pleasantly for your advantage and for the advantage of the people with whom you must live and work.

STUDENT PROJECTS

PERFORMANCE ASSIGNMENTS

Three performances are suggested for use at this point. The first involves reading, the second, speaking; the third is an "after" recording to be compared with your recording made at the beginning of the course. Prepare carefully, giving attention to all the phases of speech on which you have worked and about which you have studied. You will judge the total effectiveness of all your fellow students, and they will judge your work. This is your opportunity to use in summary all you have learned about delivery.

A. Outline a two-minute speech on a current local situation (on your campus or in your city) that might be changed. Emphasize the need for attention to the matter and perhaps suggest the person or group that should undertake to correct the problem. You will not have time to outline a solution or go too deeply into causes of the situation. You are to strive for your best total effectiveness.

B. Select a prose passage about three minutes long from a literary work. It may be a brief scene from a play, if you wish. Prepare it for reading before the class and practice it carefully, giving attention to all the phases of delivery on which you have studied and worked. You are to strive for the best possible total effectiveness.

C. Your instructor will designate a time and place for you to appear for your "after" recording. He will hand back the sheet containing the material you read at the beginning of the semester and will rerecord your reading it. When all the class has been recorded, your instructor may set up a listening period in which you and your classmates will evaluate these readings on the forms provided.

RECOMMENDED READINGS

Heinberg, P. Relationships of content and delivery to general effectiveness. *Speech Monogr.*, **30,** 1963, 105–107.

McLuhan, M., *Understanding media.* New York: McGraw-Hill, 1964.

INDEX